PENGUIN BOOKS

BABIES NEED BOOKS

Dorothy Butler first became interested in the subject of children and their reading while teaching English in a secondary school. Her interest was focused on the pre-school years when her own children (she has six daughters and two sons) were small, and she became involved with the work of the Playcentre Association in New Zealand. As her children grew up she started her own business from home, selling children's books and providing an advisory service for parents. This expanded so rapidly that she was soon forced to move to larger premises and the business has continued to flourish ever since.

She was awarded the Diploma in Education of the University of Auckland for her study of her severely handicapped granddaughter, Cushla, and the crucial part that books have played in her development; this has subsequently been adapted for publication under the title *Cushla and Her Books* (Penguin, 1987). She has also written a sequel to *Babies Need Books* entitled *Five to Eight* and published in 1986.

Dorothy Butler lectures and writes about children's books, is active in New Zealand children's publishing, and still manages to enjoy time spent with her ten grandsons, eleven granddaughters and the rest of her large family.

By the same author in Penguin

Cushla and Her Books

Dorothy Butler

BABIES NEED BOOKS

THIRD EDITION

with drawings by Shirley Hughes

PENGUIN BOOKS

PENGUIN BOOKS

Published by the Penguin Group
Penguin Books Ltd, 27 Wrights Lane, London w8 5tz, England
Penguin Books USA Inc., 375 Hudson Street, New York, New York 10014, USA
Penguin Books Australia Ltd, Ringwood, Victoria, Australia
Penguin Books Canada Ltd, 10 Alcorn Avenue, Toronto, Ontario, Canada m4v 3b2
Penguin Books (NZ) Ltd, 182–190 Wairau Road, Auckland 10, New Zealand

Penguin Books Ltd, Registered Offices: Harmondsworth, Middlesex, England

First published by The Bodley Head, 1980
Published in Pelican Books 1982
First published in Penguin 1988
This edition published 1995
1 3 5 7 9 10 8 6 4 2

Set in 10/12.25 pt Monophoto Baskerville
Typeset by Datix International Limited, Bungay, Suffolk
Printed in England by Clays Ltd, St Ives plc

For Roy

Acknowledgements

I am grateful to Methuen Children's Books Ltd and to the Canadian publishers, McClelland & Stewart Ltd, Toronto, for permission to use lines from A. A. Milne's poem 'The End' from *Now We Are Six* as headings for Chapters 3, 4, 5, 6 and 7; and to G. P. Putnam's Sons for the Poem 'Little' by Dorothy Aldis for the heading to Chapter 2. The poem is reprinted from *All Together* by permission of the publishers, copyright © 1925, 1926, 1927, 1928, 1934, 1939, 1952; renewed 1953, 1954, 1955, 1956, 1962, 1967 by Dorothy Aldis.

The author and publishers would like to thank The Bodley Head for permission to use material from *Five to Eight* by Dorothy Butler in Chapter 7 of this book.

My thanks are also due to the publishers who have supplied information about books mentioned in the text. My publishers have done their best to ensure that all details and attributions are correct; however, any errors will naturally be rectified in any future reprint.

D.B.

Contents

Preface to the Third Edition

Babies Need Books has been in print for fourteen years. During that time, many people from all over the world have written to tell me that it has helped them to steer their babies and small children through the wide and wonderful, but often dazing, sea of books around them. If *Babies Need Books* can go on working as a boat – a life-raft, it seems – to a new generation of such people, I shall be satisfied.

Babies and children need, as they always have done, adults to love them, to care for them, laugh with them, and help them learn. But many adults themselves find the world a bewildering place in which to function. Meeting children's needs, even if these can be identified, may seem impossibly difficult. As never before parents need encouragement, information and support.

This third edition has been revised, but not in essence changed. Altogether, 485 books are described, 256 titles have been retained from the second edition, and, 229 titles added. There are even some titles which, omitted from the second edition because they had gone out of print since the first, have resurfaced to reclaim their places in the third. Obviously, you can't keep a good book down.

Wherever possible, I have left anecdotes from the first edition in place. They have become an integral part of the book, I feel, and have not dated. You will have to accept my assurance that the children and grandchildren mentioned have, in the years between, grown into splendid men, women, and young people, even allowing for parental and grandmotherly bias!

As before, each new recommendation has been tried and tested. But some of the old books are still the best. In the preface to the second edition I mentioned a two-and-half-year-old grandson's affection for *Caps for Sale*. Joseph is nine now, but his cousin, my granddaughter Emily, at two-and-a-half obviously shares his view of that fine old book, and many others.

It was Emily who offered, recently, reassurance that today's children have lost none of that shining virtuosity which sets them apart from the earnest adults in their lives. With deadly efficiency she went through *The Tale of Peter Rabbit*, expunging Mr McGregor with a red felt-tipped pen wherever she encountered him. 'Don't like Mr McGregor,' she explained, and neither her parents nor her three older siblings were inclined to contest this most reasonable opinion. (I am told, however, that a degree of vigilance has been introduced. There is some evidence that Emmie looks with disfavour also on Mr Benjamin Bunny.)

Children don't change. The best equipped of them seize the world in both hands and explore it with purpose and vigour. The language of their culture is the best possible equipment for this task. Let us give it to them.

Story still reigns supreme as a source of language. If we offer children the best, they will come to recognize it unconsciously, and be nourished by it. It is likely, as well, that they will become readers.

Introduction

I believe that books should play a prominent part in children's lives from babyhood; that access to books, through parents and other adults, greatly increases a child's chances of becoming a happy and involved human being.

The dedicated involvement of parents and other adults is, of course, an essential part of the process. Without the help of adults, a baby or small child has no chance at all of discovering books, of starting on the road to that unique association with the printed word which the mature reader knows and loves.

It is in the hope of persuading parents and others of the truth of this proposition that I have written this book. I want it to be of use to parents in much the same way as a car manual is of use to the motorist who aspires to give personal care and attention to his vehicle.

Fortunately, this need not mean encumbering parents with yet another onerous duty. Children's books these days are things of beauty and delight. Adults who become convinced that they should share them with their children have presented themselves with passports to fun, quite apart from the opportunity to stay in touch with their children through the years when their minds are daily expanding.

Children are, of course, different from cars. In an extremity, you can hand your car over to the care of an expert mechanic and be reasonably sure that his attention and skill will solve your problems. Delegation does not work so well for the young child. As society is now constituted, no agent seems to be as effective with the very young human being as one loving adult. Two, if possible, but one certainly.

A reassuring truth, in these days of increasing female involvement in the world outside the home, is that quality, not quantity, is the keynote of any relationship. Any two partners profit from a break, and this is as true of parent and child as it is of two adults. Over-exposure to the developing young, however well-loved they be, can lead to irritation (if not desperation!), with all the damaging effects this implies for both parties.

But a note of caution must be struck; if contact-hours are to be reduced, ways must be found for parents and children to experience one another joyfully during the time they are together.

It is my belief that there is no 'parents' aid' which can compare with the book in its capacity to establish and maintain a relationship with a child. Its effects extend far beyond the covers of the actual book, and invade every aspect of life. Parents and children who share books come to share the same frame of reference. Incidents in everyday life constantly remind one or the other – or both, simultaneously – of a situation, a character, an action, from a jointly enjoyed book, with all the generation of warmth and well-being that is attendant upon such sharing.

A great deal is written and said these days about the breakdown of communication between adolescents and their parents. All around us we hear adults complaining:

'He never tells us anything.'

'She doesn't even want to know what we think about anything.'

'Discuss the problem with him? You must be joking!'

In most of these cases, the give-and-take of shared opinion and ideas has never been practised before adolescence. The only reason some parents ultimately want to talk with their sons and daughters is that a very real problem has arisen. Adolescence is certainly the time for real problems – problems that can't be ignored, concealed, or smoothed over. But all too often, a parent is the very last person to whom the adolescent wants to talk. Not only has the line of communication never been set up, but all sorts of tensions and awkwardness have.

All this can be avoided by the early forging of relationships, by establishing the habit of verbal give-and-take. This does not mean that problems won't arise. It merely means that the human beings concerned will have ways of coping with difficulties, ways which may lead to the deepening rather than the damaging of relationships.

And books can play a major part in this process. Because by their very nature they are rooted in language, and because language is essential to human communication, and communication is the life blood of relationships, books *matter*.

Well then: How do we introduce books to babies? Which books? When? There may be some rare individuals who can cope unaided when they decide to adopt a new approach, but most of us are mere mortals, and need help. I will remember my own 'groping' days as a young parent. I know that I made mistakes, worried and felt guilty (often about the wrong things), steeled myself to behave in ways that were later revealed as not only useless but potentially damaging . . . and that always, always, in every area of parenthood, I could have used more informed advice than seemed available.

I'm still learning. My grandchildren keep teaching me things about small children that my own children left untaught, not least in the field of language and books. My love for them is tinged with gratitude, and constant wonder.

If this book can offer a little support to adults who are a bit further back on the learning trail in the book field than I am, I shall be pleased.

ABOUT THIS BOOK

I've made Chapter 1 a 'Why?' chapter, in case anyone reading this is sceptical of the whole proposition: that is, that involvement with books from babyhood is one of the greatest blessings and benefits that can come to any child.

If you are convinced of this already, and merely seek advice about ways, means and materials, you may prefer to begin with Chapter 2, which plunges into the mechanics of the thing. But read Chapter 1 later, if only to fortify yourself for encounters with sceptical friends.

It would be impossible, in a book such as this, to attempt to cover the whole field of publishing for young children. This has never, indeed, been my intention. In *Babies Need Books* I have tried to convince parents and others that books *matter* in children's lives, and that taking action on this belief can be enjoyable as well as rewarding. To a degree 'what to read' – once the answer to 'why' has been accepted – is easier to ascertain than 'how' and 'when'. Information about titles is readily available through libraries, children's book groups, published journals and (though still rather frugally) newspapers. A book which has been revised twice in fourteen years could not compete.

And yet I believe that a book has an advantage. Whereas magazines and newspapers must concentrate on the brand new, a book is able to find a balance between the new and the old; and endurance, in the literary world, is proof of worth. I have scrupulously honoured my belief that a book which has remained in print since 1928 (such as Wanda Gag's *Millions of Cats*) and still, in humble black-and-white, lights up the eye of any three-year-old who is lucky enough to encounter it, must be given precedence over an unproven new title, however sumptuously produced.

About non-fiction: I have included several titles for the very young on general, almost universally attractive subjects: fire-engines, tractors, aeroplanes and the like. Speed and noise seem to hold perennial fascination for the young! And of course, 'word books' may be seen as non-fiction. Otherwise, I have not attempted to survey the scene. Many near six-year-olds will certainly be developing specialised interests, and parents should seek out material that will fill their needs. And perhaps there is another book waiting to be written by an enthusiast in the children's *non-fiction* field.

The Book Lists between the chapters are to be regarded as important sections of the whole. Long lists are very daunting, so I have selected titles with great care. Nothing is included which I have not used myself with babies or small children. I have tried to describe each in such a way that you will understand my reason for suggesting it, and the way in which you might use it.

It goes without saying that there are other books available which might do just as well. I make no apology for including *my* favourite books, and hope that you will compile your own list in the years ahead.

A list is useless if you cannot get hold of the titles it suggests. The following details are intended to help you to use the Book Lists in a practical way; that is, to get your hands on any particular book that you want to try out with your child.

To begin with, note the details given about any book carefully. Title, author and publisher are the most important. If you are not familiar with these terms, examine the title-page at the beginning of this book. The title-page gives the full title, and the names of author, illustrator and publisher. In this case, you will see 'PENGUIN BOOKS' at the foot of the title-page. The publisher's name, sometimes in abbreviated form, or their logo (in this case, the Penguin) will also be found on the spine of the book. Compare the two if you need to check.

On the copyright page, which is usually found on the back of the title-page, are printed the full address of the publisher and the printer's name. The latter is not important in obtaining a book. Understanding the difference between publisher and printer may help you to avoid confusing them. The publisher creates the book. He either engages an author to write it, or accepts a manuscript already written. In either case, he works with the author to get the book into suitable form for publication. He arranges for illustrations if necessary, designs the layout, and manages all the business details. Then he sends the whole thing to a printer, who uses sophisticated modern machinery to print it. Last of all, it is bound into covers and delivered to the publishers, who must then distribute it to booksellers and try to make sure that people know of its existence. The printer is no longer involved at this stage.

Let's assume, then, that you have noted the details of a particular title, and understand their significance. The next step is to ask at your library, giving all these details. Your librarian will find the requested title by reference to either title or author if the library owns it already. Libraries are often happy to buy a requested title if they do not already have it, in which case they will be helped by knowing the publisher and the International Standard Book Number, or ISBN. Since 1970, every book published in the world has been given its own ISBN; you may find *this* book's ISBN on the spine and the back cover.

You may decide that you want to buy the book, either before or after borrowing it from the library. A well-stocked children's bookshop should have most of the suggested titles in stock, and you may find it more convenient to browse in a bookshop. If the bookshop does *not* have your title in stock and you want to order it, the bookseller will need to know the publisher's name. A really considerate customer provides all three vital facts – title; author; publisher – and may even know the ISBN. A really considerate bookseller, of course, will have catalogues, directories and, these days, electronic equipment to help with the search for elusive titles. Better still, booksellers may have human qualities of imagination, determination and interest.

Many of them have amusing tales to tell of their own brilliance in identifying titles from customers' hazy details. 'Something about a Chinese duck . . . ?' (*The Story of Ping*), 'Daniel's garden . . . ?' (*Joseph's Yard*), and 'This guy called . . . Gardenia?' (*Mr Magnolia*) spring to mind from my own bookselling days.

The bookseller may know the title but not have it in stock at that moment. In this case, he should be prepared to take your order for it, and advise you when it is available. There is always the possibility that the title is out of print and therefore not obtainable, unless you are lucky enough to find a secondhand copy. This is worth trying and can, in most towns and cities, be accomplished by telephone. Most local classified directories or yellow pages list secondhand bookshops.

If you have any reason to suspect that the title *is* in print, regardless of the bookseller's statement that it is not, you might like to write direct to the publisher. All publishers are deeply interested in the public's attitude to their books, and find it hard to get enough feedback. You never know – your letter may even contribute to a decision to reprint.

Don't hesitate, even if you feel slightly self-conscious, to request details from either librarian or bookseller. Be polite and friendly, but firm. Both exist to give you service. You have a right to the information.

Be sure, also, to include your children in the 'finding out' game. They will quickly start using the terms themselves: 'copy', 'title', 'in stock', 'out of print'. Some years ago I was explaining to my family my inability to procure a particular brand of toothpaste. 'Must be out of print,' said our five-year-old!

Children feel more sure of themselves, less buffeted by fate and grown-ups if they are included. They will grow into adults who ask questions, if, as children, they come to expect answers. Bring them up to believe that finding out – about anything – is not only possible, but fun.

Why Books?

I

Why Books?

From the moment a baby first opens her eyes, she is learning. Sight, sound, and sensation together spark off a learning process which will continue to the end of her life, and determine in large measure the sort of person she will become.

Although the process is continuous, however, it is not even. At certain times learning will proceed at almost reckless pace; at others it will seem to have stopped, or at least to be in recess.

Currently, scientists stress more firmly than ever before the importance of the early years for learning. A decade ago, they were prepared to state that certain proportions of intelligence were established by certain ages (one half by age four, for example). Now, they merely claim that one cannot overestimate the vital nature of children's experiences before they ever enter school. What happens in this crucial learning period *matters*.

In families where little thought is given to the need for early stimulation, it is quite common for parents to become concerned later about a child's poor progress at school. All too often, this leads to the negative reactions of urging, nagging, blaming . . . usually to no avail. The days when the child's whole being radiated a joyful and receptive enthusiasm for learning have passed, unrecognized and little used.

Perhaps this sounds overdramatic. But it is true that the first three or four years are still seen by many people as a time when children are most tiresome, rather than as a period during which learning proceeds at almost breathtaking speed. Toddlers want constantly to touch things which may break, to attempt skills which are beyond them. They ask 'why?' and 'how?' repetitively and infuriatingly. They shout with rage when thwarted in their destructive purposes, and will not learn that this behaviour is antisocial and cannot be allowed. These are the constant complaints of some parents. Understandably, they want this stage to pass as quickly as possible.

But take heart! The same period may be seen in another way altogether. How about this?

'Early childhood is a time when children are at their most engaging, when the learning process may be seen with utmost clarity. They want to explore everything, discovering for themselves how things feel, how they work, how they sound when banged together, or dropped. They want to poke knobs and press switches and have a hand in everything. They naturally resent any attempt to curb this interesting experimentation, and protest in the only way they know, with vocally expressed rage.'

Which interpretation will *you* have?

I've long believed that a parent's only hope for real living (as against mere survival) during this period is to 'opt in'; to become personally involved in the youngster's learning life, so that triumphs and satisfactions, as well as defeats and reversals, feature daily. If you can believe that the latest atrocity is based on a desire to experiment, rather than to torture *you*, you'll feel better. You may be able to devise a harmless game which fulfils the same (apparently diabolical) purpose; but at least your dismay need not be coloured by the suspicion that you are raising a monster.

I well remember our consternation when a small son, still under two, discovered that objects could be prised off out-of-reach shelves with a toy spade, an umbrella, a broom. It was bad enough to have one's precious books crashing about; a heavy vase or a potted plant might have killed him. I don't recall any neat solution, but he was not our first child and we managed to avoid the worst excesses of parental outrage. We had learned real humility by the time this child turned into the very constructive and enterprising boy that was lurking beneath the two-year-old horror.

The other outstanding conclusion of scientists which relates to our present purpose is that language stands head and shoulders over all other tools as an instrument of learning. It takes only a

little reflection to see that it is language that gives humankind its
lead in intelligence over all other species. Only people are capable
of abstract thought. Only people can stand back and contemplate
their own situations. No other creatures can assemble, mentally,
a list of ideas, consider them, draw conclusions and then explain
their reasoning. Human beings can do this because they possess
language; only the most rudimentary thought would be possible
otherwise.

Just a little more reflection produces the conclusion that if
thought depends upon language, then the quality of an individual's thought will depend upon the quality of that language.
Language is, indeed, in the centre of the stage as far as learning
and intelligence are concerned.

How *do* children learn to use language?

From their earliest days, unless they are deaf, babies will be
listening to language. At the same time, they will be producing
their own sounds, those familiar cooing and gurgling noises which
are characteristic of all human babies. At other times of course,
the noises they produce are strident and angry, making known
their hunger, their discomfort, or their need for human contact.
But always, from the beginning of life, the sounds babies produce
are extensions of themselves. They are their way of expressing
feeling, making known their needs to other human beings.

These early noises are, simultaneously, the raw material from
which speech will be forged, and the first, instinctive attempt to
communicate. Even at as early as a few weeks or a month, a baby
will be soothed by a human voice uttering comforting words close
by. This essentially emotional response provides early evidence of
a truth which has emerged in the field of language study: feeling
is an important component of language learning. A child learns
to use language in interaction with other human beings, and this
learning proceeds best against a background of affectionate feedback from the person who is closest to the child. This does not
have to be the mother, but it does seem that a child's greatest
hope of having her language needs totally and joyfully met in the
first few years lies in the almost constant presence of one person
who loves her, and wants to communicate with her. For it is

through such caring, verbal interaction that the child learns best to use language.

At first, her attempt to name an object may be an approximation only. Her parent will accept her utterance with pleasure, often repeating it in correct form, or supplying the rest of the sentence which was so clearly implied.

'Ninner!'
'Yes, I know you are hungry and want your dinner.'

Long before she utters her first word, however, the child is involved in a two-way process which is steadily and surely building a foundation for her later performance in the language game. Constantly surrounded by language, she is building structures in her mind into which her speech, and later, reading, will fit. The form of these structures will depend on the amount and complexity of the speech she hears. The fortunate child in our society listens to articulate adults using language fluently. She will be accustomed to hearing ideas expressed and opinions defended. She will know, long before she can contribute herself, that relationships are forged through this two-way process of speaking and listening; that warmth and humour have a place in the process, as have all other human emotions.

It seems that language learning has a great deal to do with emotion and the development of relationships. This is seen to perfection in the interaction between parent and baby; eyes locked together, the adult almost physically drawing 'verbal' response from the baby, both engulfed by that unique experience of intimate and joyful 'connecting' which sets the pattern of relationship between two people.

For the baby, the experience is vital. It has long been believed that the tone of this first relationship carries over into all subsequent relationships, so that the child is equipped (or not) for successful emotional encounters. That language learning also gets its start, for better or worse, during this process is clear.

From this point there seems to be a circular process in operation which determines the direction which the child–parent relationship will take. Ideally, the baby's joyful response to the parent's approach sparks off delight and satisfaction in the adult, and ensures the continuation of the process. If the adult already uses language fluently, as a major tool of relationship, the baby's language development follows as the night the day. Surely, in every generation since the dawn of civilization, fortunate children and the adults who cared for them have demonstrated this truth.

Why, then, do we need to worry about it, or bother describing the process?

Because there is sadly irrefutable evidence that millions of the world's children have no chance at all of finding an adult partner in the early language game. And of these millions, a very large proportion are deprived by ignorance and the circumstances of their lives, rather than the absence of adults who care for them. All too often, language impoverishment is an established fact by the time a child starts school. And language is, undeniably, essential to learning. Tragedy has already entered the life of the five- or six-year-old whose early years have not provided him with the tools of learning.

It must be admitted that the ideas about using books that such a volume as this offers are inaccessible to many of these children and their parents. But this does not mean that these parents are uncaring. In my experience, the vast majority of parents of babies want to do the best they can for their children. Identifying 'the best', however, may be difficult, if not impossible.

Persuading such parents to read to their babies is not as unlikely an idea as it may seem at first. It is one which I offer constantly to the young mothers who make up the groups which I am asked to address. These are seldom 'educated' young women; more often, they are working-class wives, prey to all the modern ills of loneliness, boredom, strain and uncertainty which suburban life engenders.

It is difficult to persuade parents to read to nine-year-olds, or even six-year-olds, if the practice has not been established early. The children may resist, suspecting the adult's motive, or be unprepared to believe that the experience will be enjoyable. Many adults are keenly aware of their own shortcomings in the reading-aloud field. But babies are quite uncritical and utterly accepting of adult attention; they provide a totally captive audience, accomplishing marvels in parental self-esteem. And practice does make perfect. The assured adult presenter of *Alfie Gets in First*, three years later, will have quite forgotten his stumbling performance on *b is for bear*, all those years ago.

It is my firm belief that giving the parent the idea of 'the book as a tool' will do more for the dual purpose of establishing the parent-child relationship and ensuring the child's adequate language development, than any amount of advice on *talking* to babies. None of us can endlessly initiate speech; we run out of ideas, or just plain get sick of it. The lives of babies and toddlers, even favoured ones, are limited. The experience just isn't there to provide the raw material for constant verbal interaction, without inevitable boredom on the child's part, and desperation on the adult's. But if books are added . . .

It is not possible to gauge the width and depth of the increase in a child's grasp of the world that comes with access to books. Contact with children of very tender years − two and three years of age − engenders a sense of awe at the way their understanding outruns their capacity for expression, the way their speech strains constantly to encompass their awareness, to represent reality as they see it. Shades of meaning which may be quite unavailable to the child of limited language experience are startlingly present in the understanding − and increasingly in the speech − of the 'well-read-to' toddler.

I recall a small grandson whose command of language impressed us some years ago. Preceding me up the stairs on one occasion, and straining to reach the handrail, he stumbled and recovered himself. 'Nearly fell,' he said. Then, fearing that perhaps this failed to cover the situation exactly, he added, 'Almost!' This little boy looked like a two-year-old and certainly exhibited the full range of two-year-old characteristics (by turning engaging and enraging). But his range of reference, his appreciation of degree, and in particular his consciousness of language and the way it *works* was impressive.

He lived with his parents in a very isolated area, several hundred miles away. When he first arrived on holiday, he spoke beautifully, saying 'yes' whenever the affirmative was called for. Under the influence of the teenagers in the family, he converted 'yes' to 'yeah' in no time at all. At dinner one night someone mentioned this. Our two-year-old gave every sign of appreciating the difference and its significance. 'Not yess-ss!' he shouted, banging his spoon and laughing. 'Yeah!' He seemed to understand the general merriment in an uncannily mature way. Earlier he had corrected his mother when she referred by name to a character encountered for the first time in a new book that morning. 'Doctor *Crank*,' he said firmly, in response to her tentative 'Doctor Shanks?' Earlier still, in a department store, he had been whisked without preparation on to an escalator, a totally new experience. His dismay was fast turning to panic by the time his mother's reassurance came. 'Remember? Corduroy went on an escalator.' One could almost see his reinterpretation of the experience as familiar. If his good friend Corduroy could go on an escalator, so could Anthony!

In this family, mother and small son spent many hours alone together, in near blizzard conditions for much of the year. Anthony's father was often away until the little boy was in bed, and company was difficult to provide. His mother's way of filling the long hours always involved books. He was read to constantly, as much for his parents' needs as his own, from birth.

At nearly two, he was one of the most 'experienced' toddlers I have ever known – and yet a huge proportion of this experience had been at second hand. His first visit to the zoo was a journey of rediscovery. 'Zebra!' 'Giraffe!' 'Lion!' Let no 'expert' persuade you that small children should be introduced, in books, only to those objects which they have experienced in the flesh. Anthony made joyful acquaintance with countless people, animals, objects and ideas, all between the covers of books, in his first two years of life, to his own incalculable advantage.

To strike one last, I hope conclusive blow for the introduction of books to pre-schoolers, let me establish the connection between early book-usage and later skills in reading.

It is useless to deny that there are, here and there, children who will have difficulty in learning to read despite having been surrounded by books from an early age. Such children probably have some 'specific learning difficulty' which may be impossible to diagnose except in the most general way. But they do have some rare but *real* disability.

For every such child, there are thousands whose reading failure seems unrelated to any specific handicap. They just can't read, at an age by which reading has usually been mastered. These are the children who are, almost inevitably, 'short' on language; short on concepts, on the 'patterns' of the tongue of their culture. Book language is an unfathomable mystery to them. It is a foreign language, not their own. I believe that these children need, more than anything else, a crash course in listening; to people who have something to say to them, and want to hear their ideas in return; to stories which will expand their view of the world; stories that will stir their emotions and quicken their curiosity. Then there may be some chance of these children reading for themselves – if caring good-humoured people will only guide them through the mechanics, and show them that most of what they need for reading they have already, in their own minds, and bodies, and hearts.

There is nothing magic about the way contact with books in early years produces early readers. One would surely expect it to. A baby is learning about the way language arises from the page each time her parent opens a book, from earliest days. She is linking the human voice to the print at a very early age. Given repeated opportunity, she notices how the adult attends to the black marks, how he can't go on reading if the page is turned too soon . . .

Skills come apparently unbidden as the toddler advances into three- and four-year-old independence. Print is friendly and familiar for this child. She is already unconsciously finding landmarks, noting regular features, predicting patterns . . .

Unbidden? Not a bit of it! This child has had her reading skills handed her on a golden platter.

Too Little to Look?

2

Too Little to Look?

I am the sister of him
And he is my brother,
But he is too little for us to
Talk to each other;
So every morning I show him
My doll and my book,
But every morning he still is
Too little to look.

Ideally, a small pile of good books awaits the new baby's arrival. Friends and relations often request suggestions for presents, and gift money can be earmarked for books. In my family, we have a habit of sending a book for the 'displaced' baby. *Mr Gumpy's Outing*, 'For Jane, and Timothy when he is old enough,' is of much more use in a delicate family situation than a pair of bootees!

Keep the baby's books within reach, and make a practice of showing them to her from the day you first bring her home. The covers will be brightly illustrated, and at first you can encourage her to focus her eyes on these pictures. You can teach your baby a lot about books in the first few months.

To begin with, she will learn that a book is a thing, with different qualities from all other things. For many babies, the world must flow past in a succession of half-perceived images. Until their own physical development enables them to lift and turn their heads and focus their eyes, they must rely on obliging adults to help.

As early in her life as possible, start showing your baby successive pages of a suitable book. If you don't believe that this is making a start on her learning life, at least you'll believe that for both of you it is an agreeable way of spending time. Babies love to be held, and you will be getting your hand in early.

You will need books which have clearly defined, uncluttered pictures, in bright primary colours. The work of a Dutchman, Dick Bruna, is worth knowing about. Bruna books are simplicity itself. An apple, in *b is for bear*, is a bright red sphere, slightly indented where a green stalk is attached. The whole is outlined in black on a white page. I have yet to meet a very young baby who is not arrested by Bruna's apple.

Give her time to soak it up, meanwhile pointing to the black 'a' on the opposite page and saying anything that comes to mind; 'a is for apple' to start with, then any other cheerful and relevant comment. 'Look at the big, red apple.' Don't worry, when you come to successive pages, that she may never see a real live Eskimo or that castles are remote from her experience; 'e is for Eskimo' and 'c for castle' will be accepted in good faith, and their representations savoured. Other 'first' Brunas are listed in the relevant section at the end of the chapter. Not all titles are suitable for the earliest listener, and the standard varies considerably.

At this very early stage, before babies can snatch and grab, you can safely use any book of your choice for read-aloud sessions. Before long, however, you will probably find yourself involved in a wrestling match unless you develop defensive tactics.

Some parents feel that a retreat to undamageable 'board' books is the only possible solution, but I feel that a compromise is possible. Later in this chapter I have touched on this subject in a paragraph on the physical handling of read-aloud sessions (see page 18).

The last few years have seen an explosion in the production of 'board' books. To augment the traditional article have come examples which are toys rather than books. In every conceivable shape and size, many of them make delightful and ornamental gifts, but need hardly concern us here. They tend to disappear as they are supplanted by even more original or outlandish varieties. Meanwhile the traditional book form endures.

I believe that certain criteria should be used in choosing board books, and that these are often overlooked. This, of course, does not really matter if the book is well produced and you want to try it, but it is sensible to apportion family 'book' money with an eye to maximum benefit, and the crucial question to ask is: 'Will this book stand repeated readings?'

Here are my suggestions.

First, although I fully recognize the value of board books, I feel they should be provided only for true babies – and then only as an addition to a collection, never as the sole source of read-aloud material. By the time the children are eighteen months old they need a much wider range of style, subject-matter and art form than can ever be supplied by board books; and surely, parents have their rights, too!

Next, I would hesitate to buy a board book which has no text. This is a personal preference, certainly, and one you may happily ignore, if you *like* talking about pictures. (There's nothing to stop you doing this anyway – and I am happy with a single letter, as in Bruna's non-board *b is for bear*.) Believing as I do, however, that babies are attending to print, noting its shape – what you might call its 'conventions' – from the time they are first given the chance to do so, I feel that this exposure may as well begin at birth.

My next rule of thumb: given that board books are for babies only, they should not explore themes which are not babyish. (A recently seen example shows a child of three or four lost in a supermarket: a relevant topic, with imaginative potential. Why not ensure that the story reaches its appropriate audience? It seems unlikely to do so in a babies' board-book series.)

I note with some irritation that a variant of the old-fashioned 'rag book' has resurfaced recently. Certainly, the modern examples, with foam-stiffened pages, are more like real books than the originals, which looked and behaved like limp dish-rags (and before long smelt like dirty dish-rags), but I see no reason to revive them in these hygiene-conscious times. The near glut of wipeable board books surely renders rag books redundant. A useful addition to the baby book scene is a type of spongy-to-

touch, brightly coloured little volume which can even be taken into the bath. Methuen publishes two series, each featuring the work of an artist who is already famous in the field. There are four '*Soft Spots*' by Eric Hill, who has also produced the *Little Spot Board Books* described below. Dick Bruna is responsible for four *Bruna Soft Books* in the same tradition; and these resilient little plastic books behave like books.

To conclude: as board books will be used often by babies without parental supervision, they should be brightly coloured, and use an art style which is clear and uncluttered. It should hardly need stating that they should be strongly bound, with pages which will resist the attempts at demolition that will surely be their lot. Above all, they must not grow soggy when sucked!

Mog and Me and *Mog's Family of Cats* present the inestimable Mog (see Book List 4, page 127) in board form, suitably under-played for the very young. Judith Kerr manages a text which is brief but never boring: a bonus for deserving parents. 'I have to get dressed, but Mog wears her fur all the time.' These are square, satisfying little volumes which will appeal to children and adults alike.

Helen Oxenbury's 'Baby Board books' – and the second series, somewhat bafflingly entitled just 'Board Books', but retaining the same size, format and level – are utterly engaging little books which will have parents chuckling from first opening to last. Depicted are babies, divested of the prettiness often accorded them by unobservant adults, but accorded that diabolical inno-cence in the face of which parental or other grown-up ammunition is powerless. (An all-too-familiar quality to those who actually *live* with babies.) The pictures themselves are so clear, so unclut-tered, the situations so recognizable, that we need not feel guilty about the books' appeal to ourselves, for children love them too. Here is true sharing of that 'slice of life' which constitutes a good book.

Both Peter Rabbit and Pooh Bear (and most of their friends) now feature in attractive board book form, as *Beatrix Potter Board Books* and *Winnie-the-Pooh Chunky Books* respectively. Fortunately, no attempt has been made to trivialize the stories. In each case, faithful reproductions of the famous little characters are accompanied by simple captions. Each publisher has further extended its range to simple 'shaped' board books. Both fulfil their purpose admirably, but the Beatrix Potter example is enchanting. Each of the four titles is devoted to a theme: *Dinner Time, Farmyard Noises, Happy Families* and *Animal Homes*. Each durable spread is delicately edged with a suitable border (food, for *Dinner Time*), with a short sentence placing the scene in the context of the appropriate story.

Helen Oxenbury's four *Big Board Books* − *Tickle, Tickle, Say Goodnight, Clap Hands* and *All Fall Down* − have been described as 'multi-ethnic', and certainly they all feature multi-hued babies (yellow, pink and two shades of brown), in exuberant if somewhat staggery celebration of the brief, jaunty texts: 'Clap hands, dance and spin . . . blow a trumpet, bang a drum, wave to Daddy, wave to Mum.' The vibrant tone of both colour and theme is striking, and the books, with their rhyming texts, will serve through the second year, too.

Before I leave the subject of board books I should perhaps point out an obvious fact: babies themselves, much less concerned with durability than their parents, cannot be expected to prefer board books to the true variety, if exposed to both. At six months, my granddaughter Bridget reserved her greatest enthusiasm for *Teddybears 1 to 10* and *Home Sweet Home*. Both books narrowly survived Bridget's babyhood, and were loved for some years after, in their grubby, much mended state. Would she have liked them as well in board form? There is no way of knowing.

To return to the world of 'real' books − in all their rustly, crinkly, delectable vulnerability!

Alphabet books seem to be particularly useful at this stage, probably because so many of them are very simple. Brian Wildsmith's *ABC* is a feast of rich colour, a delight for any age. It has become, deservedly, a modern classic. John Burningham's *ABC* will be favoured by some parents, and is loved in my own family. Burningham's king and queen are masterly and majestic; and the sooner babies start making the acquaintance of the monarchs of fiction, in word and in picture, the better.

Helen Oxenbury's ABC of Things, a tall, narrow book which offers a number of 'things' connected in cheerful, nonsensical fashion, is transformed by this artist's unique and humorous drawings into a masterpiece. Her *Numbers of Things* is equally satisfying.

'Number' and 'colour' books seem made for the under-ones, too, and remember that these, like alphabet books, all come into their own again once the child is learning to read, to count, and to recognize colours.

There can be no artist working in the field at present whose style speaks more directly to the very young than Emilie Boon. Clear outline, bright but not garish colour and an overall quality of warmth without sentimentality produce pictures which are instantly received as exactly right, one suspects, by the youngest viewer. *1 2 3, How Many Animals Can you See?* is an excellent example. Each left-hand page presents a simple sentence using the appropriate number in word form:

> *Duck paddles up,*
> *That makes three.*

Below, a large clear numeral in bright colour takes the eye with its clarity. Opposite, the named animal joins the existing band, its members making their jaunty way through a landscape which offers points of focus without any clutter. Altogether a buoyant book, which will retain the child's interest for several years.

Ten, Nine, Eight by Molly Bang uses a 'counting down' device to follow the progress of a sleepy little black child to bed. From '10 small toes all washed and warm' to '1 big girl all ready for bed', the gentle action is depicted in vivid colour, in pictures which are nonetheless restful. The officiating parent here is a father: a welcome touch.

Start *now* running your finger casually under the text as you say it. Not always, but occasionally. By the time your baby is old enough to connect the black marks on the page with your voice, the knowledge that the meaning arises from the writing will have lodged in her bones. A book such as *Ten, Nine, Eight* is ideal for this purpose, with its clear print against a white page.

Jan Pieńkowski as an artist has many moods, but nowhere has he more clearly met a real need than in a set of small books covering such topics as colour, size, number and the alphabet. Several of these – notably *Colours* and *Sizes* – are probably more useful than others at this stage, though all arrest the baby's eye with that same brilliance and clarity which characterizes Bruna's work. Some of the titles are also produced as tiny board books; but the originals, still small enough for easy handling, are my choice.

There is another useful category which my family calls 'noise' books. These are loved by very small children, not least because they demand adult performance.

Trouble in the Ark, by Gerald Rose, though ostensibly an 'early reader', is also an excellent 'noise' book. It begins with the animals crowded together in the ark. A fly starts the trouble; 'he *buzzed* at mouse, who *squeaked* at rabbit, who *squealed* at rhinoceros . . .' Inevitably, wolf howls, hen cackles, lion roars . . . until 'just then dove flew in with an olive twig', at which stage Noah himself adds to the rumpus with a 'Yahoo!' and 'Yippee!' which can be relied upon to delight the young, accompanied as it inevitably will be with wild bouncing-on-parental-knee! Here is language which is rich, action which is headlong, and humour which is compelling. Vigorous, clear and colourful pictures of each animal annoying his neighbour render the whole a joy.

Peter Spier has produced several 'noise' books, each astonishingly comprehensive in its field. I remember emerging from a prolonged and enforced performance of *Gobble, Growl, Grunt* with racked vocal cords and ruined throat while on holiday with several grandchildren some years ago. The tyrant of the piece was a grandson of two-and-a-half whose enthusiasm for this book knew no bounds. His sister, aged six, disapproved strongly of it. 'It's not a real story at all,' she declared firmly, and I agreed. But I was no match for her brother. No one else offered to perform, and I weakly continued. (The children's parents pointed out with some justification that I had given it to him for Christmas. They also contrived to leave it behind when they left a few days before we did!)

Noisy Noises on the Farm, by Julie Lacome, is an excellent noise book and provides a simple repetitive text which will be enjoyed in the second year, too. The colours are brilliant and basic, and the eight double spreads offer scope for extensive vocal performance. Mechanically minded babies may prefer the same author-artist's *Noisy Noises on the Road*, which makes even greater demands on obliging – or victimized – adults.

'Noise' books are almost, but not quite, gimmicky; but they are fun, and may be used with babies long before their 'point' is understood.

This is probably the place to insert a few hints about the physical management of read-aloud sessions.

The baby is, as mentioned earlier, totally captive only while he is still unable to use his arms and hands for batting and snatching.

Thereafter, you will have to find some course which is acceptable to both of you; that will neither totally frustrate him, nor so thwart *your* purpose that you give up.

To begin with, you must accept that any baby worth his salt *will* want to grab the book as soon as his physical development renders this possible. This does not mean that he is not interested; on the contrary, he is *so* interested that he wants to experience that delectable object (the book) in the way he likes best of all. He wants to grab it and cram it into his mouth. (If you find this kind of reaction too exasperating, try to imagine what it's like to be a parent whose baby, for some tragic reason, cannot use his hands to grab anything.)

Your best course of action is to play for time. If you can arrange for him to experience real visual and aural satisfaction from contact with books, you may find that he modifies his snatching behaviour at a surprisingly early age. Be sure to give him a rattle or similar toy to suck while listening and watching, and remember that, even at this early stage, a dramatic performance, with actions and changes of voice tone, will be more entertaining than a monotonous one.

Many of the books suggested in this chapter have been written for young children, rather than babies. This reflects my own preference, rather than any lack of very simple books – and certainly relates to my own habit of reading aloud to babies, established long before the appearance of special 'baby' books. Over the last decade publishers have responded to an upsurge of interest in very early education by an increasing flow of such books. While I applaud this trend, I still insist that any book *you* happen to like will serve as well; it is your involvement with your baby that matters most. And why worry if the characters in your baby's books are operating at a level she will not reach for several years? This is true of the people around her, who walk, talk, and conduct their lives in complex ways before her sponge-like contemplation. How much could she possibly learn from the boring company of other babies?

Babies need people: talking, laughing, warm-hearted people, constantly drawing them into their lives, and offering them the world for a playground. Let's give them books to parallel this experience; books where language and illustration activate the senses, so that meaning slips in smoothly, in the wake of feeling.

For your own sake, read aloud an interesting, lively story from time to time. Endless improvisation on the near-textless page can be tiring and boring. One of my daughters read *The Elephant and the Bad Baby* which is, strictly speaking, suitable for older children, to her small son, frequently, from five months, as this book was available and she enjoyed it herself. Shortly afterwards, *The Very Hungry Caterpillar* was introduced for the same reason, a varied selection of any-age picture books following soon after. This young mother mentioned a point that hadn't occurred to me in this connection: it is possible to feel quite self-conscious, carrying on an endless one-way conversation with a very young baby, whereas reading aloud is a *performance*. And to this performance, as to any other, you can bring spirit and individuality. Don't hesitate to move in time to the rhythm, to accentuate rhymes, to tickle or cuddle the baby at appropriate points (which she will come to anticipate), to turn over the page with a flourish . . . in short, to perform with style.

Your reward will come with your baby's response. You'll be

astonished at how early she gives signs of knowing that, any minute now, the image will change. As your hand moves towards the top right-hand corner of the page, the baby's eyes will brighten. A flick – and a totally new vista is presented for her delight. You are staying in touch with her in the best possible way, if you can share her pleasure.

And please – please! – don't give up because your baby snatches at the book and appears to want only to eat it or throw it away. Cancelling the whole programme in the face of a few setbacks is like deciding to keep your child well away from the water until she can swim. There is ample evidence that three- and four-year-olds who meet books for the first time in their lives are inattentive and destructive. Your baby can put this stage behind her in the very early days, if you are patient. A little and often, is the rule of thumb.

A common mistake on the part of new parents is the assumption that for young children photographs of objects and scenes are preferable to drawings, paintings, or other art forms. This is seldom true.

Have you ever wondered why botany textbooks – or seamen's manuals – use *drawings* of plants and ships rather than photographs to illustrate their points? This is because an artist can include the features he needs for his purpose, and just as importantly, exclude those features which would distract the human eye, or mar the clarity of the intended impression. It is essential, in a serious textbook, that the shape, outline and detail of the represented object be shown in a way which permits no mistake. Thus, the author arranges for drawings, not photographs, to illustrate his points.

If students and adults find pictures simpler to follow than photographs, surely one would expect the young child to show similar preference? The three-dimensional quality of a photograph is a complication to a small child. There is a feeling abroad that it is important that small children recognize and name objects in their books. Even in this connection, flat representations win out.

*

And now to nursery rhymes.

Don't even consider facing parenthood without a really good collection. We all think we can remember them, but how many can we call to mind, offhand? Modern teachers tell us that many children come to school without knowing any.

You may ask: 'Of what value are nursery rhymes in today's world?'

To begin with, nursery rhymes are part of our children's heritage, in an age when too little is handed down. There is a world of security and satisfaction in knowing that children don't really change from generation to generation; that some of the best things are still the oldest. We feel part of a great human progression as we see our children swept into the dance as we were before them. We convey our own deep satisfaction in this process, and rejoice in our children's in return.

And the rhymes themselves? Many of them began as political jingles concocted by adults, but over the years the children have taken them for their own. They have been polished and shone and their corners smoothed, until their form is, in many cases, perfect. If children are to love poetry later, they need to discover early the peculiar satisfaction which comes from experiencing form in language. This is not something which can ever be taught; how can a sensation be taught? But it will be there, in their repertoire of response, if it has been kindled in babyhood.

You may have to take this assertion on trust, if poetry has meant little to you in your own life. You may even doubt that it matters anyway, and this doubt is understandable. Fortunately you can relax, and use nursery rhymes and other poems with your baby without examining their long-term effects at all. The evidence will be undeniable that the baby loves them *now*. They are a real aid when you and your child are obliged to make the best of one another's company (as when you are driving and he is strapped into his car seat) or when you find yourself temporarily stranded without a book. You will certainly notice the way the rhymes bubble out of him once they are entrenched. You can hear the way his flow of language is improved with this constant repetition, see the way he moves joyfully to the rhythm, sense the satisfaction he feels in the rhyme. Patterns are being laid down here; patterns into which every sort of later literary and musical experience will fit.

You may still feel that some of the nursery rhymes are too nonsensical for modern use. In this workaday world, shouldn't our children be hearing only good sense?

Not a bit of it! An element of lunacy has always been cherished by children, and words which are not completely rational, but which offer an experience to the senses rather than the mind, help them towards a feeling for language itself, in all its diverse trappings. We are surely hoping to raise imaginative children, children who tap all the available resources, without and within? At all events, over-seriousness has no place in childhood.

The nursery rhyme edition you choose matters less than your own willingness to perform. It is better to have no book at all, if you are confident about your off-the-cuff talent, than to invest in an expensive volume and leave it on the shelf. The essential factor is your determination to surround your child with the jingles and rhymes of his culture; to invite his response to rhythm and rhyme, to gladden his heart and enliven his imagination.

The Mother Goose Treasury by Raymond Briggs is unlikely to be surpassed as a comprehensive, popular collection. The illustrations achieve a superb compromise between the 'traditional' (which is usually Victorian) and the modern, and have a clarity and robust vigour which appeal to child and adult alike. You may prefer the meticulous dignity and quiet colour of Kathleen Lines's *Lavender's Blue*, or the lavish purples and scarlets of Brian Wildsmith's *Mother Goose*. Your baby won't protest, so you may as well buy with your own pleasure in mind. You'll be more likely to use the book if you love it, and this is what matters.

Tomie de Paola's Mother Goose has now joined the ranks of these outstanding books, and sits very comfortably beside them; like *Lavender's Blue* and the collections of Briggs and Wildsmith, de Paola's book has a distinct and individual character and charm. There is both elegance and sensitivity in this artist's work. His pinks, blues and greens are soft and yet luminous, his line strong, his sense of design impeccable. Those who demand dignity and grace in their nursery rhymes need look no further. Two paper-back collections from the anthology, *Three Little Kittens* and *Diddle Diddle Dumpling*, make good 'extras' for car and picnic bag, but do not together replace the big, hard-covered book.

Beatrix Potter's Nursery Rhyme Book appeals especially to grandparents in my experience, but their enthusiasm is echoed by children once Peter Rabbit and his friends become part of their listening and looking repertoire. And the collection itself is enchanting! Some of the rhymes are from the tiny collections *Appley Dapply's Nursery Rhymes* and *Cecily Parsley's Nursery Rhymes*, and some are classic verses, with suitable illustrations uplifted from Potter's other work. New reproductions were made especially from the original illustrations, and are as clear and fresh as they are charming.

My own current favourite – the one I keep on the shelves adjacent to the big old couch in the living-room, for easy access – is *The Orchard Book of Nursery Rhymes*, compiled by Zena Sutherland and illustrated by Faith Jaques. This elegant yet sturdy volume is large, and almost square (24 cm by 26 cm). The text is clear and well-set, encouraging 'real reading' when the time comes, and the illustrations have character, consistency and a feeling of total rightness for this particular book.

This arises, I think, not only from Faith Jaques's capacity as an artist, but from her scholarly approach to her work. In five pages for adults at the end of the book she explains her reasons for setting the rhymes 'mainly in rural England towards the end of the eighteenth century' and depicting accurately '. . . clothes, houses, domestic detail, gardens . . .' In this fascinating appendix, Jaques refers the reader to specific verses, explaining her use of a particular setting in such a way that interest in all the pictures is intensified, as one reads later. (She has even researched and used authentic breeds of domestic animals!)

When I first encountered this book I went straight to my shelves and searched out several of Leon Garfield's *Apprentice* novels, all twelve of which are not only set in London in the eighteenth century, but are brilliantly illustrated in black and white by Faith Jaques. Obviously, this is a special interest, and the gain is ours. The youngest children will love this book for its lilt and colour alone; but as they grow, a wealth of historical detail is there to be discovered and savoured, if parents will give the lead.

Of course, you can swing to any extreme in this fascinating field; the material is there for your choosing. *The Little Dog Laughed And Other Nursery Rhymes*, with pictures by Lucy Cousins, almost assaults the eye with bright primary colour, and looks as if it has been produced by an enthusiastic band of children (all of whom had an advanced eye for design). This is a big book, with big pictures. In some cases, a small object – for example the dish that ran away with the spoon – occupies a whole page, with staggering impact. I would acquire this robust version as well as a more traditional one, I think. It would cheer up any small child on a dull day!

You may search out any of these established versions, or find one of your own. It may even seem (and be) good sense to start with a cheap, mass-market version, or a paperback, while you make up your mind – or until Grandma resolves the matter by producing one that you hadn't encountered in your browsing.

I have heard a parent say, when shown one of the 'big' collections of nursery rhymes, 'It seems such a big book for such a little child,' and I understand this feeling. Briggs's *Treasury* certainly has to be supported by table, floor, or bed while being read, and a small child could hardly carry it safely. Ideally, the collection of one's choice should be kept on table or shelf, and produced for shared sessions, until the child is old enough to handle the book alone. You need not feel that supervised sessions are repressive if the toddler has free access to plenty of books of his own – which would do well to include at least one paperback collection of nursery rhymes.

First Nursery Rhymes, from Rodney Peppé's adroit pen and brush, would fill the bill nicely here; its twelve well-known verses each occupy one double spread, which is ideal for the attention of the very youngest child. The colour is bright, the design both clear and pleasing. The two Tomie de Paola paperback titles mentioned earlier (page 23) could serve the same purpose, though each has a proportion of longer rhymes and might better be kept for use beyond two.

A natural extension of the nursery rhyme collection is the song book, complete with music. If you can play the piano, and have one in your home, your children will be especially lucky; but supplying such a book is a good idea, anyway. Most of us are familiar with the tunes for 'Jack and Jill,' 'Three Blind Mice' and 'The Farmer in the Dell', and learning that the little black dots and handles on the five-barred fence tell your voice where to go will do the baby no harm. You will almost certainly have a relation or friend who can demonstrate – perhaps on a guitar or recorder if no piano is available – with subsequent increase of interest in this different and fascinating book.

Sing Hey Diddle Diddle is an outstanding song book for home or school use. Containing '66 nursery rhymes with their traditional tunes', it will give years of enjoyable wear. The spiral binding allows the book to lie or sit flat for easy reference and its energetic, arresting pictures invite a small child to use it also as a picture book. Tunes are learnt easily, at this stage. Lack of an instrument need be no handicap if parents will perform vocally, however unskilled they feel. Audio tapes, easy to obtain and inexpensive, constitute an excellent source of tunes which, once learned, can be used with any book, or alone.

Songs, of course, are for any and all age groups, as long as they are lyrical and uncomplicated. A. and C. Black, publishers of *Sing Hey Diddle Diddle*, have won a well-deserved reputation as the producers of superb song books for children. *Okki-tokki-unga*, *Apusskidu* and *Sing Nowell!* are intended for older children, but any one might be acquired at this earliest, or any stage.

This may be a good time to state a belief I hold about duplication in books for the young. Far from rejecting a rhyme or poetry book (or later, a story collection) because it contains material available in already-owned titles, try to make sure that this repetition does occur. The child whose own familiar Humpty Dumpty resides between the covers of Briggs's *Treasury* will greet his prototype in other collections with cries of joyful recognition. This is an essentially human reaction; we all have it. If the version is slightly different, read it as presented. The sooner small children become interested in the fascinating tendency of rhyme and story to vary from time to time and place to place, the better. Of course no one parent could afford to buy five or six editions to facilitate this process, but perhaps the major family collection of nursery rhymes could be augmented – and given new life – by one of these shorter gems? If you add library borrowing, reciprocal arrangements with friends and the odd paperback, you could raise a connoisseur!

It is hard to draw the line between nursery rhymes and what I call 'jingles'. Where, in your classification, do 'This Little Pig Went to Market . . .' and 'Frère Jacques . . .' belong? No need to decide. Several thoroughly competent editors have taken the matter into their own hands and provided staple editions which ensure that the field is covered.

This Little Puffin, compiled by Elizabeth Matterson, should be provided as a matter of course. 'Revised and updated' since the last edition of this book – and equipped with a jaunty, colourful cover – the collection remains unmatched. It describes itself as 'a remarkable treasury of finger plays and singing and action games . . .' and goes on to prove this claim incontestably.

Hand Rhymes, collected and illustrated by Marc Brown, is an outstanding book, and would make a lovely present for any baby, new or old. (Ever since our son Simon, aged three-and-a-half, more than thirty years ago, welcomed a guest with a flourish and, 'This is our new baby Josephine, and this is our old baby Susan!' we have always, in our family, talked about 'old babies' as well as 'new'.) *Hand Rhymes* presents fourteen simple verses – some counting, all rhythmical – in fourteen exquisitely designed and illustrated double spreads. One can merely read, or use the pictured illustrations to perform appropriate actions. Whichever way, enjoyment is assured.

Round and Round the Garden, compiled by Sarah Williams, has everything: forty thoroughly usable rhymes, instructions for adults which are pictured as well as described, and illustrations by Ian Beck which are clear, colourful and expressive. The same author and artist have combined to produce *Ride a Cock-Horse* which, divided into sections entitled 'Knee-Jogging Rhymes', 'Bouncing and Dancing Rhymes', Patting and Clapping Rhymes', and 'Lullaby and Rocking Rhymes', provides a wealth of material for parents and willing friends and relations.

Ownership of one or more of these splendid books will increase your confidence in the field. But private rehearsals will be necessary if you are to manage baby and book together. And remember that mastering both rhyme and action ahead of time is the ideal in the case of finger plays and rhymes requiring physical performance. The book can be used for reference and for reading, but is best cast aside for energetic action games. Fortunately, most babies prefer one single action rhyme performed a dozen times to twelve separate offerings, so you need not feel pushed. And each book gives explicit directions, telling you not only which rhymes and jingles to use with your baby, but, in detail, how to handle him, tickle, pat, rock and jog him, enlivening the performance with the words. The jingle is the pudding and the actions are the sauce, or vice versa . . .

You will find that you sing some of the rhymes, always, and say others. Respond in your own individual way to jingles; follow the suggestions given for actions if you wish, or invent your own. Before long, rhymes will come unbidden, to accompany the mundane round of life. Your baby's days will be enriched, and your task lightened.

Human response to touch and sound gets its start here. Too many of our children grow up lacking the capacity to use *all* their senses, physical, emotional and intellectual. 'It is the world's one crime its babes grow dull . . .' said the poet Vachel Lindsay nearly fifty years ago. We have done little to negate this charge since then.

Make sure that both you and your child emerge from the years of babyhood with all the old rhymes tucked safely away, as familiar as nappies and teddybears, and just as essential. You will both be well armed for the years ahead.

Book List 1

Books to Use in the First Year

The titles listed here are suitable for introduction in the first year of a baby's life, but will be in use for years. For ease of reference, titles have been grouped in categories.

Those titles which are mentioned in the previous chapter are marked with an asterisk (*). The name of the hardback publisher is given first in the brackets, followed by that of the paperback publisher, where there is one.

Please use this list in conjunction with the one at the end of the next chapter. There is a great deal of overlap between all the lists.

ALPHABET BOOKS

ABC John Burningham (Cape)
ABC Brian Wildsmith (Oxford)
b is for bear Dick Bruna (Methuen)
Helen Oxenbury's ABC of Things (Heinemann)

NUMBER AND COUNTING BOOKS

I can count   I can count more Dick Bruna (Methuen)
   Brilliant slabs of primary colour in the tradition established by
   b is for bear. Small, comfortable format makes these, with the
   next titles, real 'first' books.
Numbers Jan Pieńkowski (Heinemann/Puffin paperback)
Numbers of Things Helen Oxenbury (Heinemann/Picture Lions
paperback)
One Bear All Alone Caroline Bucknall (Macmillan)

This sure-footed book will be enjoyed for years, once acquired. Its simple couplets are easily and quickly read aloud, and its agreeable, graphic pictures faithfully depict the action: factors which make it especially suitable for first-year use. From

> *One bear all alone,*
> *Sitting by the telephone*

to

> *Ten tired bears have gone to bed.*
> *Can you count each sleepy head?*

the growing group is revealed in all its furry and lovable bearness. This author-artist has avoided over-cleverness and yet produced a book which adult, as well as child, will find both endearing and funny.

*123 How Many Animals Can You See? Emilie Boon (Orchard/Corgi paperback)

Ten, Nine, Eight Molly Bang (Walker Books/Puffin paperback)
From '10 small toes all warm and warm' down to '1 big girl all ready for bed', this richly coloured, quietly worded counting book is a delight. The small nightgowned black child and her father are both weary ('4 sleepy eyes which open and close . . .'). With luck, listening bedtime toddlers may be induced to close their eyes, too.

BOARDBOOKS

Animal Shapes (four titles) Gerald Hawksley (Treehouse)
Kitten
Frog
Puppy
Duck

'Kittens grow into cats . . . and cats say 'Miaow!'
Four simple double spreads per title, with appropriate shaping on the right-hand side of each cover, render these very small

board books ideal for the first year. The pictures are enchanting, and clear.

At Home, Colours, Going Out, My Clothes, My Toys, Noises, Numbers, Sizes Sian Tucker   (Orchard Books)

Tiny 'chunky' board books which fit neatly into small hands. *At Home* and *Sizes* are outstanding, providing examples of my advice, on page 108 of this book, to examine individual titles, rather than assume uniformity in a series. However, all are bright and attractive enough to ensure attention and enthusiasm.

*A variety of boardbooks by Helen Oxenbury available from Walker Books

Bang and Shout

Blue Hat, Red Coat

Boo Baby Boo!

Yum Yum!   all by Clara Vulliamy   (Walker Books)

All requirements of books for the very youngest are met splendidly in these engaging, well-produced board books. Each double spread – five to a book – is a small tale in itself: 'Who's there, under the chair? Boo!' (with child appearing in time-honoured fashion). White backgrounds for the bright but not garish illustrations encourage recognition of small, familiar items. Two titles feature the same child throughout, the other two using a variety of toddlers, both fair and dark-skinned. (*Blue Hat, Red Coat* is especially fetching: a plump, crawling baby divests itself systematically of all its clothes and is revealed bare on the last page. Opposite, just waiting to be identified and named, is every garment – right down to a 'white nappy'.)

*A variety of boardbooks by Dick Bruna available from Methuen

Let's Do it

Let's Go

Let's Make a Noise

Let's Play

Let's Pretend

Let's Try   all by Amy MacDonald, illus. Maureen Roffey   (Walker Books)

Suggestions for shared fun, each in one simple sentence – 'Let's pretend to jump like a frog . . .' 'Let's go tickle-tickle . . .' – on left page, with clear, bright picture on right, together produce six admirable 'double-purpose' board books which will delight both parent and baby.

Mealtime

Playtime

Bathtime

Bedtime   all by Janine Amos, photographs by Sandra Lousada and Geoff Dan   (Heinemann)

> Four small-but-not-tiny, strongly bound volumes which faithfully document daily life as experienced by a variety of toothsome babies, of different skin colours. Seven double spreads each present a single familiar object (ball, mug, book) on the left side, with the same object in use on the right. Colours are bright, against a white background. Excellent presents for a new-born!

*Mog and Me

*Mog's Family of Cats   both by Judith Kerr   (HarperCollins) (there are other available Mog titles)

*Pieńkowski Chunky Books (sixteen titles)   Jan Pieńkowski (Heinemann)

*'Soft Spots' (four titles)   Eric Hill   (Methuen)

Spot Goes Splash

Spot's Toys

Spot's Friends

Sweet Dreams, Spot!

NOISE BOOKS

*Gobble, Growl, Grunt   Peter Spier   (World's Work)

*Noisy Noises on the Farm   Julie Lacome   (Walker paperback)

*Noisy Noises on the Road   Tony Wells   (Walker paperback)

Old MacDonald had a Farm   William Stobbs   (Oxford)

> This is the old rhyme, which may as well be mastered by the parents of babies in their first year; it will crop up at many points during childhood. This well-established artist has enjoyed

himself here, producing expansive spreads of astonishing brilliance and complexity, which are never jumbled. Mercifully, in this version, one is not invited to include every animal already mentioned every time another is introduced, although this exhausting formula is provided for the hardy on the endpapers, along with music. Babies will love the quacking and oinking – and later pore over the pages.

* *Trouble in the Ark*   Gerald Rose   (Bodley Head)

JINGLES, ACTION RHYMES AND FINGER PLAYS

Baby Games and Lullabies   Sally Emerson, illus. Moira and Colin Maclean   (Kingfisher)

Here are 'toe-counting rhymes and knee rides . . . bedtime verses and soothing lullabies' to placate and entertain the most fractious infant. Lovely pictures, and brief instructions where appropriate.

Clap Your Hands: Finger Rhymes
Stamp Your Feet: Action Rhymes   both by Sarah Hayes, illus. Toni Goffe   (Walker Books)

Both of these attractive books can be used successfully as read-aloud rhyme books, or for their stated purpose. The rhymes range from simple counting jingles through appropriate nursery rhymes, to traditional poems and games. All have in common adroitly designed settings, with something new to find at every perusal. Dozens of robust, cheerful little characters pursue their affairs in and around the text, with compelling effect.

* *Hand Rhymes*   Marc Brown   (Collins)
* *Ride a Cock-Horse*
* *Round and Round the Garden*   both by Sarah Williams, illus. Ian Beck   (Oxford/Oxford paperback)
* *This Little Puffin. . .*   Elizabeth Matterson   (Puffin paperback)
Tickle Toe Rhymes   Joan Knight, illus. John Wallner   (Lion paperback)

'One little monkey (or piggy, or lamb. . .)'. Thirteen colourful double spreads, with jaunty rhymes, plenty to look at, and lots of action.

SONGBOOKS

The Kingfisher Nursery Songbook   Sally Emerson, illus. Moira and Colin Maclean   (Kingfisher)
> A fine collection of songs and nursery rhymes, with suggested activities. Musical scales for piano and guitar are provided and the illustrations are full of colour and vigour.

*Sing Hey Diddle Diddle   Beatrice Harrop (ed.), illus. Frank Francis and Bernard Cheese   (A. & C. Black)

NURSERY RHYMES

*Beatrix Potter's Nursery Rhyme Book   (Warne)

The Collins Book of Nursery Rhymes   Jonathan Langley   (Collins)
> Jaunty illustrations in bold colour embellish double spreads which are sometimes devoted to one long story rhyme (*The House That Jack Built*) and sometimes given over to a theme (*Kings and Queens*, and *What's for Dinner?*). Some spreads have decorated borders, and all will bear lengthy perusal. Langley's work is rich in detail, but never over-busy. The collection has been divided and produced also as two paperbacks, *Nursery Rhymes Book One*, and *Nursery Rhymes Book Two*.

*First Nursery Rhymes   Rodney Peppé   (Little Mammoth paperback)

The Helen Oxenbury Nursery Rhyme Book   Brian Alderson, illus. Helen Oxenbury   (Heinemann Children's paperback)
> This handsome volume would make a wonderful present for a second, or subsequent baby; the omission of many favourites rules it out as a family's only *Mother Goose*, I believe. However, its complement of less-known but attractive rhymes gives it an individual charm – and Helen Oxenbury's illustrations have a balanced elegance which is still robust.

Jack and Jill: A Book of Nursery Rhymes   Gwenda Beed Davies, illus. Betina Ogden   (Oxford)
> With one rhyme to a page, and delectable pictures of Victorian

children engaged in every imaginable game and activity against uncluttered backgrounds, this is an especially suitable collection for the youngest child. The artwork has grace and life, and the book's squarish format is satisfying to both eye and hand.

The Kingfisher Book of Mother Goose Rhymes   illus. Colin and Moira Maclean   (Kingfisher)

An unusually large format renders each opening a veritable feast of colour and action. Fragmentation is avoided by the depiction of one scene only per opening. For example, a jolly outdoor picnic spreading across two pages incorporates 'Polly Put the Kettle On', 'Pat-a-cake, Pat-a-cake', 'Jack Sprat', 'Pease Porridge Hot', and as many more rhymes again. The Maclean's work has strength, charm and humour.

Lavender's Blue   Kathleen Lines, illus. Harold Jones   (Oxford)

The Little Dog Laughed   Lucy Cousins   (Macmillan paperback)

Mother Goose   Brian Wildsmith   (Oxford)

The Mother Goose Treasury   Raymond Briggs   (Hamish Hamilton/ Puffin paperback)

Nicola Bayley's Book of Nursery Rhymes   Nicola Bayley   (Cape/Red Fox paperback)

This book has the air of a collection of prints; I have yet to meet an adult who is not simultaneously astonished and enchanted by it. The hardcovered version is perfect for holding in one hand and reading aloud, but its almost indescribable beauty may make you reluctant to risk impetuous little fingers. The paperback version may suffice; but the original book is incomparable.

The Orchard Book of Nursery Rhymes   Zena Sutherland, illus. Faith Jaques   (Orchard Books)

Over the Moon: A Book of Nursery Rhymes   Charlotte Voake (Walker/Walker paperback)

A book of satisfying shape and size, in many ways easier to handle, and yet just as comprehensive as most of the 'big' collections. This is a well-balanced book. Charlotte Voake's delicate watercolour paintings have spirit, grace and humour, and her black-and-white line illustrations provide variety.

There is something to be said for not having too many rhymes on each page; a feature which may well make this collection a favourite.

*Tomie de Paola's Mother Goose Tomie de Paola (Methuen)

INDIVIDUAL TITLES

Brown Bear, Brown Bear, What Do You See? Bill Martin Jnr, illus. Eric Carle (Hamish Hamilton/Lion paperback)

This is a long-established favourite which never fails, in my experience, with the very young. The author uses a repetitive device to tie together, in rhymed couplets, a list of likely and unlikely animals – a black sheep, a blue horse, a purple cat:

> *Brown bear, brown bear, what do you see?*
> *I see a yellow duck looking at me.*
> *Yellow duck, yellow duck, what do you see?*

The same clear, bright, no-background illustrations and jaunty rhyme have been used in a second title, *Polar Bear, Polar Bear, What Do You Hear?* with similar result; but the original title retains a slight edge.

*Colours

Sizes both by Jan Pieńkowski (Heinemann/Puffin paperback)

Naughty Henry

Henry in the Park both by Rod Campbell (Campbell Books)

Henry is a rumbustious puppy whose escapades, recounted in no more than six to eight words on nine successive double spreads (with speech balloons supporting, tersely), are predictable: he digs holes, chews slippers, and chases pigeons. On the last page we find Henry asleep in his basket exhausted. Stroking his 'real' woolly coat is an unexpected bonus at this point. A companion volume, *Misty*, presents the family cat (at whom Henry barks in *his* book) in centre stage, with *her* misdemeanours catalogued and described – and her sleek grey fur is available for stroking on the last page. Satisfying stuff, in your first year of life, when cats and dogs, way down there with you, are fascinating to contemplate. These are 'mini' stiff-paged books, ideal for the very young.

Home Sweet Home   Maureen Roffey   (Bodley Head/Macmillan paperback)

'Does a cat live in a kennel?' asks the cat on the first page in this striking book; and indeed' the bright green kennel on the opposite page reveals, through its door (which is a real hole in the stiffish page), part of a furry animal. Turn over and 'No!' we are told. 'A dog lives in a kennel, of course.' Now we are *inside* the kennel with the big furry dog, while the cat peers through the door. And so on, to the end. Four further titles: *How Do We Get There?*, *How Many?*, *What's the Time?*, and *What's the Weather?* are equally attractive, and will appeal as the baby grows into a toddler.

The Owl and the Pussycat   Edward Lear, illus. Jan Brett   (Simon and Schuster)

'The sooner the better' is the rule for introducing children to Lear's incomparable nonsense rhymes, and, because the verses are old enough to be out of copyright, modern illustrators can be relied upon to keep trying their hand at the task of fresh interpretation. Jan Brett's version of this best known of all Lear's story poems is a triumph of colour and design, with an amusing personal touch which in no way conflicts with the main tale: a desperate little goldfish can be detected beneath 'the beautiful pea-green boat' hotly pursuing his or her love, who is imprisoned in a glass bowl being borne on the voyage as part of the baggage. Their delighted reunion turns this into a double love story . . . and the pictures turn it into a celebration of life, love and lunacy. You will know the rhyme by heart in no time, and can use it, along with familiar nursery rhymes, in a host of different situations.

The Owl and the Pussycat   Edward Lear, illus. Helen Cooper (Hamish Hamilton)

This hard-covered edition of the famous story-poem has exquisite illustrations in elegant borders (with appropriate theme for each opening), endpapers which document the romantic sea-journey irresistibly, and the added attraction of its size: it is a mere 115 millimetres square – just the right size for handbag or pocket!

Welcome, Little Baby   Aliki   (Bodley Head)

One cannot imagine a better present for new parents than this enchanting and yet realistic little book. Ten double spreads and one last single page combine to welcome a new baby, tell her what to expect from the world in the way of basic satisfactions ('You'll learn to walk, to run, to talk, to read . . .') and guarantee, implicitly, the love and support of family and friends. Sharing such a book with a small child who has just turned into a big brother or sister could help understanding and acceptance, as well as give pleasure. The delicate, gently detailed pictures are totally complementary to the minimal text; and the endpapers are perfect.

When I was One . . .

3

When I was One,
I had just begun

In the second year of life, children are transformed from babies into people. With minimal help or direction, normal children arrive at their second birthday able to move around their world, manipulate objects, and make their needs and feelings known. Any group of two-year-olds demonstrates the capacity of the human being to develop, apparently spontaneously.

But the similarity of two-year-old children is more apparent than real; a startling diversity is revealed on closer contact. There was a stage, about forty years ago, when experts would have told us with confidence that IQ, a supposedly inborn and unchangeable quality, was responsible for these differences. Nowadays, opinion is more guarded. Children are certainly born with a 'potential', although this is impossible to assess and, the psychologists assure us, never fully realized even in a superbly successful life.

The real differences relate to the individual conditions of the children themselves, and in each case this condition is the product of inherited factors *and* upbringing – 'nature and nurture' as the combination is often called. For all working purposes, we can assume that 'nature' has equipped the normal child with all he or she needs. It is 'nurture' that concerns us, because this is what *we* provide.

What next, then, for the year-old baby who is already used to nursery rhymes, jingles, 'naming' books and anything else that we have wanted to try?

Increasingly, she will want and need to handle her own books, as well as to look and listen while others perform. In fact, the more opportunity babies have to develop and refine their handling skills, the more cheerfully will they accept the role of passive listeners and observers during read-aloud sessions.

It is a sensible scheme, once the baby is toddling, to keep a number of books on horizontal surfaces – low tables and ledges – as well as to preserve some larger, more expensive books by consigning them to the safety of shelves. It should be expected and accepted that the accessible books will be used by the baby. This means that she will sort through them, carry them around, pull some on to the floor to 'read', and generally make this book-contact part of her life. This is important; ideally, the adults in the house will have their 'everyday' books within arm's reach, too. At a very early age 'passing Daddy's book' can be an exercise which gives both adult and child a glow of shared satisfaction, reinforces the notion that everyone reads and gives the baby practice in visual discrimination.

It is natural for some parents to be apprehensive about allowing the toddler such free access to books. If books have featured in their own lives as objects to be handled with great care, as expensive, luxury items rather than as everyday necessities, they may find it almost impossible to leave them lying around where the baby can get them.

If you feel like this, try making a connection in your mind between books and food. All parents know that children need nourishing food if their bodies are to grow lithe and healthy. They also know that older babies and toddlers must start to learn to feed themselves and that this will certainly lead to messiness, waste of food, and even damage to property. None the less, they allow the child to learn; to embark on the bumbling practice which will lead to that dexterity with knife, fork and spoon which our society expects and demands.

Books are as essential for the developing mind as cereal, fruit and vegetables are for the growing body. In an environment where books are valued and used, competence is achieved early.

When Anthony was exactly thirteen months old, his mother wrote in her diary: 'Today, for the first time, I saw Anthony go through a book turning over one page at a time. Formerly, he has turned several together, with the occasional separate one. He seemed to know exactly what he was doing . . .' The day before he had, for the first time, spontaneously 'spoken' a word from the text. Opening *The Animals of Farmer Jones* – an early Little Golden Book which was a staple in our family for years – he had come upon the picture of the cow, underneath which is written:

'*Moo, Moo*', *says the cow.*
'*I am very hungry.*'

'Moo-oo,' said Anthony, gazing earnestly at the page. Later, his mother asked him to 'go and get your book about Farmer Jones'. He found it, even though the floor was littered with books, and brought it across the room for her to read to him.

Of course there will be some damage, even the odd catastrophe. We still talk about the time one of our own staggering babies hurled not one but *two* valued picture books into the bath where his older sister was being scrubbed. He had the best of intentions, we assured our tearful daughter. He knew she loved those books! Expectation of wear and tear is part of the contract we all make when we embark on parenthood. Why should books – essential family equipment – be seen as 'different' in some way? Or, even worse, as unnecessary equipment!

Recollection of my own family's involvement with books convinces me that books are surprisingly durable, given minimal adult supervision. Somehow, years after the dolls and cars and tricycles have all disappeared, there are Mike Mulligan, Little Tim and Babar standing shoulder to shoulder on the shelf, welcoming the renewed life which visiting grandchildren offer.

And of course you can include some sturdy board books in this accessible collection. Lynne Breeze has produced a series of eight stout, wipeable books which reflect the everyday life of the just-over-one baby. *This Little Baby's Morning* and *This Little Baby Goes Out* have simple rhyming texts over four double spreads, with clear, bright pictures in uncluttered settings. These are large books which *look* like books.

'Little books for little hands' is a maxim worth testing at this point. It is almost impossible for a baby to turn a large page without some damage, whereas a small, squarish leaf seems to flip over safely. The Pieńkowski and Bruna titles mentioned earlier are heaven-sent for beginning book-handlers and there are several other series worth investigating. The best of these are listed at the end of this, or the next chapter. Series should never be used indiscriminately, however. Often, the standard varies surprisingly from book to book, and levels are similarly unreliable. The titles may appear to be of equal difficulty, and yet be widely different in the demands they make on a child's understanding and maturity.

When considering material for this early age group, it is as well to recognize the distinction between 'theme' and 'story' books. Stories, for any age group, have narrative; the characters are established, and then the action starts. There is a plot, with some sort of climax and resolution, and it is necessary for the reader to carry the action step by step in the mind as the tale unfolds. This requires considerable mental expertise, and this expertise cannot be assumed to be present automatically. Why should we imagine that the baby of fifteen months will naturally know that the teddybear on the second page of the book is the same as appeared on the first? I learned this early: 'More teddybear!' (meaning another teddybear, or rabbit, or puppy or whatever) said my first child every time I turned the page. This was the same child who, at three (see Chapter 4), was dismayed and upset by the apparent disappearance of Patapon the sheep's 'seven little lambs'. For some children, what is pictured is real, always.

'Theme' books are less demanding, but are still a step ahead of 'naming' books, which depict unconnected objects. A 'theme' book depicts objects, activities and situations which are connected in some way. Pieńkowski's *Sizes* with, on successive pages, 'big lady little boy', 'big whale little fish', 'big mountain little hill', is a good example, as are other titles in this series, mentioned in Chapter 2. In each, a theme is explored, but the reader does not need to know what went before to make sense of any one opening.

Mick Inkpen's two titles *If I had a pig* and *If I had a sheep* fall deftly into this category too. In these simple and satisfying 'first' books, two chubby toddlers contemplate the joys of having, as pets, a pig or a sheep. The pictured animals are as plump and disarming as the children themselves, and co-operate eagerly in the innocent fun. ('I would hide from him and jump out. Boo!') This author-artist has the knack of producing utterly winning children and animals, and never tips over into sentimentality. The pastel-tinted pictures, against a white background, have a lucid charm. These are true second-year books. (The Orchard board books mentioned in Book List 1 fall into the 'theme' group, too, with their concern, in each book, with a single subject: shopping, clothes, homes.) Since this book was last revised Helen Oxenbury's *Tom and Pippo* have burst upon the toddler scene, and are not to be missed. Tom is obviously rising two, and his activities reflect second-year concerns. Accompanied by his toy monkey, Pippo, he goes for a walk, listens to a story, looks at the moon, and makes a friend. Each title (eleven currently) pursues a simple narrative through five double spreads and one last, single page. Made from stiffish card, the leaves are robust enough to stand lots of toddler rough usage, and the pictures themselves are enchanting. Helen Oxenbury contrives to show both child and adult reaction in the tilt of a head, the position of an arm. These are totally uncluttered books – and their generous squarish size and shape seem just right for their purpose.

Anxieties, both real and imagined, assail the parents of most babies and small children. If your particular worry happens to be a much publicized one, you will be justified in your concern to 'get things right' before the greater cares of childhood descend on both you and your youngster. The subject of adoption warrants attention.

In earlier editions of this book I referred adoptive parents to an excellent little book, now out of print, called *I Am Adopted*, by Susan Lapsley. Its intention was merely to familiarize the child with the word 'adopted' and it was, in its own right, a good book: an enjoyable experience for any child. In the years between, the subject of adoption has undergone scrutiny in most parts of the world. It would be a brave publisher who attempted a picture book on the subject at the moment – though a spate of teenage novels has explored the effects of adoption on older children.

There will of course always be a need for some children to find adoptive homes, and new practices are emerging which are designed to shield children and parents (natural and adoptive) from the worst effects of the brutal separation which frequently attended adoption in the past. My suggestion is to forget about 'a book on the subject' if your baby is adopted, as there is unlikely to be the perfect book to suit your particular circumstance. Any apprehension you have about your capacity to forge a lifelong relationship with your child will dissipate as you see and feel your growing closeness and interdependence. And books will be your firmest ally: books of every sort, on every subject.

Another theme which is likely to demand coverage at this (or any other time) in a youngster's life is the imminence of a new brother or sister. It is desirable to try to prepare the child for this intrusion, however young he may be; and fortunately, babies figure prominently in picture books.

The simple fact of the new baby growing inside the mother is easy for the youngest child to accept, especially as the mother's size increases over the months. One doesn't need a book about the process – but one does need help to fortify the about-to-be-displaced child against the invasion!

Jan Ormerod's *101 Things to Do with a Baby* will certainly familiarize him with things babyish; it suggests, literally, 101 ways in which one might engage a baby in activities, from saying good morning to him, bathing him, playing peepo and 'putting him in his cot for a quiet time' (for the family, also: mother is seen reading to the older child in a typically bestrewn baby-in-residence living-room), to taking him on a picnic, letting him meet big dogs and other babies . . . This author-artist has, clearly, had intimate experience of family life – and has a true talent for drawing babies, and their older relatives.

The Trouble with Babies, by Angie and Chris Sage, vastly amused three-year-old Emily when her baby sister was born some months ago. The baby in the book is not brand new – in fact is seen in a high chair irresponsibly throwing food around, in true six-months style – but accordingly provides scope for more active entertainment. And the principle is the same: babies are trans-

ported, whereas *you* have to walk, they have lots of toys, but
always want yours, and they hog an unfair share of everyone's
attention. But in the end they smile when you talk to them . . .
and they look lovely when they are asleep . . . 'But the trouble
with babies is . . . They soon wake up again!' An unromantic,
bald baby and its family are depicted in flat, muted colour which
is somehow right for this successful exposition of babyhood, as
perceived by a displaced sister. In Catherine Anholt's *Aren't You
Lucky?* the small girl tells her own story. 'At first it was just me, on
my own. Just Mummy and Daddy and me.' The arrival of baby
brother brings changes, but these are neither dwelt upon nor
exaggerated. The gradual metamorphosis of a brother whom she
can help and enjoy, so that the original visitor's comment 'Aren't
you lucky!' turns into 'Isn't *he* lucky!' is delightfully depicted in
the author's own illustrations, which are lively and colourful.
Full-page pictures are varied by the use of wide double spreads
divided into eight small pictures, each with a simple caption
beneath, allowing a small child to 'read' with ease. This is a book
to be enjoyed, whether or not the theme has relevance.

Welcome Little Baby, by Aliki, also springs to mind as a useful
introduction for the next-up child. It is fully described in Book
List 1.

There is a useful category of books which sits on the fence
between the pure theme book and the true story. It has a
confident foot in each field, and is indispensable as a launching
pad for the story proper. One might perhaps call these 'descriptive'
books. Sarah Garland has made an outstanding contribution to
this category with a series of short, splendidly earthy books with
titles such as *Doing the Washing*, *Going Shopping*, *Having a Picnic* and
Doing the Garden (see Book List 1). Each volume depicts a calm-in-
the-circumstances Mum of gratifying ordinariness, a small girl,
younger toddler and large dog, all engaged in the everyday
pursuits of the titles. The toddler works with dedicated originality
to sabotage constructive accomplishment on all fronts, and the
dog clearly does not know its place. The little girl is superb, a
match for any situation; and the toddler will come up trumps
too, one feels. How could he fail, with a mother whose strength

and humour shine through all? As good for parents as children, these brisk and eloquent books. Sarah Garland's art style has a kind of fly-away vigour which is none the less generous in detail and always comprehensible, and her use of colour is sure and generous.

Translating everyday life into print and picture for the very, very young seems, at the moment, to be largely the preserve of a small but growing group of women author-artists, of whom Sarah Garland is one. Jan Ormerod, Janet Ahlberg and Helen Oxenbury are others, and their books are described in end-of-chapter lists. One suspects that most men still lag in that total awareness of small children which women in our society have traditionally shown; an awareness which reveals itself as much in depiction of physical attitude − the set of a leg, the tilt of a head, the way a child's body works when it sits, crouches, or runs − as in careful attention to features. One can believe that, as more men take over the everyday (and every night!) care of their young children, the field will be more equally served by the sexes. One never knows; perhaps the trend may even be reversed. (After all, no one draws children from whom more feeling emanates than Quentin Blake − and Edward Ardizzone, born in 1900, has left behind him an army of real, live, *feeling* children, from babies up.)

Undisputed modern master in the field is Shirley Hughes; and she is seen at her best in her 'Nursery Collection', published by Walker Books. I would buy all of these incomparable, fortunately inexpensive little volumes. With titles such as *Bathwater's Hot*, *When We Went to the Park*, *Noisy*, *All Shapes and Sizes*, *Colours*, and *Two Shoes, New Shoes*, each is a celebration of child- and babyhood. The paraphernalia of family life, indoors and out, invades each page; the children are enterprising, honest, ordinary and full of that heartbreaking charm which is the true quality of childhood, and which has nothing to do with prettiness and good behaviour. As always, design and use of colour are masterly.

A Japanese author and artist team, Shigeo Watanabe and Yasuo Ohtomo, have produced, over recent years, a series of very simple picture books which are just right for children between one and two. With titles like *I'm going for a walk!*, *I can build a house!* and *How do I put it on?*, these are uniformly satisfying books. Between the covers, a very young bear faces the physical and social problems common to the second year of life – as well as revelling in its satisfactions. The clarity of Ohtomo's illustrative style is hard to describe: his colours are quiet and few, his background the consistent white of the page. A gentle warmth is conveyed – and the subject matter is totally appropriate.

I wonder who first thought of using a small flap attached to a page to conceal and then reveal a person, animal or object, to the delight of the viewer? We will probably never know, though I suspect that early examples have passed without the acclaim accorded several modern ones. The device is simple, and the resulting book more durable than the complicated 'pop-up', with its tabs to pull and wheels to turn.

With the creation by Eric Hill of an appealing puppy called Spot, the technique sprang to public attention, so that 'Spot' books are now found, appropriately translated, in the far corners of the world. Spot books are instantly recognizable; square in shape, with sensibly stiff pages, they present animals and objects in pleasing and simple clarity against a white background. Best of all, there is the expected flap at every opening, to be lifted triumphantly, revealing such delights as a monkey eating a banana (in a wardrobe, where we are expecting to find Spot himself) or a tortoise, under a rug (where we were *certain*, from the shape of the bump, that we would find the errant puppy at last).

Subsequent titles show the guileless puppy in a variety of situations, from school to the circus. All are successful and the large, clear, simple text is excellent for early reading at a later stage. To my mind, the original *Where's Spot?* has never quite been equalled, but each new book has adult enthusiasts rushing to acquire it for the young devotees in their care.

The recipe has, predictably, been copied, and several of these 'flap' books have achieved (lesser) prominence. My grand-daughter Charlotte, at just two, found *Oh Dear!* by Rod Campbell so uproariously funny that I was amazed, all over again, at the way in which children do not change. A small boy, sent to fetch an egg from the farmyard, finds instead a succession of other objects behind and through the doors and windows he hopefully opens. Charlotte's shriek of delighted hilarity at the raising of each flap would have warmed the heart of the author, could he have heard it. One can, of course, see the child's point: given that she knows that eggs come from chickens, the suggestion that a cow or a pig might produce one is likely to raise a laugh. But ten times over? 'Oh yes,' the parents of second-year babies will tell you resignedly. If it works once, it will work *fifty* times.'

Emilie Boon has used the same 'flap' device to bring life to simple texts by Harriet Ziefert in *Mummy Where Are You?* and *Daddy Can You Play With Me?* On a typical page, a toothsome hippo toddler asks, 'Mummy, what are you doing?' On the opposite page, swinging kitchen doors open to reveal a genial hippo mother saying, 'I'm cooking supper.' Emilie Boon as an artist understands the very young child's need for clear line, warm colour and lack of clutter. These are utterly engaging books.

You will, of course, come to feel that these simple little books are all very well for the baby, but ultimately a little boring for you. Such parental rebellion is to be encouraged. This is the right time to join the local library, if you don't belong already.

Membership of a library allows you to experiment, and experimentation often leads to the emergence of unexpected truths. Be reckless; bring home anything that you fancy, or want to investigate. You'll have to bow to your child's choice in a year or two, so you may as well have fun while the field is yours. You may find that your toddler's gaze is held compulsively captive by bold, dramatic slabs of colour in a book which is still several years beyond her understanding. On no account be persuaded that the text, because it is 'too hard', should not be read aloud. Modern research shows that children who are exposed to complex speech patterns learn to express themselves earlier and more fluently than those who are spoken to in careful, simple sentences. But the child's willingness to listen, meanwhile enjoying the pictures and the special feelings of warmth and sharing which read-aloud sessions evoke, must call the tune. If she doesn't enjoy the experience, your persistence will do more harm than good. But don't form hasty conclusions about what is suitable without trying a variety of types.

Rhyme and rhythm are real strengths at this early stage, and an impressive number of artists have conspired to exploit their undoubted appeal. One can believe that the opportunities presented by 'The House That Jack Built' might prove irresistible to an artist who longed to indulge his passion for colour and line and at the same time communicate with the very young. For freshness and enthusiasm, this audience is unmatched anywhere.

William Stobbs has elevated the old tale of Jack and his house – malt, maiden, priest and all – to the ranks of high artistic and literary achievement; and a new 'rebus' version by Elizabeth Falconer (in which certain words are represented by pictures, instead of text) is a delight, its pictures sparkling and sprightly, its overall design innovative and yet beautifully clear.

'Over in the Meadow' is probably the most lulling number rhyme ever composed – and one supposes that it must have been composed originally, though its modern forms are diverse. The factor they all have in common is a wonderfully warm, drowsy contentment.

> *Over in the Meadow in the sand in the sun*
> *Lived an old mother turtle and her little turtle one.*
> *'Dig' said the Mother,*
> *'I dig' said the one;*
> *So he dug and was glad in the sand in the sun.*

'Over in the Meadow' is not to be missed. An old version by John Langstaff, with illustrations by Feodor Rojankovsky, was a favourite in my own family for many years; it must have endured hundreds of read-aloud sessions and is, indeed, still in our library. And Ezra Jack Keats's version is superb, too. The warm colours of a summer afternoon drench 'the little crows six' and 'the little crickets seven' in a haze of peace and plenty, and communicate their glow to reader and listener alike. Sadly, both of these versions are out of print at the moment, but the library may be able to help.

Fortunately, the old rhyme continues to attract artists, and publishers obviously recognize its merits. An attractive version by Olive A. Wadsworth, with pictures by Mary Maki Rae, is bolder in presentation than the older books, with brilliant slabs of colour as background to engaging, easily discerned and counted animals. But I miss the eloquence of the wording in the old, Langstaff edition. Why 'dug all day' when 'dug and were glad' invites the young listener to share in the joy of living experienced by 'the little turtle one', 'the little ducks nine'? Perhaps this is to split hairs; the endpapers of this book are a joy to peruse, with a centrally placed picture of the meadow ringed with, in turn, the boxed numerals from 1 to 10, each followed by its appropriate animal. This allows the child to recap the listening experience with '1 turtle, 2 fish, 3 owls, 4 rats. . .' and, in all likelihood, to begin to recognize numbers in their written form.

At this early stage, rhyme helps in yet another more practical way. Once the baby has mastered the art of page-turning, he will be intent upon demonstrating his accomplishment. You'll be lucky if you *can* read the text before the page is turned! Knowing it by heart is almost essential, and rhymes are the easiest to learn. Of course, traditional rhymes are usually known at least in part beforehand.

This is the stage when one-page-per-rhyme *Mother Goose* books have a clear advantage over the bigger type. The Peppé and de Paola versions mentioned on page 24 are useful here, and Lady-bird and Little Golden Books are likely to have editions for every day access.

This second year is the time, too, for wordier ABCs and counting books, and there is an agreeable and increasing number of these available.

The Very Hungry Caterpillar cannot fail to delight and amaze. It has everything. At the first two openings, we meet a little egg, which quickly hatches a 'tiny and very hungry caterpillar'. The rest of the book tells the tale of the caterpillar's increasing and cheerful gluttony, as he eats his way through three plums, four strawberries, five oranges . . . to final repletion. At last, stomach-ache and all, he builds a cocoon around himself, retires, and after 'more than two weeks', emerges as a 'beautiful butterfly'.

This extraordinary book (which has been imitated but never, of its type, approached in excellence) is simultaneously a counting book, a nature lesson, a painless Monday-to-Sunday exposition, and to cap it all, a 'manipulative' book; the finger-sized hole in each edible object on successive sturdy pages invites immediate exploration. But the whole is more than the sum of the parts. Its impact is sobering in its force. An argument for acquiring the hard-cover edition lies in the certainty of its endurance among front-line family favourites for years. *The Very Hungry Caterpillar* demands to be learned by heart. Performances will still be given at five and six, when 'by heart' material plays a valuable role in learning to read.

Less spectacular, but just as innovative, is Susanna Gretz's *Teddybears 1 to 10*. Why are teddybears so enduringly appealing? Successive double spreads devoted to '1 teddybear, 2 old teddy-bears, 3 dirty old teddybears . . .' with the described characters depicted in colour against white backgrounds, sprawling dazedly or whirling dizzily (in a washing machine – nothing Edwardian about *these* bears) enchant utterly. At eighteen months, Sam, my eldest grandson, used to gaze as if mesmerized until the last page, on which '. . . 10 teddybears home for tea' pose for their photo-graph in a large armchair . . . except for one, who has fallen down the back and is seen as two desperate eyes and a pair of clutching paws. 'Peep-bo!' Sam would shout in glee, bringing his face to within an inch of the discomfited bear!

The bears reappear in *Teddybears ABC*, in which they are seen 'arriving in an aeroplane,' 'climbing', 'dancing', 'finding fleas in their fur' and 'mucking about in the mud'. Wonderful, alliterative phrases to be absorbed now, and laughed at later.

Dr Seuss's ABC might well be acquired in the second year of life (preferably in hard covers; it lies flatter, that way). The jingly nonsense will appeal to the baby's sense of fun and encourage you to bounce, tickle and generally indulge her; and it is never too soon to start using the sounds of the alphabet in a way which is likely to stick:

> Big R
> *little r*
> *Rosy Robin Ross*
> *Rosy's going riding*
> *on her*
> *red rhinoceros.*

Dr Seuss's clownish little characters have a determined affability about them which is hard to resist. This will become a much used and quoted book.

Years ago I used to read to my children the Lear Alphabet which begins 'A was once an apple pie' from the old *Faber Book of Nursery Verse* (of revered memory.) In time I had it by heart and would often say it without the book, with family chorus supporting lustily. Over the years since, several illustrated versions have been published. And how well the old rhyme sits in picture book format!

A recent and welcome edition is illustrated by Julie Lacome in brilliant primary colours, guaranteed to take and keep the eye of the youngest child. The letters of the alphabet are given in capital and lower case, and the generously large pages are models of clarity and sound design. The wonderfully nonsensical, rhyming alphabet will evoke sure response from second-year babies – and their elders. There is no 'suitable' age for such a book; its appeal is to the senses, not the intellect.

> *A was once an apple pie*
> *Pidy*
> *Widy*
> *Tidy*
> *Pidy*
> *Nice insidy*
> *Apple Pie!*

Such an earnest undertaking as 'learning the alphabet' need never feature consciously, for the child exposed to Lear's robust fun.

Several double spreads in this lovely book feature one letter only, and would grace any nursery wall. 'N', for example, expanding on the properties of 'a little needle', presents threaded needle, pincushion and spools of thread in a sampler-like frame, with the beginnings of a patchwork quilt, cobbled together with childish stitches: an engagingly domestic image. But there is still spirit and action, too, with an enormous whale cavorting, and 'Great King Xerxes' brandishing a sabre and leering (cheerfully, it must be admitted). The great Xerxes made his mark in our family; when he was about eleven, one of our sons came home after a history lesson at school one day and said to me, 'We've just met up with Great King Xerxes. I always thought you made him up!'

This sort of book illustrates the superior effect of rich, flowing sound over mundane *sense* for babies and toddlers. There is a tendency among publishers to produce, in response to a growing demand for titles for the very young, books which are over-earnest to the point of dullness. We need to remember that the sound rather than the sense of language is all important if babies are to be 'hooked'. Later, at nearly two, they will be enthralled by the evidence that life goes on between the covers of a book. Meanwhile rhythm, rhyme and the peculiar satisfactions which arise from sound used resonantly will evoke a ready response, arousing an expectation of satisfaction, even joy. Compare Lear's Alphabet ('Waddly-woosy Little Goose!') with 'Sally likes to skip. The boys fly their kites.' Neither text can mean much to the year-old baby – but Lear's will set her feet jigging and her senses soaring – and bring her back for more.

But Where is the Green Parrot? is a phenomenon; it does not belong in any category. Each page shows a different background (a train, a toy chest, a table set for tea), lists the objects pictured therein, and asks in capital letters: 'BUT WHERE IS THE GREEN PARROT?' There he is, in each case peeping from behind, below, above or through, a unifying and satisfying character who elevates this book to a level far above the earnest little volumes which in their dismal dozens invite children to 'point' and 'name' as a way of learning. Thomas and Wanda Zacharias do not hesitate to present their tree 'heavy with red apples . . .', to equip their horse with 'tight curls, a blue bridle with yellow tassels, a rider in the saddle with high boots . . .' But then, they probably had no intention of 'teaching' children anything.

There is another comparison to be made between those books which are intentionally instructive, and those which imaginatively represent the world. The former state, page after page, bold, boring and obvious truths about shops, sunshine, school or any other natural or man-made phenomenon. The latter establish atmosphere through interrelating picture and language, evoking response on several fronts: emotional and artistic as well as intellectual.

Two matching volumes by Shirley Hughes spring to mind: *Bouncing* and *Giving*. Each title explores, in eight evocative double spreads, the activity of its title: 'I gave Dad a very special picture which I painted at play-group . . . And he gave me a ride on his shoulders most of the way home . . .' 'In the morning I bounce on my bed, and the baby bounces in his cot.' As usual, Shirley Hughes's illustration of these everyday occupations conveys not only their actuality, but their spirit. This is a rare capacity; I cannot think of any other artist who demonstrates it to a similar extent. For good measure, there are no fewer than *twenty* extra pictured activities across the endpapers of each book: waving, singing, crying, skipping, digging, reading, painting, hugging . . . forty in all! Any adult who is looking for a 'language teaching' book for a small child would be well advised to go no further than *Giving* or *Bouncing*; information comes in on the wings of sensation in both titles.

And this is the time for the old woman and her recalcitrant pig! A modern version by Priscilla Lamont, *The Troublesome Pig*, retains the original rhythm of this rousing old tale, and demonstrates the power of unrhymed verse to enthral:

> *'Please water, quench fire,*
> *Then fire will burn stick,*
> *Stick, will beat dog,*
> *Dog will bite pig,*

> *The pig will jump over the stile*
> *And we shall get home tonight!'*
> *But would the water quench the fire?*

IT WOULD NOT.

The pictures in this book capture the spirit of the story and impart true individuality to all the characters. The text makes compulsive listening, and unfamiliar words – stile, harness, quench, gnaw will be stored up for future reference, as more and more traditional rhymes and tales are encountered.

You may notice that the artist has used a delicate rather than vigorous style to embellish the old tale; the colours are muted and sensitive rather than bright and brash. You may wonder if very young children will attend to such pictures; have we not established that they prefer brilliant colours and likely pictures? I believe that this is like saying that, as young children obviously prefer ice cream to vegetables, we may as well defer to this taste and abandon our intention of providing them with good, nourishing food. In my experience, children increasingly enjoy a wide range of art styles if we give them the chance, and the example of our own appreciation.

In the years that have elapsed since its appearance, *The Baby's Catalogue* by Janet and Allan Ahlberg has become an established feature of the 'Books for Babies' scene. The first page of this truly enchanting book introduces the six babies whose lives become its subject, in catalogue form; They represent five families; two of the babies are twins. Each successive page is appropriately labelled: Toys, Brothers and Sisters, Dinners, Games ... In each case one can differentiate the babies and their families, with details compounding as the book proceeds. Endless perusal is rewarded by discovery, the 'Books' page strikes a blow for the right cause and 'Accidents' ought to become a poster for framing. These babies are babies, in all their messy and appealing innocence. They are celebrated gloriously here, in a book which seems certain to survive into the next century.

An occasional book, being tried out with a particular child, is immediately recognized as a winner in the toddler – or any –

stakes. Such a book is *Cock-a-doodle-doo*, with words by Franz Brandenberg and pictures by Aliki, his wife. One might call this a farm book, a noise book, a family book . . . light, warmth and happiness arise from its pages, with animals and humans pursuing their active course through an early morning stint of milking, chicken-feeding and breakfast preparation. There is much more in the expansive, truly enchanting pictures than the simple text reveals, but no over-cleverness, no contrivance. The small child's eye will find plenty to look at, nothing to confuse in these pages. (I read it aloud to Bridget at fourteen months. Her usual determination to help turn pages was in total abeyance for once, her eyes straying with attention across the wide, landscape double spreads. My loud 'oinks' and 'neighs' were received soberly, and, I think, appreciatively.)

Such a book is an experience, from which a child will derive immediate and lasting benefit. Experiences lodge in the mind and heart, and enrich the spirit – unlike lessons, which as often as not, bounce off and are lost. Spend your baby's second year of life entrenching and expanding the book habit you have established in the first year. If you have been really successful, of course, it won't feel as if you are implementing any policy; you and your child will both know, with assurance, that books are indispensable and that the good life you are leading together is immeasurably enriched by their cheerful and comforting presence.

Book List 2

Books to Use between One and Two

Remember to use this list in conjunction with Book List 1 (page 28) and to consult Book List 3 (page 83) for very bookwise children.

**A Was Once an Apple Pie*   Edward Lear, illus. Julie Lacome (Walker)

All Gone!

Oh, No!   both by Sarah Garland   (Puffin paperback)
> In style, akin to the Garland titles mentioned on pages 45–6 but with less story content. Each opening reveals a baby involved in a neatly conveyed situation – 'Red balloon. All gone!' Minor domestic upsets are entertainingly depicted in *Oh, No!*, with this author's usual earthy realism.

Animal Friends

Wild Animals   both by Betty Paterson   (Little Mammoth paperback)
> Brilliantly coloured and exceptionally clear, these simple little books depict one animal per page. Informative as well as entertaining, for the youngest child.

**Aren't You Lucky?*   Catherine Anholt   (Bodley Head/Red Fox paperback)

**The Baby's Catalogue*   Janet and Allan Ahlberg   (Viking Kestrel/ Puffin paperback)

**Bathwater's Hot* (and *When We Went to the Park, Noisy, All Shapes and Sizes, Colours* and *Two Shoes, New Shoes*)   Shirley Hughes (Walker)

The Big Blue Truck (and *The Busy Orange Tractor, The Little Red Car, The Noisy Green Engine* and *The Strong Yellow Tug Boat*)   Rosalinda Knightley   (Walker)
> Appropriately called 'On the Move' board books, these are robust little volumes with a strong noise component: 'Hiss!

went the air. Slurp! went the oil.' One line of text only, at the foot of each page, bold colour, brisk and assertive little characters: formula for success.

*Bouncing
Giving   both by Shirley Hughes   (Walker)
Busy Monkey
Enormous Elephant
Roaring Lion
Tall, Tall Giraffe   all by Emily Bolam   (Orchard Books)
These are board books, but each, in five double spreads, tells a simple story. Brilliantly coloured, and shaped to follow the cover illustration, the books would be ideal to prop in a cot, or on the floor or window ledge – or to hand to a second-year baby to 'read' to herself.

*But Where is the Green Parrot? Thomas and Wanda Zacharias (Bodley Head/Pan, Piper)
*Cock-a-Doodle-Doo Franz Brandenberg, illus. Aliki (Bodley Head)
*Dad's Back (also *Messy Baby, Reading* and *Sleeping*)   Jan Ormerod (Walker/Walker paperback)
*Dr Seuss's ABC (Collins/Collins paperback)
*Doing the Washing (also *Coming to Tea, Doing the Garden, Going Shopping, Going Swimming, Going to Playschool* and *Having a Picnic*) Sarah Garland   (Bodley Head/Puffin paperback)
Each Peach Pear Plum Janet and Allan Ahlberg (Puffin paperback)
An 'I Spy' book in which the child is invited to find familiar nursery rhyme characters hiding in the deftly drawn and neatly framed illustrations.

> *Tom Thumb in the cupboard*
> *I spy Mother Hubbard*
> *Mother Hubbard down the cellar*
> *I spy Cinderella*

The interiors are meticulously drawn, the exterior scenes filled with the light of summer afternoons. Each left-hand page has not only text (framed, like the illustrations), but an engaging little picture-heading.
Farm Counting Book Jane Miller (Macmillan paperback)

This is a photographic picture book in which considerable care has been taken to keep backgrounds clear and uncluttered. The objects themselves, from 'one kitten to 'ten geese', with splendid red numerals supplied as well, are distinct and attractive. Bright yellow borders lend colour and clarity. (See Book List 4 for companion volume *Farm Alphabet Book* which is more complex in concept.)

Four Fierce Kittens   Joyce Dunbar, illus. Jakki Wood   (Orchard paperback)

A perennial theme, engagingly invoked. Mother cat is asleep on her mat, and her four babies go exploring. Each in turn challenges one of the other farm animals, but in the event can '. . . only go miaow, miaow' (and the pig went OINK OINK OINK!). In the end they jointly chase off the puppy with their hissing and spitting. ('We didn't know we could do THAT!') and go happily home. Peaceful farmyard scenes in gentle colour provide appropriate backgrounds for the ridiculously saucy kittens.

The House That Jack Built   illus. Emily Bolam   (Macmillan)

A singular version of the old cumulative tale which, we learn on the back cover, was first printed in 1775. (For how long before that it had been chanted, we will never know.) The artist in this case has abandoned the traditional Old English setting, and we have a hero who looks like a modern teenager in shorts and T-shirt, a house which looks like a Roman temple, and flat, brilliantly coloured pictures which might have been done by a (talented!) child. But it has charm, and the text has not been tampered with, and is well and clearly set. And the endpapers are dazzling!

**The House That Jack Built*   illus. William Stobbs   (Oxford)

How Many?   Fiona Pragoff   (Gollancz)

It is almost impossible not to exclaim aloud at the clarity and beauty of the photographs in this arresting, spiral-bound, wipe-clean little book. Successive double spreads range from one (solid, old-fashioned) key, to twenty (youthful, tanned) toes. Everyone will have their favourite. Mine are five pairs of vividly coloured, variously patterned socks for '10' and fifteen

round, square or triangular buttons, in a perfect, flat pyramid.
'17 teddybears' belie description (and would certainly be hard
to count – but who cares? Babies can't count anyway).

If I had a pig

If I had a sheep   Mick Inkpen   (Macmillan paperback)

I'm going for a walk! (and *Hallo! How are you?*, *How do I eat it?*, *How do I put it on?*, *I can build a house!* (all Red Fox paperbacks) *I can do it!*, *I'm having a bath with Papa!* *I'm the king of the Castle!*, *I'm playing with Papa!* (Puffin paperback) and *Ready, Steady, Go!* (Puffin paperback)   Shigeo Watanabe, illus. Yasuo Ohtomo   (Puffin paperback)

In Our House   Anne Rockwell   (Heinemann paperback)

> *This is my family –*
> *my mother, my father*
> *and me.*

Three cheerful bears embellish the first page. Their house and
its various rooms are shown on successive double spreads,
alternating with Scarry-like vistas of bear activity in kitchen,
living room, garage and bathroom. Finally, 'This is my very
own room. It is full of nice things.' And it is. Clear outline,
bright colour, easy identification.

Just Like Jasper   Nick Butterworth and Mick Inkpen   (Knight)
A cheerful little cat is on the way to the toy shop to spend his
birthday money. What will he buy? A succession of attractive
possibilities are pictured in bright primary colour against
white backgrounds: A car? A doll? A ball? His final choice – a
little cat, just like Jasper!' – will please everyone; and Jasper
himself is a joy.

The Kingfisher Nursery Treasury   Sally Emerson, illus. Moira and
Colin Maclean
This large, handsome book provides a wealth of resources for
reading aloud and playing games, and would enrich any
family's life. There are six sections: *Baby Games, Nursery Songs,
Dancing and Singing Games, A was an Apple Pie, Story Rhymes* and
Lullabies, and a well-laid-out index. The selection is admirably
balanced, and the colourful illustrations are expressive without
being intrusive. This is definitely a book for using with a child,

between babyhood and schooldays. (One can imagine fives
and sixes discovering with joy that they can *read it themselves*!)

The Little Car
The Little Plane
The Little Boat
The Little Train Sian Tucker (Orchard Books)
These are board books, and so will stand lots of unsupervised
use. Each has a simple one-line-to-a-page text, and glossy
pictures in primary colour. Each little vehicle goes out – and
comes home. The beginnings of a narrative!

Mummy Where Are You?
Daddy Will You Play With Me? both by Harriet Ziefert (Puffin
paperback)
My Cat Likes to Hide in Boxes Eve Sutton, illus. Lynley Dodd (Puffin
paperback)
A succession of jaunty couplets about the cats of the world,
with some elegant and understated illustration, make this a
successful modern rhyming book.

My Day Rod Campbell (Collins/Picture Lions paperback)
This simple 'naming' book devotes ten double spreads to
framed pictures of objects which very young children will
recognize. Each page is divided neatly into quarters, so that
eight objects are revealed at each opening. Ten categories are
covered, among them 'inside the house', 'going shopping' and
'at the park'. At each end of the book a toddler is shown
getting up, and going to bed. Treatment is representational
rather than imaginative, and colour is bright and clear.
Single-word captions may be indicated usefully by adult and,
later, child. Such a book has a place at rising-two, when most
children like playing the recognition game.

Nandy's Bedtime Errol Lloyd (Red Fox paperback)
The gentle account of a small West Indian child preparing for
bed – having a bath, listening to a story, playing with her
father. Softly coloured pictures are at one with the quiet text.

Nursery Rhymes
Who Does What?
Animals

Opposites   all *Peek-a-Book* titles by Eric Hill   (Puffin paperback)
   'Hickory dickory dock, what ran up the clock?' asks the text in
   Nursery Rhymes. Behind the flap lies the whole rhyme, with, of
   course, the scampering mouse herself. The other titles invoke
   the device according to their differing needs. Engaging little
   books for the 'Again!' brigade.
Oh Dear!   Rod Campbell   (Pan, Piper)
*101 Things to Do with a Baby   Jan Ormerod   (Viking/Puffin
paperback)
One Hungry Baby   Lucy Coats, illus. Sue Hellard   (Orchard paperback)
   A one-to-ten book with a significant difference. The cover
   shows one cheerful crocodile baby, bib-adorned, sitting on a
   cushion eating a sandwich. Within, at each opening, another
   animal baby (hippo, rabbit, panda, pig . . .) joins the fray,
   while the rhyming text proceeds:

> *Four bubbly bathtimes,*
> *To wash off the crumbs.*
> *Five sploshy splashers,*
> *Five wet Mums.*

   Second-year babies will love the jingle and the clear, bright
   pictures, and with help, spot the extra species on each page.
   Two-year-olds will do it alone.
1, 2, 3 to the Zoo   Eric Carle   (Hamish Hamilton/Puffin paperback)
*Over in the Meadow   Ezra Jack Keats   (Scholastic) Out of print.
Over in the Meadow   John Langstaff, illus. Feodor Rojankovsky
(World's Work) Out of print.
*Over in the Meadow   Olive A. Wadsworth, illus. Mary Maki Rae
(Puffin paperback)
A Peaceable Kingdom: The Shaker Abecedarius   illus. Alice and Martin
Provensen   (Viking Kestrel/Puffin paperback)
   'ALLIGATOR, Beetle, Porcupine, Whale,
   BOBOLINK, Panther, Dragonfly, Snail . . .' begins this old
   (1882) and very individual animal alphabet. By the time the
   whole irresistible cavalcade has been inspected, more than one
   hundred animals, birds and fish (everyday, exotic and imagi-

nary) have proceeded sedately across its wide, shallow pages. Dignified ladies, gentlemen and children, all clad in Shaker dress, reflect the sobriety and industry of this stern – but clearly not dull – sect. The illustrations, against a buff-coloured background which evokes parchment, are sheer delight. Warmth and good humour temper severity, and the details demand endless perusal.

A second-year baby, lucky enough to be introduced to this 'abecedarius' on parental knee, might well keep it in his head and heart for life.

**Teddybears 1 to 10*
*Teddybears ABC   both by Susanna Gretz   (A. & C. Black)
**The Troublesome Pig*   Priscilla Lamont   (Hamish Hamilton)
**This Little Baby's Morning*   (and seven other titles)   Ann Morris, illus. Lynn Breeze   (Orchard)
**Tom and Pippo's Day*   (and ten other titles)   Helen Oxenbury (Walker)
**The Trouble with Babies*   Angie Sage and Chris Sage   (Viking/ Puffin paperback)
**The Very Hungry Caterpillar*   Eric Carle   (Hamish Hamilton/Puffin paperback)
**Where's Spot?*   (and twelve other 'Lift the Flag' titles)   Eric Hill (Heinemann/Puffin paperback)

When I was Two . . .

4

When I was Two,
I was nearly new

One can imagine a six-year-old, in retrospect, feeling with A. A. Milne that two was indeed a 'nearly new' time of life.

In fact, two-year-olds have learned more in volume 'since birth than they will ever learn again in a similar period. And they are ready for life. They want to open every door, take the tops off *all* the bottles and press *all* the switches. Successful parents of two-year-olds are identifiable by the ease with which they connive and conspire: to get their two-year-olds into bed, out of the bath, on to the pot, away from the fire, into a jersey, out of the china cabinet . . . They develop a line of frenetically cheerful, non-stop patter which astounds and dismays their childless friends. It is of course aimed at diverting the young from occupations of their choice to occupations of their parents' choice. Just as naturally, the young resist diversion with vigour and outrage; there is nothing hypocritical about the noises *they* make during the exchange.

The average two-year-old is athletic, voluble and determined. She assesses herself totally unrealistically, and can see no point of view but her own. Other people's rights do not exist, and she has no feeling for the relative importance of different people, places and things. Your best course is to hold on with as much good cheer as you can while she grows a little; and a little growth at this stage takes her a long way. She will, when you have all but given up, start to co-operate occasionally, modify her 'crashing through the jungle' life-style, show signs of understanding the rudiments of cause and effect, and even be prepared to wait a little while you make her a sandwich.

I have purposely avoided description of her attractive qualities.

Parents are inclined to smile through clenched teeth when their two-year-old's friendliness, and her deceptive appearance of shining and beautiful innocence, are remarked upon by visitors (who are not staying long, and are known to be returning to peaceful, tastefully arranged houses where books and music and good food mingle in pleasing and orderly proportion . . .).

Can you believe that *books* may make all the difference?

What the two-year-old lacks (particularly the first child in the family) is colour in her life. What *can* a two-year-old do to satisfy her burgeoning need for experience – for finding out how things look, how they feel, how they can be manipulated – *except* explore the possibilities of her surroundings? Her apparently diabolical intentions are, in fact, innocent, and her outrage at our interference (*she* thinks!) justified.

Constant recourse to books has, at this stage, as many advantages for the parent as for the child.

To begin with, book sessions fill in time, and time hangs heavy for both custodian and child in the early days. Granted, the adult has plenty to do, especially in a busy domestic situation, but the deterrent of a resident two-year-old may make productive accomplishment impossible a great deal of the time anyway, unless some way is found to meet her obtrusive needs. And you may as well, if you are going to be interacting with her most of the time, make the interaction as pleasurable as possible from your own point of view, as well as from hers.

And two-year-old books are fun!

In our family, a habit of taking to the sofa with books and babies after breakfast ('in the middle of the muddle') seems to have carried on into the second generation. By the time those who are departing to school or work have actually left, a break is needed; the toddler has had to defer to the pressing needs of older family members and is ready for attention. Half an hour of her own with her mother and a pile of books will set the tone for the rest of the morning, and make the mother's work not only easier to face, but less interrupted once begun. If there is a baby in the family, it may prove possible to feed her while this session proceeds, thereby ensuring that *her* earliest memories are of the associated warmths of milk and story. And be sure to include a special 'baby' book for her, consulting the older child about its choice and suitability. *Feeling* like an older brother or sister can have a lot to do with *behaving* like one.

Don't worry about leaving the dishes, or any other chore undone at this point; nothing is more certain than that the dishes *will* be washed and the next meal prepared, whereas no certainty at all attaches to the inclusion of story-sessions unless they are placed firmly at the top of the list. I've never been able to understand people who doggedly do the so-called 'essential' things first. If you have undertaken to assume a housekeeping role, you must, before all else, capitalize on the advantages; you are, after all, saddled with the drawbacks. And the one advantage that you have over most of the working world is that you can plan your work to suit yourself. Train yourself to smile confidently at neighbours' and relations' surprise or disapproval; tell them, if you need explain yourself at all, that you would be ashamed to neglect your children whereas you don't feel emotionally involved with the breakfast dishes. You will get through as much work as they, in the end, and the profits of your good sense will be as obvious to your critics as to yourself. With any luck, some of them, at least, will join you.

A word about the classic notion of 'the bedtime story'. This is usually envisaged idealistically, even sentimentally: dreamy child and adoring parent locked in a situation of wonder and rapport, with lights low and the rustlings of night all around.

You may achieve this (if you have household help, no other children, take the phone off the hook, and decide to relate *only* to this child, regardless of your own and other people's emotional and social needs). More probably, bedtime will be a fairly hectic period, with other family members making demands, nerves a little frayed all round, the child himself overtired and crotchety. If books have featured prominently during the day, you will have no need to feel any guilt about deciding to omit bedtime stories from your repertoire, at least temporarily. Once the child is old enough to accept that a story in bed is sometimes, but not always, possible, all will be well; but two-year-olds are not like this.

Bedtime requires ritual – so be sure that you *can*, easily, perform the ritual every night before you institute it in an immutable form.

You might also, at this stage, consider looking about your neighbourhood, town, or city, for a book group to join. The name and nature of such groups vary (Books for Your Children Groups, Children's Literature Associations, and so on) but most of them are simply clubs whose members share an interest in books which their children might enjoy. Don't feel that you need to know about books already. All groups want, more than any other sort of member, young (or older) parents who *don't know*, and want to *find out* about books for their children. You will have something of worth to contribute by reason of your current dealings with a baby or small child. You are *really* 'in the field'! Even if you can't attend meetings, joining is worthwhile. All such groups send out material, accounts of meetings, lists of good books, and arrange the occasional address by authors and artists. The more solitary your life, the more you need to belong to organizations of people who, like yourself, are tied up with child care, and concerned about children's needs. Your local librarian should have information about such groups; or ask at the nearest school.

And so to books.

Between two and four the world opens up to the child. Whereas before this time her curiosity was confined to her actual surroundings, she now wants, increasingly, to go out into the world, to learn about everything, to become involved. She is able now to follow a simple story through a book, and involve herself with the characters. At two she will still love her 'old' books – repetition is going to be savoured for a long time yet – but will need new and different stories constantly.

Books like *Doing the Washing, How do I put it on?* and *Pippo Gets Lost* will have shown her that life goes on between the covers of a book. Now she is ready to advance into other situations, to hear about other people and things, likely and unlikely events.

With the growth of wider understanding, of course, many of the earlier books will assume new roles. Pleasure at the jingly rhythm and bright pictures of *The House That Jack Built* and *Brown Bear, Brown Bear, What Do You See?* will be increased, as more of the action is understood, and the people and objects 'tied up' with their counterparts in real life, or in other books.

Fortunately, there has been an increase in the publication of simple but sound stories for two- to three-year-olds in the last few years; but you may still find difficulty in obtaining such books in any quantity. Appropriate books for this age group are often not seen by those who must market them as potentially successful; publishers, constantly on the lookout for a new *Where the Wild Things Are* or *Dogger*, may need to be persuaded that an apparently mundane little book about events in the restricted daily life of a two-year-old is not only well conceived and executed, but also likely to sell. The form of this type of book is, certainly, a demanding one, requiring as it does the provision of characters who come alive in situations which are believable, and action which *happens* – all within the experience or imagination of a human being whose knowledge of the world and its ways is only just beginning to widen.

Some of the best books are old or middle-aged and may seem, to the adult who encounters them alongside the more glossy, colourful volumes of today, rather dull and dated. It is salutary to reflect that *Harry the Dirty Dog* by Gene Zion was published in 1956 and has been in print ever since. If one considers only colour and that indefinable 'modern' factor which seduces the eye before discernment intervenes, one is obliged to admit that Harry suffers by comparison. But look a little further: read *Harry the Dirty Dog* to a young child and you will recognize excellence.

Harry eclipses all dogs of fiction for the very young. The briskly related activities which transform him from a 'white dog with black spots' to a 'black dog with white spots' are rollicking in the extreme; this is how the small 'reader' would spend *his* day, given a temporary relaxation of adult supervision. Harry's 'family' is an anonymous group which exists only to support him, and provide a backdrop to his adventures.

Only Mr Gumpy has a name in the two books which celebrate his cheerful relationship with a large and irresponsible group of animals and humans (the pig, the rabbit, the boy, the girl). In the first title (*Mr Gumpy's Outing*) they all set out by water in Mr Gumpy's boat; in the second, *Mr Gumpy's Motor Car*, they are packed uncomfortably into a small ancient 'tourer'. In both books they all (the guests, that is) behave badly, with predictably catastrophic consequences, but all is well in the end ... Mr Gumpy's affability is unfailing. Both stories end with a joyful gathering of all the friends at Mr Gumpy's home.

I almost decided, in this third edition of *Babies Need Books*, to abandon mention of the work of one of my favourite author-artists the Frenchwoman Françoise Seignobosc (known always as 'Françoise' only.) Working in the middle years of this century, Françoise produced a handful of picture books which, travelling first to America and then to England, delighted a generation of children. Several have attained classic status, and should not be allowed to sink without trace.

The characters Jeanne-Marie and Jean-Pierre, Patapon the lamb and Madelon the duck certainly established their power to captivate the young, including my own children, in the fifties and sixties. An American expert, describing the pictures in *Jeanne-Marie Counts her Sheep*, said, 'they are as fresh and pretty as a garden of pink petunias', and one has to agree. But they have style too, and a sort of earthy frivolity which is not often seen among books at this level. The impact of the clear, colourful, doll-like figures against their white backgrounds is arresting and satisfying.

It is interesting to note that this particular title, *Jeanne-Marie Counts Her Sheep*, confused and upset our eldest child at first encounter when she was nearly three – an illustration of different children's diverse (and usually unexpected) reactions to the same book. Our later children had no such difficulty. Catherine was clearly enchanted by Jeanne-Marie's plans for the seven little lambs Patapon was expected to produce – they are shown on successive pages, in growing numbers. But predictably, the little sheep gives birth to only one lamb, and Catherine was not only mystified, but disturbed. 'What has happened to the other little lambs?' was never answered to her satisfaction at three, and we gave up. A year later, all was well. Catherine's daughter Nicola gave evidence of exactly this confusion, years later. At a little over three she told friends happily, 'Our new baby is inside Mummy, and we don't know if it is a boy or a girl. If it's a girl it will be Maria, and if it's a boy it will be Samuel.' In due course, Samuel appeared and we all assumed Nicola's total understanding. After all, she was both intelligent and well informed. One day several months later she looked at her mother with tragic eyes and asked 'Whatever happened to Maria?' Obviously, Nicki could manage alternatives *verbally*, but not *actually*.

Early difficulties of this sort are not consistent from child to child. Some (but certainly not all) children are confused by the depiction of only part of a person or object, and most prefer everything mentioned to be pictured, a near impossible undertaking once themes begin to expand. But it is surely reasonable to require authors and artists to give care to such matters; and quite shocking breaches are common. Sometimes the illustrations give the secret away and destroy the climax utterly. At other times pictures are blatantly incorrect, and show characters wearing the wrong clothes: shoes when the text has them barefooted, day clothes when pyjamas have been mentioned.

There is some evidence that with the growth of informed criticism, greater care is being given to these considerations. And yet the best of the old picture books – the ones which have endured – have always given meticulous care to the matching of text and illustration. (This factor is, of course, related to their endurance. I remember reading that Margaret Wise Brown, an inspired and abiding author, would change a word in her final text, if need be, to achieve union with her illustrator.)

Other problems are encountered as soon as we move into the realm of 'story'. How are we to know what will terrify and what amuse? We can't; each of us must find our own way through this maze, and none of us is likely to emerge without having turned into a wrong alley, and been obliged to back out hastily. Sometimes we can use our experiences to avoid later traps, but not always, and we run a risk in applying any rule too firmly. One of the greatest of these is that we will transfer our own trepidation to the child by our careful screening of situations and characters. Another is that we will become so assiduous in shielding the child from any situation which we suspect may frighten him, that his literary diet will become more and more insipid as the months roll by. And we cannot tell! I well remember one of my children always turning the page quickly to avoid listening to 'I had a Little Pony' (who was 'whipped' and 'slashed') and just as regularly shouting with delight when we reached 'Taffy was a Welshman' in which '. . . I took up the marrow bone and beat him on the head!' Clearly, for this child, violence against humans was less disturbing than violence against animals!

Another of our children, in the middle years of childhood, used to ask me to read *The Little Mermaid* aloud to her and then, half-way through, be so overcome that she would beg me to stop. By contrast, she showed nothing but gleeful enjoyment of ghosts, monsters, and the everyday violence which seems to invade the life of the modern child, regardless of parental vigilance. No conclusions have ever seemed possible in the light of such contradictory evidence.

Children between two and three are almost daily increasing their contact with the world and its fears, as well as its wonders. We cannot know how impression is building on impression to create the individual set of finely tuned reactions which will dictate their tolerance to events, people and circumstances. Certain simple precautions are sensible and easy to apply; beyond these, we must feel our way, using as guides our own sensitivity to the child's response and temperament.

Back to Françoise and Jeanne-Marie. *Springtime for Jeanne-Marie* has always been my favourite, and will surely return. *Springtime* is a prototype for all two-to-three-year-old tales; it embodies the age-old lost-and-found theme. Jeanne-Marie, her pet sheep Patapon and her white duck Madelon go to pick flowers. Madelon, heedless of her mistress's warning, swims away down the river and is lost. Jeanne-Marie and Patapon pursue the little duck, meeting a succession of people who cannot help – and then a boy, Jean-Pierre, who can, and does. All is heart-warmingly resolved, the errant Madelon discovered unrepentantly alive, and a new friend made.

There is a substantial but jaunty air about the characters in all
the Jeanne-Marie books. They give themselves over to unashamed
emotion. Their behaviour is wholehearted. They are never devious or undecided. The page-sized pictures have a lucid, almost
festive quality. They follow the action faithfully, and are beautifully complemented by the text, which is designed, rather than
merely placed on the page. First published in the 1950s, *Springtime
for Jeanne-Marie* demonstrates the power of certain books to
captivate, certain characters to take on immortal life. This book,
with its singular mixture of innocence and wisdom, joins *Harry the
Dirty Dog*, *Mr Gumpy's Outing*, *The Tale of Peter Rabbit* and *The
Elephant and the Bad Baby* at the top of the list. Each serves to
demonstrate the rareness of the talent that can speak in real
terms to this age group.

The under-threes like their characters to be consistent and
dependable; and Jeanne-Marie, Harry and Mr Gumpy demonstrate these qualities to perfection. One knows, when the next
title is opened, that Harry will embark upon another adventure
in which his own energetic pigheadedness will lead him into
trouble, Mr Gumpy will yet again allow his good nature to
complicate his life and banish his comfort and Jeanne-Marie will
once more plunge into some innocent and joyful celebration
which, while its consequences may temporarily dismay her, will
always renew her faith in life and its goodness in the end.

This is how stories for the under-threes should be; they should
move smoothly in a steady direction to a predictable outcome.
The best of them will contrive to achieve a sort of virtuosity
which has the adult exclaiming, 'Yes. Just right,' to himself, the
child listening and looking with that intent absorption which is
reserved for the rare and superlative experience.

For this is what contact with a fine book can give to a very
young child. Through it, he can experience the capacity of good
English words to evoke emotion, to create place, and to usher the
reader into that place. If this experience is offered him as a
normal human right in childhood, he will expect repetition of it
to the end of his life, and make sure that it is always available. In
other words, he will become a reader.

Illustration interacts with text to produce this effect, of course, but it is the story and its telling on which the book stands or falls. Make no mistake about this. An adult may open a picture book at random and be so carried away by the quality of its illustrations that he must borrow or buy it; but it is the story that will captivate the child or leave him cold. All too often the language of picture books seems to exist for the sole purpose of justifying the binding together of a series of impressive pictures. This may be well worth doing; but why try to disguise the resulting product as a children's book? At its best, the picture book demonstrates the capacity of illustration to support and extend language, and of language to interpret illustration. It is easy to imagine that this will be achieved more commonly when author and artist are one and the same, but this is not necessarily so. Many fine artists, no doubt under the delusion that the short, simple texts they have been asked to illustrate must be easy to produce, have tried writing their own texts and failed. A master hand on both is needed, and producers of outstanding texts for the two- to three-year-old seem to be in shorter supply than able and sensitive artists.

When one person possesses a combination of talents, of course, heights are sometimes reached. This is the case with John Burningham's Mr Gumpy, and Judith Kerr's superb story *The Tiger Who Came to Tea*. Here, picture and text seem to, and indeed have, sprung from the one source. Near perfection of form is embellished by clear and expressive illustrations. The pace is exactly right, the resolution totally satisfying.

Sophie and her mother are having tea when there is a knock at the door. Sophie answers it, and admits a 'big, furry, stripy tiger', who plainly (but cheerfully) intends to join in their meal. Sophie is enchanted and her mother admirably calm as the tiger eats his way steadily through all the food on the table and, ultimately, all the food in the house. Her mother evinces growing dismay as excess piles upon excess, but Sophie remains enchanted. In the end, the tiger departs, Daddy comes home, and there is nothing else for it; they must go out to a café. This they do, Sophie consuming a marvellous meal of 'sausages and chips and ice cream'. How better could we leave her?

Pat Hutchins is an author-artist who has produced an impressive number of picture books in little more than a decade. Her work is *for* children, in the best possible way. Text and illustration are mutually supportive, language simple and expressive, pictures a celebration of clarity and colour.

Rosie's Walk has already become a classic. In twelve double spreads, two single pages and thirty-two words, it describes Rosie the hen's sober and purposeful journey through the farmyard '. . . across the yard . . . around the pond . . . over the haycock . . . past the mill . . .' At each point she is almost, but not quite, overtaken by a fox who is hungrily pursuing her. He, poor animal, is himself overtaken by a series of related catastrophes, unmentioned in the text, but documented in the illustrations (he lunges at Rosie, misses, and lands in the pond, the haycock collapses on top of him, a bag of flour from the mill engulfs him . . .). Rosie stomps stolidly on, unseeing.

For fun, read *Rosie* to your two-year-old without mentioning the fox. It is, after all, a straightforward story. Repeat the performance at regular intervals (or as asked), and note the age at which he does notice the predatory fox and his ill-starred antics. You may be surprised, one way or the other!

The Wind Blew won the Kate Greenaway Medal for the year of its publication. For the young child, it is pure joy. Wide landscape pictures reveal, as the pages are turned, a growing succession of people pursuing their escaping possessions – all wrenched from their hands by the boisterous wind.

> *It plucked a hanky from a nose,*
> *And up and up and up it rose.*

The last few openings show a mad mixture of jostling people and flying paraphernalia, all of which is suddenly abandoned by the capricious gale. An even more muddled mix-up naturally results. Two- and three-year-olds will love finding and matching people and possessions in these vigorous and detailed pictures.

Good-Night, Owl! is even simpler, and is bound to succeed. It uses 'noise' words and the repetition so loved by the young, and has illustrations of extraordinary impact.

> *The woodpecker pecked, rat-a-tat! rat-a-tat!*
> *and Owl tried to sleep.*
>
> *The cuckoo called, cuckoo cuckoo,*
> *and Owl tried to sleep.*

Predictably, Owl, who likes to stay awake at night, finds the perfect way to retaliate . . .

Pat Hutchins speaks directly to small children. Her themes recognize their concerns, the limits of their understanding, their natural taste in humour. That her individual art style works so well to support and extend her stories is every child's good fortune.

Beatrix Potter's *The Tale of Peter Rabbit* naturally serves as the prototype for author-artist picture books. Peter is firmly instructed *not* to go into Mr McGregor's garden, does so, is pursued, almost caught, escapes without his 'blue jacket with brass buttons' and reaches the sanctuary of home – to incur his mother's disapproval and the punishment of no supper, and bed, with camomile tea. There is a breathlessness about Peter's adventures that is not often matched; certainly, no tangents or sub-plots interfere with its course and the tiny, now classic illustrations are a new delight and wonder to successive generations of children.

The 'well-read' two-and-a-half-year-old will be ready for this and several other Potter stories – and *Appley Dapply's Nursery Rhymes* is not to be missed at this stage, if not already known. This is a small gem of a book and can be read in three minutes: three minutes of enchantment. Could any three couplets, with facing illustrations, tell a more complete story than this?

> *Now who is this knocking*
> *at Cottontail's door?*
> *Tap tappit! Tap tappit!*
> *She's heard it before?*
>
> *And when she peeps out*
> *there is nobody there,*
> *But a present of carrots*
> *put down on the stair.*

> *Hark! I hear it again!*
> *Tap, tap, tappit! Tap tappit!*
> *Why – I really believe it's a*
> *little black rabbit!*

A word of caution about the indiscriminate use of Beatrix Potter at this time. There is a very wide language and interest range among the stories, and some of them have complex and sophisticated themes. *The Story of a Fierce Bad Rabbit* is certainly the shortest of the stories proper, but somehow lacks the cosy detail of the other tales. Before three-and-a-half, I would use only *Jeremy Fisher*, *Tom Kitten* and *Miss Moppet*, in addition to *Peter Rabbit* and *Appley Dapply* – and *Cecily Parsley's Nursery Rhymes*, which, while less distinguished in content, has the usual pictures. But do use them! Don't risk overlooking their capacity to captivate, and the opportunity they offer to familiarize the small child's ear with precise, Victorian-parlour language ('I am affronted,' said Mrs Tabitha Twitchit.). As an antidote to the banalities of television utterance, Beatrix Potter's easily available little books should not go unused.

Repetition is a never-fail ingredient in stories for this age group, and Eve Rice's book *Sam Who Never Forgets* is classic in its progression. Sam, the zookeeper, loads his wagon and feeds bananas to the monkeys, fish to the seals, oats to the zebra . . . and then induces anxiety in the elephant's breast by departing. But all is well – he has merely gone off to re-load his wagon with golden hay because '. . . you do eat *such* a lot – so I've brought you a wagon all your own'. Sighs of satisfaction from the elephant and two-year-old listener-looker! Eve Rice demonstrates in this simple story her own familiarity with this age group and its still tentative grasp of reality. Over-cleverness, and ignorance of the concerns and limitations of young children are the twin banes of picture books for the rising threes. Custodial figures, whether parents or zookeepers, should be reliable, supportive and accepting.

I feel that a word of caution is appropriate at this point. The modern conviction that the first few years of life are of prime importance for intellectual development sometimes produces a 'teaching' note in books for two-year-olds. Somehow, learning has become confused with fact-gathering. 'Let's teach the children the difference between up and down, black and white, fast and slow,' many over-earnest educators seem now to be saying. And so we have a dreary progression of series called 'Learning about . . .' or 'What Do I See?' or 'How Does it Feel?'

I have never had any patience with these books; most of them are as dull as they are demeaning. They may have some usefulness for school beginners whose language development has been inhibited by their backgrounds, but even here, the superior claims of simple, spirited stories to inform and inspire can be, and have been, demonstrated. And surely, the meaning that emerges from words used in context, and the lift that comes from language which in itself has life, colour and novelty, is what such children always need? I would give them only such language – beginning with nursery rhymes and jingles and proceeding by way of *The Owl and the Pussy-cat* to *Where the Wild Things Are*. To activate the brain, prod the emotions and stir the imagination every time!

Fortunately, some of the most inspired and able illustrators continue to give attention to the old rhymes and jingles. Penny Dale has used the repetitious counting game of my distant childhood to produce a picture book which two-year-olds – and their elders – will love: *Ten in the Bed*.

> *There were ten in the bed and the little one said 'Roll over, roll over!'*
> *They all rolled over and one fell out . . . there were nine in the bed . . .*

Here, the 'ten' consist of the obligatory 'little one' (a typically irresponsible two-year-old) and nine stuffed toys who do not take their one-by-one ejection from the bed lying down. Each glorious double spread shows one of their number falling (or being thrown) out, to join a riotous game with the other exiles. Unfortunately, the 'little one' is devastated – 'I'm cold! I miss you!' – and they all come back, and are soon, predictably, 'fast asleep'. An utterly satisfying outcome for an engrossing tale, which combines wonderful domestic chaos with warmth and humour; and the pictures are beautiful. For good measure Penny Dale has followed the first book with a second: *Ten Out of Bed*, which, unlike many sequels, achieves the same standard and flavour of the original and yet is different enough to hold the interest.

> *There were ten out of bed and the little one said*
> *'Let's play!'*

In turn, the cheerful band invent expansive games of trains, seasides, theatres, pirates, dancing, ghosts, flying, camping and monsters, the company diminishing steadily as exhaustion sets in and yet another to character returns to bed. In the end . . .

> *'There was one out of bed and the little one said*
> *'I'm sleepy now!'*

The final double spread with ten in the bed, all sound asleep, is a joy.

Hairy Maclary from Donaldson's Dairy succeeds before the cover is ever raised. In fact, the title itself will be repeated with relish, even if incorrectly, by the nearly three-year-old whose ear for the satisfactions of language is developing fast. A quite singular list of friends accompanies Hairy Maclary on his walk into town:

> *Schnitzel von Krumm*
> *with a very low tum,*
> *Bitzer Maloney*
> *all skinny and bony,*
> *Muffin Mclay*
> *like a bundle of hay,*
> *Bottomley Potts,*
> *covered in spots,*
> *Hercules Morse*
> *as big as a horse . . .*

All prove to be equally fainthearted when confronted by

> *SCARFACE CLAW*
> *the toughest Tom*
> *in town . . .*

with a verbal outcome which scatters the cowardly band and delights the small listener. Lynley Dodd has followed the original title with no fewer than five more, all featuring the chequered canine band. Several explore situations which two-year-olds will not totally comprehend, but this will not matter; the language gives an almost physical pleasure:

> *There were miserable dogs,*
> *cantankerous cats,*
> *a rabbit with pimples*
> *and rickety rats . . .*

and will go on doing so throughout early childhood. The simplest are, certainly, the first three: *Hairy Maclary from Donaldson's Dairy*, *Hairy Maclary's Bone* and *Hairy Maclary Scattercat*. I have included the subsequent titles in List 4, where they are joined by a pair of titles about a rascally cat who features in the earlier books: Slinky Malinky!

This is the Bear is a phenomenon that those readers who develop keen discrimination will come to recognize: an outstanding title which rears its head up from an 'easy reading' series which, while competently written and illustrated, is otherwise unexceptional. There is nothing unexceptional about *This is the Bear*. It has in full measure that quality of virtuosity which marks it out for success provided it is identified, asked for individually, and manages, itself, to escape the bonds of its series origin. Of course, it fulfils its role as a 'beginning reader' beautifully; and Helen Craig's sensitive and expressive pictures complement Sarah Hayes' terse and yet eloquent text precisely. But it is more than a 'reader'. The story is irresistible. 'The bear' — helpless in his plump, inanimate bearness — is pushed into the rubbish bin by 'the dog' — well-meaning but brainless — and ultimately rescued from the dump by 'the boy' who is resourceful, courageous and determined, in the best tradition of devoted bear-owners. All this is revealed in less than two hundred simple words, which, with the illustrations (in which 'asides' to the action appear in small balloons) contrive to create a tale in which drama, humour and pathos are nicely mixed.

No one needs to apologize for writing yet another book about bears; the category is so well established that it demands – and fortunately receives – a constant supplementary flow of new titles. And anyone needing a new 'bear' idea, might well tap Niki Yektai's *Bears in Pairs* which starts, innocently enough, with pictures of 'Black bear, Brown bear, Up bear, Down bear' and proceeds to a total of forty-nine assorted characters of diverse appearance and predilection. On twelve double spreads they appear, four to a double spread and then can be seen, over two subsequent openings, trailing in a throng to 'Mary's tea party' – Mary's existence, heretofore, being quite unsuspected. And yes, on the very last double spread – a magnificent prospect – you can count, if you *can* count – fifty-one invited bears (you probably missed the delectable dancing pair on the title page) as well as two obviously in-house fellows on Mary's bookshelf. The illustrator, Diane de Groat, has continued to keep every single bear so clearly visible that you can find him or her easily and check that your favourite was not missed. Unbelievably, the formula has worked for a second book, *Hi Bears, Bye Bears*. This time a different but just as diverse row is struggling back on to the toyshop shelves because 'Sam is coming!' to choose one to buy. Rhyme and rhythm again . . . the never-fail recipe for two-year-olds.

Between two and three many children become fascinated by things that move – particularly large things that make a lot of noise. And if the large, noisy thing happens to be bright red, and equipped with personnel wearing shiny helmets . . . ! *Fire Engines*, by Anne Rockwell, provides very simple details about the operation of the dazzling monster, and presents extraordinarily clear pictures which spread across each wide opening. That the firefighters happen to be brisk, spotted dogs adds a jovial note, and the text is minimal, and precise: 'Hoses spray the water on fires.'

As I noted in my introduction, this is not a book about non-fiction for children; but Rockwell's well-aimed expositions of 'things that move' give free rein to imagination in this wide-eyed age group. Several other key titles are mentioned in Book List 2 (page 57).

The books I have described in this chapter are a varied collection: some sparkling, some quietly glowing, all inspiring or useful in their own way. One cannot possibly exaggerate the learning, of all kinds, which will proceed from their constant use with children between two and three – or older, for many of them will become staples. Those adults who are concerned to educate the very young may safely relax, if their children come to live with such books; to pore over them alone, and to hear them read aloud often. Information slips unnoticed into the mind, from such contact: varieties of people and places, shades of reaction to emergency, effects produced by action, new ways of looking at things, and people, new adjectives – their meanings self-apparent in context – all are encountered and absorbed when mind and senses are engaged in the fascinating game of story.

And this is real learning – learning that beds down and stays, because it happens joyfully, with nothing of duty associated. Anything missed the first time will be absorbed at second or third exposure as the young reader-listener grows in maturity: the best way to learn.

As her third birthday approaches, the world is opening up to the delectation and delight of the well-endowed child. She is less imprisoned by her own emotional responses than in the past. Increasingly, she is able to defer immediate gratification of her wishes; she starts to see that some things must be done before others can happen. She is on the way to becoming a reasonable being, and this factor will influence the sort of stories and books which she needs.

As children's spoken and understood language burgeons they enter a period which, for parents who themselves love books, is the best time of all for story sharing. Some of the best picture books of all time have been produced for the child over three. There is enchantment ahead.

Book List 3

Books to Use between Two and Three

Earlier books will still be in constant use, and some two-year-olds
will be reaching forward into the next list.

Ahhh! said Stork Gerald Rose   (Macmillan paperback)
Stork finds an egg and plans to eat it. However, he can't break
the shell, so the other animals join in. Simple, brilliantly coloured
pictures show how 'Hippopotamus rolled on it' ... 'Lion bit
it' ... A surprise awaits them all. Economy of text, exact
portrayal of action in illustration.

Alexander's Outing Pamela Allen   (Hodder and Stoughton)
Alexander, one of a clutch of ducklings produced by a somewhat irresponsible mother, falls down a deep narrow hole.
Getting him out requires ingenuity, but is accomplished in
style by a resolutely helpful group of bystanders. Alexander's
mother takes her brood home again ... 'Quack! Quack!
Quack!' Ducks, like bears, never fail. The illustrations typify
this author-artist's spare, expressive style, and in fact, tell the
story precisely.

Alfie's Feet Shirley Hughes   (Bodley Head/Red Fox paperback)
This is the youngest Alfie book; and Alfie will become a friend,
once met. Here, new gumboots are coveted, acquired, and
worn to the park, a resigned but good-natured Dad in attend-
ance. Alfie has fun stomping in puddles ... but something
seems to be wrong with the boots. Dad helps him change feet,
and all is well. Nothing to it, really – but near three-year-olds
identify rapturously. There is wry humour for the adults, too,
in scenes of baby-and-toddler-encumbered mealtimes and
shopping trips, with this author-artist's genius for invoking
the messy cheerfulness which is all most of us can aspire to

in the circumstances. Alfie and Annie Rose, with their likeable if unremarkable Mum and Dad are here to stay, I predict. (Further 'Alfies' in Book Lists 4 and 5 on pages 115, 118 and 197.)

The Animal Fair   Jill Bennett, illus. Susie Jenkin-Pearce   (Puffin paperback)

This collection of animal verses will do as well for three-to-sixes, but has a cheerful jauntiness which brings it into two-year-old country – and the pictures have a vivacity of their own.

*Appley Dapply's Nursery Rhymes   Beatrix Potter   (Warne)

Other recommended titles by Beatrix Potter: **Cecily Parsley's Nursery Rhymes*, **The Story of Miss Moppet*, **The Tale of Mr Jeremy Fisher*, **The Tale of Peter Rabbit*, **The Tale of Tom Kitten*.

Are You There, Bear?   Ron Maris   (Julia MacRae/Puffin paperback)

A circle of light from the torch shown on the title-page illuminates a succession of places in a bedroom where Bear *might* be hiding. Before he is finally unearthed, other toys – Donkey, Little Doll, Jack-in-the-Box – are revealed in likely spots, with the family dog curled up in an armchair. Two-to-threes love torches, and might explore their own dark bedroom, with help. The toys are engaging, the device successful. (See also companion volume, *My Book*, below, in which the same bedroom is revealed, with resident bear, donkey, the familiar cupboard, and the family dog. Joseph, nearly three, and I, searched for the cat from this title, unsuccessfully, in *Are You There, Bear?* Then: 'She's outside on the wall – remember?' said Joe. Obviously the scenario had come to life as intended, for one small listener-viewer.)

*Bears in Pairs

*Hi Bears, Bye Bears   both by Niki Yektai, illus. Diane de Groat   (Puffin paperback)

Big Wheels   Anne Rockwell   (Hamish Hamilton Puffin paperback)

The perfect book for the two- to three-year-old who is impressed by large working vehicles but dazzled by too many details. Front-end loaders, dump trucks, bulldozers and cement mixers are brilliantly and simply pictured. Colours are primary, text minimal. 'Big wheels are good. They help us every day.'

Bye Bye Baby   Janet and Allan Ahlberg   (Little Mammoth paperback)

This is a wild spoof of a book which had some over-earnest souls frowning in a doubtful way when it first appeared. It's about a baby '. . . who had no mummy. This baby lived in a little house all by himself. He fed himself and bathed himself. He even changed his own nappy.' And there he is, accomplishing all these acts of essential baby care with panache (the nappy change is delectable). Understandably, he tires of all this responsibility: 'I am too young to be doing this . . .' and sets out, purposefully, to find a mummy. In turn, he asks a cat, a teddy, a clockwork hen and 'an old uncle.' Will you be my mummy?' Predictably, they all refuse. Instead, they offer their help in finding him a mummy – a feat which is accomplished accidentally and improbably, and is ultimately extended to the finding of a daddy too, so that they all, including the old uncle, settle down and live happily ever after. Everyone in this delicious book is solemnly dedicated to the task in hand. There is no behind-adult-hand humour – and the whole thing continues to be as heartwarming as it is unlikely. Janet Ahlberg's pictures are unpretentiously eloquent.

Cars   Anne Rockwell   (Puffin paperback)

Clear colourful pictures of cars old and new, big and small, 'on six-lane motorways and on dusty country roads . . .' provide compulsive viewing for very young motor enthusiasts. The brief text seems mundane, but actually covers the material well. Several other titles (*Planes, Trains, Boats*) by the same author-artist are equally attractive.

Catch it if you can   Brian Thompson, illus. Susie Jenkin-Pearce   (Puffin paperback)

Short enough to read to a good listener at a sitting, but useful to pick-and-choose from if you have a more active two-year-old (or less time for a reading session), this is a jaunty, highly approachable collection of 'nursery' verses. The pictures are clear, colourful and vigorous.

Come Back Kittens
Come Back Puppies   both by Jan Ormerod   (Walker)

The texts of these delectable, squarish books are almost identical. In the first, a pair of cats – one black, one white – ask, at
the first opening, 'Where are all our kittens?' Most subsequent
double spreads are interleaved with stiff strong see-through
pages which have one or more kittens painted on them. This
device allows the kittens to be seen first against a background
of gardens of various sorts, and then, as the page is flipped,
restored to their parents. At the end, all are together, 'warm
and safe and dry'. *Puppies* differs only in provision of parents,
only one dog recalling her straying young. The pictures have a
collage air about them; the colours are flat, rich and clear to a
point of sparseness. The device may seem slightly gimmicky at
first, but is simple and easily operated. Small children will be
fascinated by their own power to keep moving the enchanting
little animals about!

Dear Zoo   Rod Campbell   (Puffin paperback)
The Elephant and the Bad Baby   Elfrida Vipont, illus. Raymond
Briggs   (Hamish Hamilton/Puffin paperback)

This picture book has all the factors most likely to succeed
with very young children: a racy text which calls for 'performance', an engaging and ever-enlarging list of characters, repetition, and two central figures who are bound to appeal. For
good measure, it has Raymond Briggs's spirited illustrations,
and a repeated jingle which will pass into the language:

'and they went rumpeta, rumpeta, rumpeta, all down the road.'

Fancy That!   Pamela Allen   (Puffin paperback)

Countless hens through literary history must have sat hopefully
on clutches of eggs, and rejoiced when 'six fluffy yellow chicks'
emerged. Here, the little red hen is watched throughout by
three rather disbelieving white leghorns, who are, in the event,
just as thrilled with the outcome as she is. Pamela Allen has
characteristically given her framed, spirited pictures a sparkling white background. This is a perfect book for the two-year-
old, with plenty of visual noise. The triumphant chorus of

'took took took took . . .' fills the final page in letters of brilliant red.

Fire Engines Anne Rockwell   (Puffin paperback)
Garage
House
Tools
Wheels all by Venice Shone   (Orchard paperback)

These are exceptionally clear 'word' books which positively invite perusal and discussion. Backgrounds are white, colours bright but not gaudy, and most of the objects will be easily recognized. (With a little parental encouragement, two-year-olds will spend increasing periods gazing at books alone. Even at this early stage, personal interests emerge; Alexander, a friend's very well-read-to two-year-old, is currently gripped by *Garage*!)

Good Days, Bad Days Catherine Anhott   (Orchard paperback)

'In our family we have good days and bad days, happy days, sad days . . .' Wide vistas in the artist's characteristic gentle style, her squat, energetic little people engaged in domestic and outdoor activities of every sort. Two-year-olds will love it, but threes and fours still find fresh details to savour.

Good-Night, Owl! Pat Hutchins   (Bodley Head/Puffin paperback)
Hairy Maclary from Donaldson's Dairy (also *Hairy Maclary Scattercat, Hairy Maclary's Bone*) Lynley Dodd   (Spindlewood/Puffin paperback)
Harry the Dirty Dog Gene Zion, illus. Margaret Bloy Graham (Julia MacRae Books/Red Fox paperback)
I Like Books Anthony Browne   (Walker Books)

Surely the simplest – and probably the most persuasive – celebration of books ever written. 'I like books,' says an engaging, overalled monkey-child on the first page. 'Funny books . . . and scary books. Fairy tales . . . and nursery rhymes'. One book type per page with framed picture of appropriately garbed and equipped monkey-child. Browne's gorillas, large and small, are eloquent. This book should be owned, and read aloud often, as propaganda for the cause.

Jack's Basket Alison Catley   (Red Fox paperback)

In this exquisitely illustrated book we follow Jack from birth until six. In particular, we follow the diverse uses to which the basket he slept in as a newborn baby is put through the years; a place for Mum's knitting, a boat or a car for Jack and his sister to play in, a hamper for a family picnic . . . Finally worn out and confined to the back shed, the basket becomes home to a family of mice. This is a true parent and child book. Nostalgic but not sentimental, the illustrations reflect the passing of time in evocative full-page realistic depiction of children, toys and seasons. The short rhyming text is in parts faintly stilted, but adequately supports the lovely pictures.

*Jeanne-Marie Counts Her Sheep
*Springtime for Jeanne-Marie   both by Françoise   (Hodder and Stoughton)
Katie and the Smallest Bear   Ruth McCarthy, illus. Emilie Boon (Corgi paperback)
Little Pink Pig   Pat Hutchins   (Julia MacRae Books)

Little Pink Pig's mother is doing her best to get him to bed, and he is doing his (innovative) best to follow her through the farmyard – but things keep happening to him. One by one, the other animals are invoked to help in the search, and in the end, all seems to be (well, almost) well, but . . . My three-year-old listener quickly got the idea and followed the enterprising little fellow's antics with enthusiasm. Pat Hutchins's pictures have total clarity, and shine with summer sun. A lovely book.

Lucy & Tom's Day   Shirley Hughes   (Puffin paperback)

This is the 'youngest' of the well-known 'Lucy & Tom' books, and features an energetic little girl of about three, and her typically cherubic if irresponsible little brother of eighteen months or so. Their activities throughout the day are those of many small children: they 'help' Mum with the housework, go shopping, and create predictable domestic confusion with the greatest good cheer. Their world is seen from knee height in discerning detail by this observant and understanding author-artist. (See also Book List 4, page 115.)

Me and My Cat
Me and My Dog   both by Maureen Galvani   (Puffin paperback)

These twin titles make engrossing listening for two-year-olds, but will still interest older youngsters. (In fact, either would make an excellent 'early read' for a school starter.) In one, a little girl has the sort of fun with an energetic dog which most of us have endured (if we have both children and dogs), and in the other, a small boy describes his life with his cat. The sunny pictures show only what is described, but do this completely, against a white background.

* *Mr Gumpy's Motor Car*
* *Mr Gumpy's Outing*   both by John Burningham   (Cape/Puffin paperback)
Mrs Mopple's Washing Line   Anita Hewett, illus. Robert Broomfield (Bodley Head)

A line of neatly hung washing rearranges itself entertainingly when a brisk breeze has fun. Pictures of a chicken wearing a muffler and a pig clad in a petticoat are genuinely funny. Simple text, bright colour.

My Book   Ron Maris   (Puffin paperback).

An engaging half-page device allows a small child to explore and re-explore the resources of this simple, but well-designed book – a companion to *Are You There, Bear?* (above). These excellent books should be used in combination; the overlap encourages much satisfying search and discovery.

My Old Teddy   Don Mansell   (Walker Books)

Simple, repetitive, heart-warming. 'My old teddy's leg came off. Poor old Teddy!' The 'Teddy doctor' (alias Mum) is profitably invoked – as she is when Teddy's arm comes off, then his leg ... Cheerful expressive pictures enhance the certain-to-succeed text.

My Presents   Rod Campbell   (Campbell Books)

The classic flap book, on a popular theme: birthday party, with presents. Eight separate presents under parcel-shaped flaps are revealed in eight double spreads, with minimal text on the facing page ('John gave me ...'). A brief, two-line description beneath the flap gives slightly increased wordiness, and the book is stoutly constructed.

No, No, Charlie Rascal!   Lorna Kent   (Hamish Hamilton)

Charlie Rascal is a deliciously badly-behaved cat. His misdeeds are first suspected – through a round peephole in every second right-hand page – and then revealed in all their glory when the page is turned. Brilliantly coloured pictures and jaunty, rhyming text compliment the theme admirably, for the two-to-threes.

Now We Can Go   Ann Jonas   (Walker paperback)

Bright primary colours and clear, large text (thirty-three words in all) are used to show a small child, who might be either girl or boy, packing for a trip. On the first page we see a full toy box. By the time the youngster says 'Now we can go!' the entire contents have been transferred to a large bag, ready for departure. The endpapers show a wonderful mixture of toys against a white background, encouraging the child to point and identify – and enjoy.

Peace at Last   Jill Murphy   (Macmillan/Macmillan paperback)

This story has in full measure those essential but hard-to-find qualities which make an enduring book: characters who appeal immediately, action which is believable – however singular – and a satisfying resolution. In this case, the pictures clinch the deal; they depict a family of robust, good-humoured bears against agreeable indoor and outdoor backdrops in warm colour and clear outline. This is a book for all children – and will evoke a rumble of sympathy from over-tired *human* parents.

Quacky quack-quack!   Ian Whybrow, illus. Russell Ayto   (Walker/ Walker paperback)

A mad romp of a book with wonderful opportunity for joining in the rumpus as a baby who is supposed to find the ducks instead starts to eat the bread himself. Not only the ducks, but animals far and wide protest at this outrage; only the intervention of the baby's big brother restores calm. The pictures bring a younger John Burningham to mind, but have their own charm and vigour as well. An excellent book.

Quentin Blake's Nursery Rhyme Book   (Cape/paperback)

Seventeen less-well-known – but all-appealing – nursery rhymes, all but two occupying one whole double spread apiece, each illustrated in Quentin Blake's inimitable style (Little Jumping Joan is here given immortality). An extra to the conventional, comprehensive collections – but to be sought out this year, for its whacky fun.

*Rosie's Walk   Pat Hutchins   (Bodley Head/Puffin paperback)

Sally Anne Lambert's I Spy ABC   Sally Anne Lambert   (Macmillan)
This is a beautiful book, unusual in its muted colours and exquisite design. The artist's fondness for misty greens and purples is evident in her frames and backgrounds; animals, and occasional humans, busy themselves in occupations around – and sometimes through – large, upper case letters in the centre of each page. Readers are invited, in a foreword, to find more objects beginning with the relevant letter on each page, and a list is given in the back. The smallest children will certainly not concern themselves with this factor – but they will enjoy the book's gentle, rather old-fashioned elegance.

*Sam Who Never Forgets   Eve Rice   (Red Fox paperback)

Teddy Bear Coalman

Teddy Bear Baker

Teddy Bear Postman   all by Phoebe and Selby Worthington   (also Teddy Bear Boatman, Teddy Bear Farmer and Teddy Bear Gardener, all by Phoebe and Joan Worthington)   (Puffin paperback)
This appealing little bear-in-child's-clothing (engaging in grown-up occupations) first appeared on the literary scene almost fifty years ago. His appeal is perennial in all his guises; he is cheerful, industrious and quite without pretension. A day in his life makes fascinating listening and viewing, especially when accompanied by illustrations which are bright, detailed and colourful.

*Ten in the Bed   Penny Dale   (Walker/Walker paperback)

*This is the Bear   Sarah Hayes, illus. Helen Craig   (Walker/ Walker paperback)

*The Tiger Who Came to Tea   Judith Kerr   (Harper Collins/Picture Lions paperback)

Tractors (and Diggers and Special Engines)   Paul Strickland   (Ragged Bears)
Large vehicles – whether designed to dig, carry, move or

rescue – are perennially seen as dramatic by young children. These competent, square, brightly illustrated little books present their subject matter graphically, and with a fair degree of accuracy. The text in each case makes little demand, contenting itself with a simple statement on each page, unconnected with what has gone before. Once acquired, the books will be used and enjoyed for several years.

The Very Busy Spider Eric Carle   (Hamish Hamilton)

A simple, repetitive story, with an unusual feature: the 'silky thread' which this persistent spider uses to spin her web is raised from the page, so that small fingers can actually feel and trace it. On successive left-hand pages different farmyard animals suggest that the spider join them. '"Oink! Oink!" grunted the pig. "Want to roll in the mud?"' The industrious spider does not answer; and between the chosen fence posts, her web grows and grows. Eric Carle's illustrations are, as ever, brilliantly coloured and well-designed. This is a satisfying book, certain to engage the attention of the two-year-old, who loves to touch as well as look and listen.

Walk Rabbit Walk Colin McNaughton and Elizabeth Attenborough, illus. Colin McNaughton   (Heinemann/Little Mammoth)

Rabbit, Fox, Bear, Cat, Pig and Donkey are all invited to Eagle's party, but only Rabbit decides to walk. The others, in various vehicles, suffer successive accidents in the best tradition of slapstick. The hare and the tortoise re-enacted! All is well in the end. Neat, detailed, expressive illustrations aid and abet this well-rounded story.

What I Like Catherine and Lawrence Anhott   (Walker/Walker paperback)

Likes and dislikes as experienced by six children, including several races and twins. The rhyming text is minimal, and there is plenty to look at in the delicate but detailed illustrations.

Who Sank the Boat?   Pamela Allen   (Hamish Hamilton/Puffin paperback)

The ancient 'straw that broke the camel's back' theme is a familiar one in the world of picture books. Here, it emerges as fresh as a new day, with the characters – cow, donkey, sheep, pig and tiny little mouse – achieving truly individual status, and action pulsing along at breakneck speed. It is impossible to describe the virtuosity of the pictures, except to say that the animals manifest the most ridiculous attributes of humankind and yet remain animals. They are also lovable, unjudging and wonderfully innocent. The story is simple enough for a two-year-old, will come into its own again at 'early reading' time – and be savoured thereafter at any age.

* *The Wind Blew*   Pat Hutchins   (Bodley Head/Red Fox)

Young Joe   Jan Ormerod   (Walker paperback)

Joe can count one fish, two frogs . . . up to ten puppies . . . 'and one puppy chooses Joe for its very own'. This is my favourite of four 'Little Ones' from this sensitive and capable author-artist's pen. Our own near-three-year-old Joe copies book-Joe's actions throughout. What matter that 'ten' as a concept is beyond two-to-three-year-old comprehension? 'One, two, five, eight . . .' does as well, while learning proceeds; and the small animals enchant.

When I was Three ...

5

When I was Three,
I was hardly me

Your own self, indeed, at three; or nearly so. What isn't possible, when you can make yourself understood with real language, go upstairs one-foot-to-a-step, take yourself to the toilet and pedal your tricycle?

Babyhood is behind; gone with nappies and high chairs and potties. A year ago, the world beckoned and you wanted to run at it, but clung to parental skirts instead. Now you're *there* and it all whirls around you in dazzling colour and variety.

To the uninitiated, a roomful of pre-school children is just that; the only distinction is between babies who crawl and older children who walk. To the informed, of course, the difference between two-and three-year-olds is almost as marked as that between babies and toddlers.

The parents of just-turned-three-year-olds must be forgiven for assuming, with incredulous relief and joy, that they have now mastered the art of parenthood. This totally civilized being (their firstborn: the delusion does not endure beyond this point in the family) is clearly the result of their love and care through days of best-forgotten anguish. From here on, all will be well.

They are, of course, on the three-year-old plateau well known to veteran parents. Later, with subsequent children, they will treasure just-three tranquillity while they have it, merely praying that it will endure until rising-four, rather than shattering around their ears at three-and-a-half.

Three-year-old children, give or take a few months, do seem suddenly to be all-of-a-piece; to have reached a stage of equilibrium at which conformity begins to be attractive, when giving as well as taking is possible and co-operation positively enjoyed.

People matter to them now; new friends are savoured; toys are even – joy unbounding to the adults in their lives! – *shared*. It is as if they suddenly stop shouting 'No! No!' and flinging themselves on the floor (or whatever form their own particular brand of protest once assumed) and say, clear-eyed and interested, 'Yes, yes!'

The emerging capacity to cope with life physically accounts for much of the three-year-old's feeling of well-being, of course. Whereas two-year-olds run *into* things, almost as if they count on sofas and people to stop their blundering progress, the three-year-old moves with agility and dexterity. She can dodge, turn, and wheel about in mid-flight. Think what this means to her in terms of play possibilities! No wonder she feels better about the world and its intentions towards her. For the first time in her life she feels – she *knows* – that she is not totally dependent on others for personal needs. Less need for help means reduced interference. Choice is suddenly seen as a heady privilege.

But it is her accomplishment in the field of language which confers the greatest blessing upon the three-year-old's personality. It is as if 'perhaps' has just swum into her repertoire of response, rescuing her from 'yes' and 'no' – the two terrible extremes. Shades of meaning now start to be recognized and even, increasingly, expressed. All the wonderful modifying words – later, nearly, tomorrow, almost, wait, half, lend – emerge in blessed effectiveness! But don't imagine that merely knowing such words at two would have made any difference to social behaviour. Intellectual development, yes; but not her willingness to compromise. This comes slowly, and is only in its infancy at three; but it is discernible, if you look and listen carefully; the three-year-old has a new understanding of the world and her place in it.

The responsibility of catering for the book-and-language needs of this suddenly superior being would be sobering were it not so satisfying. Ironically, though, it is both easier and harder than before. Easier, because there is such a wealth of material available for children whose language and experience at last equip them for more complex and sophisticated stories, and harder because they will, inevitably and desirably, become more and more discriminating in their tastes.

They may also, suddenly, demand complete comprehensibility from books. Whereas before they expected to listen without understanding at least some of the time, now obscurities must be cleared up as they arise.

But there is a wide range of reaction in this area and it seems to relate less to intelligence and book-experience than to temperament. Some children have a precise, step-by-step approach to the gathering of information, and these children will seldom allow an unfamiliar word or concept to pass without explanation. 'What's a gander?' 'Why did she do that?' 'What does slumber mean?'

A prolonged session with such a child may well persuade you that the book in question is too advanced. The child, by contrast, may have thoroughly enjoyed the experience. Asking questions and receiving answers may be his or her idea of an enjoyable book session, even if you find the constant starting and stopping tiresome.

Another youngster of similar age and experience will hear the story out, unfathomables and all. This child may be simply less curious, but may also love the total effect of a story; may be prepared to take details on trust, for the experience of the whole. Our youngest child demonstrated this willingness in extreme form. When only two years old, she would sit in on family story-sessions intended for brothers and sisters of the eight-to-eleven age group, listening almost endlessly to language which must have been often incomprehensible. Even when it was time for the little ones' story, the choice was almost always made by someone else; Jo herself would listen intently and without comment or question, to anything anyone chose to read aloud.

Fascinating insights into the way language develops have been made in this century. The most interesting of these from our present point of view relate to the sort of environment in which children learn to use language best. Obviously, the more information we have on this score the better.

There is clear evidence that babies and small children profit from an environment in which language is used creatively, to examine ideas, relate occurrences and describe shades of meaning. Far from needing one-syllable words combined into simple sentences to expedite their learning, children need regular access to complex speech patterns if their own language is to develop richly. A truth that is still overlooked, or at least undervalued, is that what a child understands is actually much more important than what that child can express at a given time.

Meaning exists in the mind of the listener, not in the sound waves generated by speech, a fact that becomes obvious if one thinks of the uselessness of listening to someone speaking in an unknown foreign language. To keep the comparison going: think how easily children learn a new language if they go to live in a foreign country. Adults often try to learn words, phrases and rules of grammar beforehand. Children, less tense about the business, let the new language flow around and through them, pick up a reference here and there and are able quite quickly to use the local dialect, if not fluently, at least confidently. They don't need lessons on the agreement of adjectives and nouns, or the tense of verbs; they learn by listening, and relating what they hear to meaning, which resides in their minds. Nor do they fall into the fatal adult trap of translating word by word. Children know intuitively that meaning arises from language in full torrent.

So with their native language. Ideally, it flows around them, rich in content and imagery. From it, and using it, children construct their own view of the world. At no stage can they use, aloud, all the language they understand; their speech lags, inadequate to their insights. The danger lies in adult assumption that because young children can themselves produce only simple words and constructions, they must be spoken to only in speech which reflects this pattern. By this formula, many children are condemned to a meagre language diet, fare which makes a mockery of the rich, diverse equipment of their minds.

Attending to children's minds, then, is a profitable pursuit: good for them and rewarding for us. And reading aloud is one of the simplest and most enjoyable ways of providing this enrichment. Direct teaching is boring for children and tedious for adults. But stories, in exciting and varied profusion – that's a different matter! And the third birthday does seem to usher in a period of boundless opportunity in book sharing.

To begin with, it is a suitable time to introduce the first fairy stories. The three-year-old seems prepared to accept the 'other-world' quality of these earliest tales (the 'Beast Fables' they have been called, appropriately). I would suggest for a start *The Three Bears, Little Red Riding Hood, The Three Little Pigs, The Gingerbread Man* (hardly a beast, but of the same ilk), *The Three Billy Goats Gruff* and *The Little Red Hen*. These have in common features which render them suitable for the child whose contact with stories has so far been confined to simple, progressive narratives and straightforward cause-and-effect tales.

It is important to understand the difference between these stories and the more sophisticated tales, such as *Jack and the Beanstalk* and *Snow White*. The 'Beast Fables' help children to move into an imaginary world which is quite unlike their own, but whose qualities are universal. The characters are often in peril, but the child comes to know that they will emerge unharmed in the end if they are courageous and wise. The rules are rigid; the first two Little Pigs were eaten because they were foolish, the Gingerbread Man because he was, after all, a biscuit, and biscuits are meant to be eaten.

Motive in story is important, and must be comprehensible to the reader. The Billy Goats Gruff want to go up on the hillside to eat and grow fat. The Gingerbread Man runs away because running away is fun. Goldilocks uses the bears' furniture and tastes their porridge from motives of understandable curiosity. These are emotions and reactions which the three-year-old has experienced himself; there is a two-and-two-makes-four quality about these simple plots which is utterly satisfying.

By contrast, jealousy, revenge and obsession with wealth or power are not, as motives, accessible to the young child's understanding, and this lends a degree of horror to some of the more sophisticated tales. Even though in *The Three Little Pigs* the wolf proposes to make a meal of the perky little heroes (and does eat two of them in the best versions), it is in the nature of things that wolves will hunger after pigs – and the resultant contest has a rollicking quality which keeps horror at bay. The sustained hatred of the disguised queen for Snow White is a different proposition for the three-year-old; this is a human situation, in which penetrating evil is sensed but not understood; and the unknown and unknowable is always more horrifying than the revealed terror.

Not all three-year-olds will react with fear to the more complex tales, of course, but the possibility needs to be borne in mind. Fortunately most of them are much longer and more involved than the 'Beast Fables' and their use may well be deferred for other reasons. But some children will encounter them inevitably in story-sessions intended for older children. In this case, you will soon find out whether your child is resilient to their gross horrors or not! And we have ourselves to cope with; I have never been able to bring myself to read aloud any variant of that tale in which a giant, being duped by a visiting family of children which he proposes to kill, slits the throats of his own (eight?) children by mistake. We all have our own tolerance limit, and mine is reached just before this excess.

On the other hand, I am sure that my children met this tale in some form in their own reading; censorship has never been part of the contract for reading alone in our family. It was my own blood that curdled at this atrocity, not that of my robust sons and daughters.

The variety of forms in which the 'nursery tales' have been published, and their occurrence in collections and series at every level from 'mass market' up, makes choosing the appropriate version for the young child a baffling task. Fortunately the field has attracted a number of responsible and sensitive authors and artists, and the best versions tend to stay in print because they are successful.

Paul Galdone is the outstanding name to watch for, in single-picture-book treatment of these early traditional tales. His interpretations may somethimes surprise, but seldom offend, in my experience. From Galdone's big handsome *The Three Bears*, Goldilocks emerges, startlingly, as an individual, plain in person and brash in behaviour. In his similarly spectacular *The Three Billy Goats Gruff*, the dreaded troll has such presence and personality that one almost wishes he might avoid disaster. (One of my grandchildren at three-and-a-half always responded soberly, if not sadly to the troll's well-deserved end. For this child, Galdone's rascally imp was the hero of the piece, never the villain.)

As for the retellings themselves, always be sure, even with a recommended version, that you are happy with the details before reading it aloud. In the original version of *Little Red Riding Hood* (illustrated strikingly by William Stobbs in an edition which is now out of print), both small heroine and her grandmother are gobbled up irretrievably before the tale is out. If this outcome offends you, you will certainly pass on your unease to your young listener. It might be preferable to settle for a modified version in the first place – an illustration of the advisability of reading *every* story alone, always, before you use it with a child. I do recommend, however, that you choose a version of *The Three Little Pigs* in which the first and second little pigs *are* conclusively eaten up by the wolf. After all, the predator meets a violent end himself; he must surely be seen to deserve it! You may, of course, judge the whole tale to be too frightening for three-year-olds; but in my experience they take it in their stride. (Perhaps grandmothers, being human, provoke easier identification than pigs!)

As with nursery rhymes, it is sensible to introduce different versions, buying some and borrowing others. An old friend in a new guise will be greeted enthusiastically, and comparisons made with interest. You will learn much about your child from his preferences if you watch and listen to him.

The 'original' tales (if such a description is valid) have been augmented over the years with others of the same type. Many have become classics, and keep turning up in new versions. Long may this tendency continue! A new author or artist contributes something of his own – a comment, an emphasis, a touch of humour in an unexpected place – and the tale is revitalized.

Such a tale is that of *The Enormous Turnip*. I remember loving it from my own childhood, when I met it in a school reader. This must have been a meticulous, blow-by-blow account, because I have always been faintly disapproving of the brevity of Helen Oxenbury's *The Great Big Enormous Turnip*, despite its obvious success with three-year-olds. And I will not have any version which does not end with, 'And they all had turnip soup for supper.' I add it, if it is not there.

An older, wordier version by Anita Hewett, illustrated by Margery Gill, *The Tale of the Turnip*, continues to be in successful use in our family. Here, the detail is rich and repetitive. 'The little old man the grandfather, the little old woman the grandmother, and the little girl the grandchild' together with their friends the little black cat and the little brown mouse, exert an almost hypnotic effect on reader and listener alike. Sadly, this excellent book is out of print; a casualty, no doubt, of the modern fetish for bright colour, as against the quieter charm of black and white. For Margery Gill's pictures, detailed and expressive as they are, are 'penny plain' rather than 'tuppence coloured'.

I suspect that many of the adults who demand full colour in the books they buy for very young children have not looked very closely at the way these children react to their books. To begin with, a picture book will stand or fall, in a young listener-looker's estimation, on the story and the way in which the illustrations support and interpret it. This bears repeating. *Story* comes first, with all its requirements: appropriate theme, well-shaped plot, characters who are sympathetic and who come alive, well-paced narrative which moves smoothly to a climax - and that elusive quality of 'wholeness' which is impossible to define but easy to recognize.

It is true that a five- or six-year-old who is introduced to books for the first time is more likely to be captured by bright red and blue than sober black and white. This, of course, proves only that an unsophisticated taste in any field demands impact rather than subtlety for its satisfaction (Disney rather than Sendak, shall we say). As experience widens, and taste refines, the graphic quality of a picture is tempered by other considerations. Sensitivity to line and form, and a feeling for relationship, develop unconsciously through access to the best picture books, but are unlikely to emerge spontaneously in youngsters whose experience of books has been limited. These children may need – almost certainly will need – wooing with eye-catching colour and slam-bang action if they are to be won over to books at all. The bright lights and loud noises of the modern world (even excluding the effects of television) have a lot to answer for in the impairment of children's sense of wonder.

You may feel, nonetheless, that your three-year-old is unlikely to be captivated by the apparent austerity of black and white. If this is the case, I suggest an experiment. Borrow or buy a copy of *Millions of Cats*, by Wanda Gag. In this lyrical and shapely tale a little old man sets out to walk over the sunny hills and down through the cool valleys in search of a cat, for which his wife longs. He finds, instead of one little cat:

> *Cats here, cats there,*
> *Cats and kittens everywhere,*
> *Hundreds of cats,*
> *Thousands of cats,*
> *Millions and billions and trillions of cats.*

Text and picture are one here; they are experienced indivisibly. The lettering is hand-done, pictures and paragraphs expertly intertwined. One feels that colour would intrude. *Millions of Cats* is a unified experience; it has spoken directly to those children lucky enough to encounter it for fifty years, and will surely continue.

By all means make sure that your children have the joy of rich and varied colour in their books. But don't deny them the unique experience of word and illustration which are mutually supportive in the particular and rare way of some black-and-white picture books.

To return to traditional stories for the three-year-old.

Collections of stories are to be viewed with suspicion and examined with care. There is no substitute for reading at least one story from the book before a decision is made; and even then, you may find yourself using only two stories regularly from a volume which contains twenty. The main difficulty stems from a factor mentioned already in this chapter: the wide variation in emotional response required by different stories.

Some collections brashly set *The Gingerbread Man* and *Jack and the Beanstalk* cheek by jowl and try to reduce both to a lowest common denominator by the use of a uniform language and style. This practice usually suits neither, mainly because each requires separate, sensitive treatment, with different audiences in mind. Many children are ready for *The Gingerbread Man* at two-and-a-half; not many are ready for *Jack and the Beanstalk* in its best forms until six or over.

There is, fortunately, a collection which can be acquired with confidence for three-year-olds. Several stories will be usable from two onwards if their babyhood has been bookish, and several might be left until four, but Anne Rockwell's *The Three Bears and 15 Other Stories* will be in daily use for years. This book is actually the equivalent of sixteen picture books. No page is without an expressive colour picture, and every single story is usable. There is something especially satisfying about a book which can be taken along on any expedition – a picnic, a trip to the doctor, a long car or train journey – with a guarantee of stories for all moods and moments. *The Three Bears and 15 Other Stories* is a treasure trove; sturdy, not too big, thoroughly companionable.

A more recent, but equally useful collection, *The Helen Oxenbury Nursery Story Book* will give both pleasure and value for money at this time. The choice of stories – ten in all – is impeccable, and the cover a joy in itself. This artist's overriding quality has always seemed to me to be one of entwined delicacy and robustness; a quality which produces an unlikely but radiant suitability for young children and yet appeals to adults as well. Here the pictures are generous in size as well as number and the retellings sound. The whole is a superlative book.

New since this book was last revised, and certainly not to be overlooked, is Charlotte Voake's *The Three Little Pigs and Other Favourite Nursery Stories*. Compiled and illustrated by this fine artist for her own three-year-old daughter, Chloe, it has already proved to be 'just right' for my three-year-old granddaughter, Emily. Indeed, it is hard to imagine a three-year-old who would not fall prey to its eight rousing stories, encased as they are in a large, beautifully produced book, with Charlotte Voake's distinctively evocative illustrations. Each double spread is generously embellished with pictures which intersperse the text, so that a non-reading child who has once heard the story can follow and enjoy it alone, later. The print, too, makes this book especially attractive; large, clear and well-spaced, it will be read several years later with a flourish by the young school child.

The Orchard Book of Nursery Stories has even more recently joined the ranks of reliable collections, and, with fifteen well-told tales, will be in family service for years once acquired. This book, too, has especially clear, uncrowded print, and will double as an 'early reader' later. All the 'beast fables' are included and are presented in their classic forms. (Attempts to 'embroider' the good old tales always grate, once you develop an ear for the 'real thing'.) Several stories might be left for a year or so – but by now you will be the best judge of your own child's understanding and tolerance. Sophie Wyndham's illustrations have both clarity and beauty. The eight full-page pictures would grace any nursery wall, and every opening has at least one colourful, expressive picture.

While on the subject of collections – which certainly help busy parents to find an acceptable story quickly – I should point out the contribution that Shirley Hughes has made to this category. Her 'earliest' Alfie and Annie Rose story, *Alfie's Feet*, has already been mentioned, and others occur in appropriate lists. Each of the stories in her two anthologies, *The Big Alfie and Annie Rose Story Book* and *The Big Alfie Out of Doors Story Book* (nine, between the two titles), might have made a splendid picture book alone. Each collection contains, also, four page-long poems (or perhaps 'interludes') which serve to tie the stories together in their indoor and outdoor settings.

These are big, handsome, utterly usable books. Each story reflects its author's deep knowledge of children and their ways; and as usual, the pictures are vigorously and yet sensitively expressive of their subjects. The second title has afforded an opportunity for the artist to reveal her capacity to produce country vistas and seascapes of astonishing detail and beauty. Panoramic views of countryside with houses, trees and animals make fascinating perusal for the young, as do the wonderful sweeping views of beach, sea, cliff and sky.

There is another category which appeals to this age group and must be conceded a place in its literature. It consists of big, lavish volumes, of which Scarry's *What Do People Do All Day?* is probably the best-known example. (It is certainly one of the best of its kind.) The books themselves attract attention by reason of their sheer size, colour, and apparent value for money. They are full of pictures. Great double-page spreads reveal panoramic vistas of people (or animals dressed up as people) conducting their lives in every imaginable and unimaginable circumstance, against everyday and bizarre backgrounds; going places on land, on sea and in the air. The scurrying little characters are involved in activities and accidents at once wildly unlikely and comfortably familiar.

An upsurge in the production of such 'bumper' volumes occurred in the early to mid seventies, and related, I believe, to increasing media emphasis on the importance of the pre-school years for learning. Richard Scarry became a household name in the wake of mass-marketing methods which guaranteed his fame. Meanwhile many fine authors and artists working in the children's field went unnoticed by the greater public. Many parents who, for the best reasons, were anxious to introduce their pre-schoolers to books had little or no knowledge of suitable titles or sources of information. But, almost without exception, they had heard of Richard Scarry!

Scarry began his career as an illustrator in the 1940s, later moving into writing. He can scarcely be termed, fairly, an author; his stories are at best commentaries on what is happening in his pictures. One suspects that this style speaks directly to children who are used to watching television and films regularly. There can be no doubt that Scarry's rounded, jolly little animal-humans, trotting or rushing about their cluttered world, attract and amuse them. Action is the keynote. Character and situation are stereotyped, and reaction is instant, predictable and absolute. Shock, dismay and grief abound and are invariably presented as funny to the viewer, regardless of their reality to the sufferer. In this, Scarry's work has much in common with the comic book, or filmstrip cartoon. For me, these books are all fairly shallow experiences – not usually damaging, but seldom inspiring either.

A more definite limitation of Richard Scarry's books should perhaps be mentioned. It is an important drawback, because it negates the very quality which supporters claim for his *Busy Busy World, The Great Big Air Book* and similar titles: that is, that they increase a child's knowledge of words and concepts and so expand his intelligence. I am not persuaded of this. These books set out to teach, and yet invoke a method which is hit-and-miss, if not slip-shod. Facts seem to shoot from the page of a Scarry title like sparks from a wheel; there is seldom any unifying theme or purpose to lead to cohesion.

You may ask, 'Does this matter, if the youngster enjoys the book anyway?' and I would answer, 'No – unless *all* her books use these staccato, unconnected statements to describe character and action.' We all learn best by tying newly encountered information to an existing body of knowledge. Research shows that young minds need practice *not* in the random collection of facts, but in the discernment of common factors, the recognition of cause and effect, an understanding of action, development, result. Narrative prose – a story – engages the attention in a way which guarantees concentration and the making of connections between new material and old. The patterns laid down by the sensitive, rhythmical use of language are lasting ones. Children respond later to words which flow, language which brings image to the eye and music to the ear; language which ensures that information is absorbed, apparently without effort.

These large impressive books are valuable if kept in their place: as supports to the mainstream of literature for the three-to-sevens, the central current of which is *story*. Certainly, they can widen a child's knowledge of things, activities and places, but their content is unlikely to linger in the mind long after the book itself is forgotten, as a story with real characters will do.

Most modern parents and grandparents will remember the 'Dr Seuss Beginner Books' and the impact they made on children's reading in the sixties. How do they compare now, with the wealth of picture books available?

The 'Beginner Books' were a phenomenon. Never before had a series aimed directly at very young children so caught the attention of the average parent. Beginning in 1957 with *The Cat in the Hat*, 'Beginner Books' multiplied rapidly. New and different authors were added to keep the image alive, and some of them achieved distinction in their own right. Stan and Jan Berenstein, P. D. Eastman, Syd Hoff and others all played their part in the establishment of a series which has always been known as 'the Dr Seuss books'. If you had lived through the real 'Beginner Book' era as the parent of a young child, you would remember the near fervour which greeted the appearance of each new title. Some families owned every single volume – numbering more than fifty – and used no other books at all. (I recall the barely concealed exasperation of staff in our bookshop with parents who would not even *look* at the other wonderful books on the shelves!)

As in any series, of course, the standard varies, and each title should be judged separately. And, as in the Beatrix Potter books, there is wide variation in the level of required understanding. There is no substitute for careful pre-reading of each title, with your own child's level of maturity and taste at the forefront of your mind.

And the best in my opinion? Well, all those years ago, my youngest children loved *Are You My Mother?*, *One Fish, Two Fish, Red Fish, Blue Fish*, *A Big Ball of String* and *The Digging-est Dog* – and our son Simon became positively addicted to *Green Eggs and Ham*, which I personally consider one of the silliest books ever written. (I was obliged to continue reading it aloud through clenched teeth when everyone else finally rebelled. Years later I find that its fatuous sentiments are still there, in all their absurd inanity, to torment me if my eye happens to fall upon the wretched book on shelf or in list.)

My research for this edition of *Babies Need Books* reveals that *Green Eggs and Ham* is still in print. Perhaps Simon, with true child eye, was right!

Another loved title, *Robert the Rose Horse*, has recently re-surfaced. Our own family copy has given good service over the years. This ludicrous tale of a horse with an allergy never fails. Horses that sneeze – especially as devastatingly as Robert sneezes – are, clearly, funny to the very young. And Robert's vicissitudes *are* engrossing, his ultimate triumph heartwarming. Several titles by Dr Seuss himself, rather longer and more complex in subject matter and vocabulary than the 'Beginner Book' titles, were originally published in a larger format. Their current inclusion among regular 'Beginner Books' is not altogether reasonable, as they are more suitable for the fives-and-overs. One must rejoice at their survival, however (I have included my favourites in the appropriate lists).

Astonishingly, the 'Beginner Books' are, almost without exception, still in print. They have stood the test of time. And recently, when a just-reading grandchild found *The Digging-est Dog* on our shelves and read it aloud with zest, I realized why. There is certainly a sameness about all the texts, with their jaunty rhyme and simple language, but there is style, too. These stories are as unlike school 'readers' as you could possibly imagine. The rhyme is never inept, or forced, and the plot fairly races along, in each book.

Plenty of whoosh-slash-bang ensures a constant gleam in the child's eye, and yet there is never cruelty. Even the nasty characters are won over, rather than punished. (The moral tone is, in fact, impeccable!) Nor is there any of that over-clever, behind-the-child's-back humour which mars many more modern picture books. 'Beginner Books' are all aimed fairly at children, and their aim is true.

All the 'Beginner Books', of course, make good 'read-alone' material once children launch themselves upon the serious business of 'gleaning meaning from print'. At this time *The Cat in the Hat* and all his clownish colleagues, with their jaunty and repetitive texts and funny (if sometimes vulgar) illustrations, ensure immediate attention. And *Dr Seuss's ABC*, already mentioned in Chapter 3, will remain a staple throughout toddlerhood and into early school years, if acquired early.

Over the years, I have become more convinced than ever that language, in all its resource and vitality, must become part of children's very beings long before 'official' education begins, if they are to use their minds and emotions confidently, flexibly and imaginatively. My continuing observation of young children persuades me that poetry probably gives the richest return of all in these stakes; but suggests also, that this area of children's access to language is likely to be the most neglected of all.

There is, of course, a sort of 'chicken-and-egg' pattern in evidence; most parents, having not themselves experienced the mental and emotional stimulation of rhythm and rhyme – 'the best words in the best order' – early in life, are likely to be awkward with poetry, if not actually derisive of its relevance to life. Sadly, these attitudes take root by early adolescence in all but a few children. Poetry comes to be seen as affected; effeminate, in the old, demeaning sense; even hypocritical, or bogus.

No such danger with the three-year-old! Try reading him

> *Someone came knocking*
> *At my wee small door;*
> *Someone came knocking,*
> *I'm sure – sure – sure;*
> *I listened, I opened,*
> *I looked to left and right,*
> *But nought there was a-stirring*
> *In the still, dark night . . .*

and watch his eyes grow round with wonder at the heartfelt mystery of Walter de la Mare's evocative words (from 'Someone' by Walter de la Mare). Then read:

> The pickety fence
> The pickety fence
> Give it a lick it's
> The pickety fence
> Give it a lick it's
> A clickety fence
> Give it a lick it's
> A lickety fence . . .

and see if the magical beat of David McCord's words doesn't elicit a grin, at least; a delighted shout in all likelihood – 'Read it again!' (from 'The Pickety Fence' by David McCord).

I believe that this experience is such a thing of the ear and the nerve ends that it should, much of the time, be unaccompanied by illustration. I will concede that poetry and colourful pictures can co-exist to produce an attractive and successful book; indeed I have included examples of such happy collaboration in my lists. But experience with real children over a long period of time has reinforced this belief. A poem which demands attention from the ear only, purposely allowing the 'inward eye' to operate, allows the imagination fuller rein. And what lively, passionate imaginations children have!

Television has a lot to answer for in our society, I believe – and one of its sins is that it has brainwashed several generations of human beings into thinking that there must *always* be something to look at; listening is not enough. As a result, poetry for the very young almost always comes with illustrations and I suppose I must accept this and be thankful whenever the pictures do not take over completely. Of course, if you read a poem aloud often enough, you come to know it by heart, and can thereafter repeat it anywhere, anytime, without the book. A wonderful resource in fact, if you find yourself abandoned at bus stop, or in car-which-won't-go, or doctor's waiting room – or any number of barren spots, with one or more small children. You may even, once you have become a devoted reader-aloud of poetry, find yourself astonished at how much poetry you have inadvertently taught these same children!

Poetry at this stage means rhyme, jingle, and lullaby – or any suitable song. For it is rhythm and rhyme that makes the whole memorable, with melody lending a special flavour to certain verses (surely *everyone* sings 'Here We Go Round the Mulberry Bush' and 'Old King Cole'!). Constant repetition, of course, embeds both words and associated emotions in the child's mind, often for life.

So keep on reading and singing nursery rhymes. You may, from now on, include some of the longer rhymes – *all* of 'Mary Had a Little Lamb', 'Little Bo Peep' and 'Old Mother Hubbard', as well as 'Simple Simon', 'Three Little Kittens' and a host of others (Dear old *Lavender's Blue* is a gold-mine if you are looking for longer rhymes, but almost any collection has several).

If you are keen to make a start on 'real' poetry with your three-year-old, you might like to start making your own collection. I did this many years ago, and still use my own hoard of verses with grandchildren. Some of the anthologies mentioned in later chapters and lists are worth exploring for especially young poems. Jill Bennett's is a name to keep in mind in this connection.

It is understandable that parents should feel that books about 'real' things matter. Life is a serious business, they reason; the sooner the child starts to collect facts, the better. This is true, as far as it goes, but it stops short of a profound truth. In the early years, facts and feelings are not clearly differentiated – and feelings endure longer than facts, at any age. There is a much greater chance that a fact will take root in the mind if it comes in on the wings of a feeling, a stirring of the emotions as well as the intellect.

Similarly, an interest in a subject that is kindled by an imaginative story will demand its own explanation later. As an example, let's look at Don Freeman's *A Rainbow of My Own*:

Today I saw a rainbow. It was so beautiful that I wanted to catch it for my very own. I put on my raincoat and hat and ran outdoors.
Fast as the wind I ran
But when I came to where the rainbow should have been, it wasn't there.

The illustrations show a dark, smudgy-grey sky against which the rainbow – and the small boy's bright yellow raincoat and hat – stand out in bright relief. Rapturous attention is guaranteed. By all means try to *explain* the rainbow phenomenon to your small son or daughter if you want to. Children 'catch' enthusiasms; we should all try to let them share ours. But don't expect the details to take root in their minds as the feeling of this story will in their senses. Why worry? Not knowing about the origin of rainbows until ten or twelve won't hurt them, and the magic and wonder of such a story will give the explanation, when it comes, an impact that will help it to stick.

One last word before we move on to the big world of the sophisticated over-fours. The factor which must guide you before all others is your own child's reaction to different books – and this may astonish you. It is quite common for a youngster to become almost addicted to one particular title, and to insist upon its repetition day after day, night after night, when all available readers-aloud have passed the point of no return in boredom. Clearly, such a title (and it may not even be a 'good book' by the experts' judgement) is meeting a need which will probably remain undiagnosed. All you can do, I think, is to grit your teeth and keep reading. By all means suggest – and produce – other seductive volumes, but on no account criticize the adored book. It has probably become part of him by this time, and your disapproval could be experienced as a personal betrayal. Anything as intense as this devotion *has* to be seen as important, even if the need, and its fulfilment, are not understood at all. (No use asking the youngster. *He* won't know in his head; only in his bones and all his fibres.)

And be prepared for (but don't jump to conclusions about) *real* individual differences in children. Many three-year-olds are impassioned by fire engines, earth-moving machinery, animals, or a host of other preferences. It is sensible to try to find titles which will satisfy these interests, but dangerous to cast a child in any particular mould. This happens more often to boys, I suspect. The casual onlooker might well have been convinced that Anthony, at just over three, would prefer his *Big Book of Machines* to any other title; his preoccupation with motorized lawn-mowers was intense. They would have been wrong, however. *Sally's Secret*; *Farmer Barnes Buys a Pig*; *Happy Birthday, Sam*; *The Trouble with Jack*; *The Very Little Girl*; all the Jeanne-Marie books; all the tales from *The Three Bears and 15 Other Stories* – he requested these and countless other, very different stories constantly.

An apparent fixation with a particular topic (rather than a particular title) makes it important that you offer a wide selection, taking in both reality and fantasy, and including traditionally male and female topics, for children of both sexes. It is impossible to avoid the suspicion that many supposed preoccupations are cemented at an early age by well-meaning but short-sighted parents. Let's not risk turning all our poets into scientists – or vice versa.

You needn't worry, if your policy so far has been an open one. You will in all probability be panting behind, rather than leading, your youngster as the fourth birthday approaches.

Book List 4
Books to Use between Three and Four

Many of the books from earlier lists will still be loved, and some children will be moving on to stories from the next, and last section (Book List 5, page 196).

Alfie Gets in First   Shirley Hughes   (Bodley Head/Red Fox paperback)

Alfie is every three-year-old, running ahead of Mum, intent upon reaching home first. This he does, easily; after all, Mum is encumbered with Annie Rose in her pushchair, as well as the shopping. It is when Alfie contrives to shut himself (*and* Mum's basket containing the key) inside that the trouble starts. Everyone helps on the outside – neighbours, milkman, window-cleaner – but in the end it is Alfie himself, alone on the inside, who takes action. The final double spread is utterly engaging:

Then the window-cleaner came down from his ladder, and he and the milkman and Mrs MacNally's Maureen and Mrs MacNally and Annie Rose and Mum and Alfie all went into the kitchen and had tea together.

And there they are. Warmth, concern, humour and masterly use of pen and brush have together created a book which will endure.

An Evening at Alfie's has the same cast in another domestic drama. Mum and Dad have gone out for the evening, leaving Alfie and Annie Rose in the competent hands of Mrs Mac-Nally's Maureen. All goes well, until a burst pipe fractures everybody's peace, and necessitates the summoning of first Mrs MacNally and then, as the situation worsens, Mr Mac-Nally. Good will and hard work restore order, with Alfie clearly enjoying an unexpected evening's fun. This is real life, between the covers of a book, superbly accomplished in word and picture. (See List 5 for *Alfie Gives a Hand*.)

Andrew's Bath   David McPhail   (Puffin paperback)

Picture books in which children interact with animals (or monsters, or ghosts) who just might have been imaginary are now quite common; doubtless because they serve a need, in reflecting or even suggesting children's own fantasy games. Here, Andrew goes upstairs to bath himself for the very first time, equipped with 'all his favourite toys and books'. His parents' consternation at the resulting noise – and Andrew's shouted reports – are more than justified. A frog, a hippopotamus, an alligator, a lion and an elephant have joined the watery fun. The pictures are quietly expressive.

Are we Nearly There?   Louis Baum, illus. Paddy Bouma   (Bodley Head)

Watercolour illustrations of very fine quality indeed extend and grace a text which is confined almost entirely to conversation between a father and his small son in this successful book. They are on their way home from a day's outing by train. Only on the last page do we realize that the young man is delivering the child to his mother, rather than returning with him. There is sadness but no sentimentality in the picture of the father waving as he goes. 'Goodbye, Simon.' 'Goodbye, Dad.' 'See you soon . . .' Simon himself is all confidence and tired pleasure, red balloon trailing. Almost all families are touched by separation or divorce these days. This sensitive documentation of a happy day in the life of a child and his father will speak to some children directly, and draw others into the circle. This quality, in a book which stands alone as a 'good read' without it, makes it memorable.

*Are You My Mother?   P. D. Eastman   (Collins, Beginner Books)

First published in 1960, this book has been in constant favour with small children ever since. While it is certainly simple enough for two-year-olds, its humour appeals to the three-year-old's greater sense of the ridiculous. A little bird, having hatched during its mother's absence, sets off to find her, asking inappropriate animals and machines in turn, 'Are you my mother?' The pictures, as usual in this series, are exuberant and absurd rather than sensitive. The story carries the day.

Babies Babies Babies Tessa Dahl, illus. Siobhan Dodds (Kingfisher)
An obviously pregnant mother and her two children of about five and three are shown on the left-hand page of each opening, engaged in everyday occupations. Each right-hand page is devoted to the mother's answers to her children's questions about new babies and their development. 'Do all baby animals grow in their mummies' tummies?' 'When will our baby be able to walk . . . ?' 'How long before our baby is born?' Because the mother chooses to include information about other species in her replies, the book is a mine of engrossing information. The pictures are colourful, correct and well-designed (with Dad featuring too!).

Baby Animals Margaret Wise Brown, illus. Susan Jeffers (Puffin Paperback)
The text of this lovely book was written over fifty years ago by a master in the field, and yet has not dated. The title is somewhat inadequate; this is far from being merely a catalogue of young animals, however sensitively depicted. The 'story' follows a day on a farm, the baby animals and birds, and the little girl in the farmhouse all awakening to 'the grey light that is in the sky before the sun comes up.' The new illustrations, by Susan Jeffers, are irresistibly beautiful. The design, quiet colour and detail bring animals, humans and surroundings into immediate range; the artist's work is both meticulous and original. The little African-American girl, her family and the animals all convey their quiet contentment to the reader. One can only hope that *Baby Animals* will stay, now that it has resurfaced.

A Bag Full of Pups Dick Grackenbach (Puffin paperback)
An age-old formula is here put to pertinent use. The first page reveals old Mr Mullin bearing an enormous bag which is erupting with puppies – twelve in all, every one up for offers. First a farmer and then a succession of other potential owners (from the bizarre to the average) appear. Slowly, the group

diminishes, until one small seemingly unwanted pup remains. Predictably, along comes a little boy ... The pictures are explicit and antimated, the puppies deliciously perky. An irresistible tale, deftly handled.

Bear in the Air Benedict Blathwayt (Red Fox paperback)

Bears continue to burgeon in the literature of the youngest, and one can do no less than welcome Bear, who herein inadvertently but entertainingly becomes airborne. Bear's young owner mistakenly believes that Bear, and the basket he is sitting in, will restrain the bunch of balloons tied to the handle of the basket. Quite the reverse ... The text is minimal, and there are wonderfully detailed aerial views in clear colour for the young to pore over.

Belinda's Balloon Emilie Boon (Corgi paperback)

Lucy Bear loves wheeling baby Belinda in her pram in the park, and Belinda loves the balloon Lucy buys for her. When disaster strikes, and the balloon bears the baby aloft, Lucy displays both courage and imagination in a successful rescue attempt. The bears are hearty and wholesome, depicted with style by an artist whose work is direct, uncluttered, and buoyant.

* *The Big Alfie and Annie Rose Storybook* Shirley Hughes (The Bodley Head/Red Fox)

* *The Big Alfie Out of Doors Storybook* Shirley Hughes (The Bodley Head)

* *A Big Ball of String* Marion Holland (HarperCollins, Beginner Books, hardback and paperback)

Billy's Beetle Mick Inkpen (Knight paperback)

Billy had a beetle in a matchbox, but it escaped. (We can see it on the sleeve of his jersey.) One by one he consults a girl, a man with a sniffy dog, a woman, an oompah band and sundry others, and they all set out to hunt. Meanwhile the beetle, predictably, undertakes an interesting journey of its own! The quick-eyed young can find it at every opening and the pictures are themselves robustly funny.

Can't You Sleep, Little Bear?

Let's Go Home, Little Bear both by Martin Waddell, illus. Barbara Firth (Walker Books)

The first of these titles is a prize-winning book which endears itself immediately to child and adult. It concerns a pair of bears, one huge, gentle and endlessly prepared to humour the little one's night fears, the other small and utterly appealing. The illustrations are splendidly designed; most pages are framed with a steel-grey border which suggests the mystery of the night, and lends credence to Little Bear's repeated plaint, 'I'm scared . . . I don't like the dark.' Homely domestic detail inside the bear's cosy cave contrasts with the glorious panoramic vistas outside. The story is all too familiar, but original, too. *Let's Go Home, Little Bear*, by the same author and artist, presents Big Bear and Little Bear on their way home through a snowy landscape. This time, Little Bear's apprehension attaches to sounds: Drip, drip, drip and Plop, plop, plop ('I think it's a Plopper,' says Little Bear). The same quiet humour and warmth emanates from this second book. Both epitomize the three-year-old bedtime story.

Caps for Sale   Esphyr Slobodkina   (Mammoth paperback)

Another classic, in print since 1957 (but the story is much, much, older). This book illustrates the picture-book recipe to perfection: simple but well-rounded plot, interesting characters, a satisfying climax – the whole supported by pictures which tell the story and are themselves eloquent. A pedlar has his wares (tiers of caps, which he carries on his head) stolen by a tree-full of monkeys. He gets them back, by chance rather than good management. This story works, always, even with reluctant listeners.

Cars and Trucks and Things that Go   Richard Scarry   (Collins)

Twenty-three large double spreads – taking in both sets of endpapers – will provide young two- and four-wheel enthusiasts with extended opportunities for intent perusal and identification. The text is almost impossible to read aloud, but opportunities exist for parents to share in the discovery, speculation and sheer fun of it all. Nonsensical vehicles (a hot-dog car which is clearly a modified sausage, and a toothpaste car that's a made-over tube) alternate with dazing varieties of truck, car, bus, tank, bike, ferry and tractor. A family of cheerful pigs makes its way unscathed through a succession of spectacular pile-ups, and Officer Flossy on her bicycle pursues Dingo Dog through the whole book to bag him at last on the final page. Rousing stuff; I'd tell your three-year-old that this book is for 'looking at' and hope for some peace.

* *The Cat in the Hat* Dr Seuss (HarperCollins; Beginner Books, hard-back and paperback)

Cockatoos Quentin Blake (Cape Red Fox paperback)

Professor Dupent is the epitomy of all absent-minded academ-ics – and Quentin Blake the master of depiction, in this woolly-witted field. When the confused professor's ten cocka-toos decide to quit their conservatory and hide from him (*just* out of sight, in every searched location) they find him very easy to elude. Young viewers will search all ten out though, if they hunt hard enough – and enjoy the poor man's bewilder-ment in the process. An ideal theme, ideally explored.

Corduroy Don Freeman (Puffin paperback) Out of print.

The story of an engaging toyshop bear who is longing to be bought. As time goes by, he starts to give up hope. But a little girl has her eye on him, and all is well in the end. Corduroy must be one of the most lovable of all lovable bears. The illustrations do him justice; in quiet colour, they are clear and expressive. (This notable book is out of print in England, but still flourishes in its homeland, America. I cannot believe that it will not be seen again, and so include it. Try the library, meanwhile) Also, *Corduroy and Four Other Bear Stories* by Don Freeman, Paula Winter, Robert McCloskey, Frank Asch and Sanosch is available from Watchword (Random House)

The Cow Who Fell in the Canal Phyllis Krasilovsky, illus. Peter Spier (Heinemann/Little Mammoth)

Hendrika is bored and unhappy, until the day she falls in the canal, stumbles on to a raft, and floats gently down to the town. Peter Spier's double-spread pictures of Dutch town and countryside are panoramic, meticulously detailed and utterly absorbing. Continuously in print since 1957, this splendid book must be regarded as a classic.

A Cup of Starshine: Poems and Pictures for Young Children Jill Bennett, illus. Graham Percy (Walker/Walker paperback)

A collection which is all of a piece; the gently coloured, almost textured pictures are totally in tune with the poems, but might be enjoyed alone. One has an impression of many weather poems and of how it feels to be a child. The humour is kind, rather than riotous, the whole a joyful experience.

* *The Digging-est Dog* Al Perkins, illus. Eric Gurney (HarperCollins, Beginner Books, hardback and paperback)

Emily's House Niko Scharer, illus. Joanne Fitzgerald (Heinemann/ Little Mammoth)

> *Emily lived in a little brick house*
> *With a creaky old door and a little brown mouse . . .*

Both the house, and Emily herself, are utterly winning; and the story has its beginnings in distant folklore. The creaking of the door and the squeaking of the mouse are driving Emily mad. The mouse's suggestion that they invite a succession of animals to live with them in the end has the desired effect (once the visitors are banished!)

> *. . . all she heard in her little brick house*
> *Was a small sort of creak and the squeak of a mouse.*

Peace, perfect peace, reflected in gentle, cottagey pictures.

Emma's Lamb Kim Lewis (Walker/Walker paperback)

A companion piece to *The Shepherd Boy* in the last list, with the same glowing beauty and a sense of interdependent place, people and animals. Emma 'adopts' the little lost lamb her father brings into the kitchen, but finds his care rather more extending than she had foreseen. A happy reunion with mother and son solves all problems. A read-and-read-again title. Text and picture complement each other exactly.

Everybody Said No! Sheila Lavelle, illus. Nita Sowter (A. & C. Black)

An uproarious variant of *The Little Red Hen*. Mrs Mudd buys an apple tree and asks her large, cheerful family to help her plant it . . . water it . . . pick the apples. 'But everybody said no!' Nita Sowter's illustrations sparkle. A delightful book.

Farm Alphabet Book Jane Miller (Macmillan paperback)

This book makes a visual impact, with its black pages, clear white print and eloquent photographs of farm life. A companion volume to the *Farm Counting Book* (see Book List 2, page 59), it is somewhat more complex in nature: a short but informative text supports pictures that are structurally more sophisticated than those in the earlier book. Three- to four-year-olds will pore over the subtly coloured pictures, finding more to enchant and inform at each encounter. Both upper- and lower-case letters are well placed for easy identification, and a narrow white line ties all together visually.

The Fat Cat   Jack Kent   (Puffin paperback)

A Danish folk tale concerning a cat who eats an astonishing list of people and animals before his moment of disaster arrives. The text is jaunty and repetitive and the pictures full of fun and action, in this excellent retelling.

Find Me a Tiger   Lynley Dodd   (Puffin paperback)

The reader is challenged, page by page, to discover different animals against backgrounds which disguise, but do not totally conceal them in jungle, river, desert, creek ... The last quest brings us home to the family verandah where 'Out in the sun on a rickety chair ...' a black cat (surely Slinky Malinky!) snoozes peacefully. Imaginative text, peaceful, expressive pictures, and the fun of finding tiger, crocodile, lion and lizard cannot help appealing to young listener-viewers.

Forget-Me-Not   Paul Rogers, illus. Celia Berridge   (Puffin paperback)

When Sidney, a bumbling old lion, sets off in the morning to visit Cousin Joe, he is equipped with everything he could possibly need for a day at the seaside: fishing rod, binoculars, camera, towel, umbrella, thermos ... One by one, he loses them all, with the exception of the cake he has brought for Joe; although the birthday *card* seems to have gone along the way. The framed pictures are not merely attractive; in each, a vigilant eye can find the latest of the lost articles (fishing rod left leaning against a post, hat glimpsed through the train window, still on the luggage rack ...). An entertaining saga of mishap, with built-in bonus.

The Gingerbread Boy
The Little Red Hen
The Magic Porridge Pot
* *The Three Bears*
* *The Three Billy Goats Gruff*
The Three Little Pigs
Traditional stories by Paul Galdone   (Heinemann)

> The above stories are all suitable for use with three- to four-year-olds. The books themselves are alike only in their excellence; Paul Galdone contrives to give each a character of its own, while yet preserving its age-old flavour in the retelling. Colour is clear and lines are flowing in these expansive books. All will be handled with love and read again and again.

Grandma Goes Shopping Ronda and David Armitage (Deutsch/Puffin paperback)

> *On Friday Grandma went shopping*
> *and she bought an amiable alligator*
> •
>
> – and there she is, plodding smugly along with her unlikely purchase on a lead. Before long her mounting pile of shopping includes some startlingly inappropriate items, and Grandma herself, in newly acquired candy-striped jumpsuit, is bowling along on a bicycle built for two with a variegated vicuna riding tandem! Repetitive nonsense in cheerful colour, against a background which offers endless opportunity for profitable perusal – with an entertaining twist before the reassuring 'home to tea' finale.

* *The Great Big Enormous Turnip* Helen Oxenbury (Heinemann)
* *Green Eggs and Ham* Dr Seuss (HarperCollins Beginner Books, hardback and paperback)
Hairy Maclary's Caterwaul Caper (also *Hairy Maclary's Show Business* and *Hairy Maclary's Rumpus at the Vet*) Lynley Dodd (Spindleword/Puffin paperbacks)

> Three more stories about the perky little dog described in Chapter 4; rather more complex than the first three tales, but just as diverting. Hairy Maclary's capacity for creating mayhem is impressive.

Harvey Slumfenburger's Christmas Present John Burningham (Walker Books)

Father Christmas's delivery marathon is over for the year – or he thinks it is. Just as he is climbing into bed he notices a lump in his discarded sack: a lump which is Harvey Slumfenburger's undelivered present. Delivering it on foot (one of the reindeer is off-colour) is an incident-packed sortie which becomes increasingly complex, but is accomplished triumphantly. Repetition – Father Christmas is helped in turn by a succession of people in and on a variety of vehicles – and expansive, richly hued and yet uncluttered pictures bring this very large book within reach of three-year-olds, but will be loved for several years.

The Helen Oxenbury Nursery Story Book Helen Oxenbury (Heinemann children's paperback)

Home Sweet Home Colin Smithson (Julia MacRae/Red Fox paperback)

A funny, warm-hearted book about a farmer and his wife who weakly invite animal after animal to share their fireside (and table and bed and sofa and all) during a storm. Persuading them all to leave becomes impossible; but the barn proves to be a comfortable place for Ma and Pa Gumm to set up house in! The illustrations have vivacity and humour, and the book is beautifully designed. Note: Another book with the same title (*Home Sweet Home*, Maureen Roffey, Bodley Head) is given in List 1, page 36.

How St Francis Tamed the Wolf Elizabeth and Gerald Rose (Bodley Head)

There is no more engaging saint than Francis, who loved all animals, and here he has been guaranteed endurance in the affections of modern children. This St Francis is robust and humorous. He tells Brother Wolf how wrong it is to eat people, and thoroughly enjoys the feast which celebrates his victory of kindness over violence. This old story is one to grow on, and is here very well served, both by text and picture. Out of print currently, but this must surely be a temporary state!

I'm Glad the Sky is Painted Blue: Poems for the Very Young Rosalyn Barnett (ed.), illus. Robyn Belton (Julia McRae)

This is a beautiful book, sensitively illustrated and clearly produced with loving care. Originating in New Zealand, it includes a proportion of poems by antipodean authors, but taps also into the poetry of England and America. A thoroughly usable anthology this, with an individual character, and great charm.

It's a Perfect Day Abigail Pizer (Pan Macmillan Children's Books)
Cumulative stories have been popular since − or probably before − *The House That Jack Built* arrived on the scene. This well-designed, handsome book invokes a pleasant variation on the theme: a farm, at dawn, 'As the sun rises over the hill . . .' The cock naturally begins the cacophony; in the end, ten creatures have had their say, and the left-hand page is full, each animal pictured (rebus-style) in the line of print which recounts its contribution. Right-hand pages present successive noise-makers in arresting colour and clarity. An unusual, harmonious book.

The Lazy Bear Brian Wildsmith (Oxford/Oxford paperback)
Wildsmith's use of colour is incomparable. His picture books are extravaganzas, but are balanced by the earthiness of his subject matter, and the warmth and humour of his characters. Here, Bear (who is lazy but lovable) finds a trolley and contrives to have all the fun of riding in it while his friends (who are mild but not meek) do all the work of pushing. Their ultimate retaliation is effective, without being spiteful. A heartening story, made memorable by magnificent illustrations.

The Lion in the Meadow Margaret Mahy (Dent/Puffin paperback)
An outstanding book, on the one hand very simple, on the other, thought-provoking. A little boy claims that there is 'a big, roaring, yellow, whiskery lion' in the meadow, and his mother counters with a *dragon* to chase the lion away. Both fantasies come true, the cowardly but lovable lion taking refuge, after the encounter, in their broom cupboard − from which he emerges every night thereafter to share the little boy's 'apples, stories and a bedtime hug.' Enchantingly complementary story and pictures have turned this book into a classic, already.

Lucy & Tom go to School
Lucy & Tom at the Seaside
Lucy & Tom's Christmas
Lucy & Tom's abc
Lucy & Tom's 123   all by Shirley Hughes   (Gollancz/Puffin paperback)
See also *Lucy & Tom's Day*, List 3, page 88.

The concerns of small children are universal. This likeable and natural pair make their way through six books without ageing noticeably; they play, protest, explore their world – from the delights of a day's visit to the sea, to the excited preparation for Christmas Day, and the joys and rigours of its actual arrival – with the zest of early childhood. In the second book, Lucy starts school and Tom goes to nursery school. The alphabet book, far from any sober intention to teach, provides a fascinating insight into the children's lives, with 'G for Granny and Grandpa, two other very important people', 'm' for 'moon, the most magic light of all' – in each case providing the viewer with a wealth of detail from which to identify and savour additional objects. *Lucy & Tom's 123* has the same quality; no mere counting book, this! Information and fun, in equal proportions, with that warmth and humour one has come to expect from this outstanding author-artist, abound in all six books.

Machine Poems   Jill Bennett, illus. Nick Sharratt   (Oxford)
An excellent collection, which will appeal in particular to the wheels-and-action faction among this age group – and nourish its eye and imagination at the same time. Brilliantly illustrated in full colour – the cover is a triumph – the collection comprises poems about things that function mechanically (or electronically), from space rockets through earth-moving machinery to domestic appliances. Well-known poets such as Charles Causley and Kit Wright join lesser known in a collection whose flavour is as whoosh-bang-crash as its target audience could wish. See also *People Poems* in this list and, by the same author/artist team, *Noisy Poems* and *Tasty Poems*.

*Millions of Cats   Wanda Gag   (Faber)

Mog the Forgetful Cat (also *Mog and the Baby, Mog and Barnaby, Mog and Bunny* and *Mog's Christmas*)   Judith Kerr (*Mog on Fox Night* is described in List 5, page 220).   (all HarperCollins)

Mog exasperates her human family. She cannot remember how to get back into the house through the cat-flap they have considerately made her and is forever miaowing outside the window. But in the end she helps to catch a burglar! This artist's incomparably clear, colourful illustrations tell the story exactly. A most successful book, as are the sequels.

Mr Rabbit and the Lovely Present   Charlotte Zolotow, illus. Maurice Sendak   (Bodley Head/HarperCollins Picture Lions)

A serious, straw-hatted little girl asks Mr Rabbit for help in choosing a present for her mother. Together they consider the possibilities, using colours as reference.

> *'A canary bird is yellow,'* said Mr Rabbit.
> *'She likes birds in trees,'* the little girl said.

A basket of fruit is finally assembled. 'It made a lovely present.' Here is precision, relationship, anticipation and successful resolution, all in fourteen pages consisting almost entirely of polite conversation, with pictures opposite, of course, by Maurice Sendak. To say that they are memorable, or superb, simply does not cover the situation. Each has a quality of utter beauty, and yet utter earthiness; in each, the thoughtful little girl and the helpful rabbit (who has, surprisingly, a jaunty casualness about him) are seen in different parts of a rural landscape, conferring. (If you think this sounds boring, you are in for a surprise.) *Feeling* arises from these pictures. In my experience, three-year-olds stare and stare.

My Brother Sean   Petronella Breinburg, illus. Errol Lloyd   (Puffin paperback)

Sean is every three-year-old starting playschool. He wants to go and he hates the idea, simultaneously. In these brilliant, simple, vivid illustrations, and the sparse text, his agony and his joy come across. A superb book. The sequels, *Doctor Sean* and *Sean's Red Bike* (Bodley Head), show the small hero in a series of situations which typify the everyday life of his age group.

Noah and the Rabbits   Sally Kilroy   (Puffin paperback)

A 'flap book' in the style of *Spot* and others mentioned earlier, but with a slightly more mature theme. A pair of rabbits only just make it to the Ark. 'You're a bit late,' says Noah – but he hunts for a spot to make them comfortable, and finds a rather novel one, in the end. The colours are brilliant, the brief text all that is required, the whole a most successful experience for the three-year-old.

Oh, Little Jack   Inga Moore   (Walker)

This is not the only book in print which explores the notion of being too little to do the things you want to do (*Titch*, Julia MacRae/Puffin paperback, and *Happy Birthday, Sam*, Puffin paperback, spring to mind) but it does have a special flavour of its own, and will be relished the two- to three-year-old. The illustrations will engage the attention and admiration of any age; here are people/rabbits demonstrating by stance, expression and interaction all the pleasure, apprehension, humour and concern that humankind is prey to, in quiet but harmonious colour and superb design. The last double spread reveals little Jack content at last. Not only has he proven to be exactly the right size to ride his new little tricycle, but he is 'just the right size to sit on Grandpa's knee' as well. This particular illustration has an abiding peace which seeps into the bones; Grandpa, little Jack on his knee, is reading to the children, and Mum and Dad are reading, too, all in front of the fire – *with not a telly in sight*!

One Fish, Two Fish   Dr Seuss   (HarperCollins Beginner Books, hardback and paperback)

1 Hunter   Pat Hutchins   (Bodley Head/Puffin paperback)

More than a mere counting book; this amusing volume tells a mute story which ultimately has the hero – a determined if unobservant big game hunter – in full flight before his intended victims. This artist's work is here, as ever, colourful and vigorous. The progressive theme gives full rein to her flair for design; each double spread seems to improve with examination.

Some of the inherent irony may be lost on the three-to-fours, but the action and humour will delight.

One Snowy Night Nick Butterworth (HarperCollins)

Percy the park-keeper is a generous, loving little man; a fact which does not go unnoticed by the small animals on the first snowy night of winter. One after the other they infiltrate his cosy hut – but of course, Percy can cope. Enchanting pictures and heartwarming text. *After the Storm*, and *The Rescue Party*, (both HarperCollins Picture Lion), are equally engaging. In the first, Percy helps the small animals of the wood, bereft of a home after their oak tree is felled in a storm, find a new place to settle in; in the second, Percy and the other animals set out to rescue Rabbit, who has fallen down a well. Satisfying outcomes, always, in Percy's neck o' the woods.

* *The Orchard Book of Nursery Stories* Sophie Wyndham (Orchard Books)

Our Cat Flossie Ruth Brown (Andersen Press)

This book describes, simply, the likes and habits of a loved family cat. The illustrations are beautiful in the extreme, and the combination evokes the nature of domestic cats in a gentle, unspectacular way. (She's unable to resist a box . . .) The clear text will certainly help the early reader; and the cover, with Flossie's yellow eyes staring boldly from her thick, tabby fur, is an added joy. This book could be acquired at three, read alone at six and loved forever, if cats are part of the child's family life.

Out and About Shirley Hughes (Walker/Walker paperback)

There is so much to look at in this lovely book – so many more details to find at each new perusal – that it would be worth acquiring for the pictures alone. But the text directs attention to each expansive, engrossing double spread, and is rewarding in itself. Clearly, this author-artist knows what children are like; how they see things, their total disregard for order and convention, their fascination with things close to the ground, their unconcern for tomorrow, their absorption with what *is*. My daughter Susan (whose well-worn copy I am using as reference) tells me that this book is loved by her children –

12,000 miles away from the children whose life experiences it enshrines. Some things are universal.

Pass the Jam, Jim   Kaye Umansky and Margaret Chamberlain (Bodley Bodley Head/Red Fox paperback)

A wild romp of a book, with a jaunty rhyming text:

> *Where's the bread, Fred?*
> *Bread, I said, Fred.*
>
> *Pass the Jam, Jim,*
> *Jam, Jim, Jam.*

A highly diverse group of children is preparing for a party – quite marvellously depicted in all its messy detail. Jim is deputed to fetch the jam (at regular intervals) but can be seen in every picture disposing of it very creatively instead. There is no target audience for this book. *Anyone* would love it!

People Poems   Jill Bennett, illus. Nick Sharratt   (Oxford University Press)

Twelve characters of diverse and diverting type are here celebrated in twelve brilliant double spreads. From Ella McStumping (who was fond of jumping) to Gregory Griggs (who had twenty-seven different wigs, all depicted) they will entertain and astonish. Good fun; and one poem per opening lends clarity, and incentive to concentrate.

Peter's Chair   Ezra Jack Keats   (Bodley Head)

Peter's apprehension about baby Susie's tendency to take over all his possessions reaches the limit when it comes to his little chair. Only his ultimate realization that he really is a big brother – far too big for the chair – and Dad's wise suggestion that Peter help paint it for the baby, defuse the situation. Keats is an enterprising artist. His work, a combination of collage and vivid colour, is arresting. There is a masterly matching of word and picture in this book.

The Pig in the Pond   Martin Waddell, illus. Jill Barton   (Walker Books)

This is an exuberant, joyful, full of summer story which will bear a thousand readings. A perspiring pig, envious of a pondful of smug ducks and geese, joins them with a gigantic SPLASH (Wonderful to observe – the pictures are enchanting.) Complaints to the farmer (from the outraged birds) merely give *him* the idea, which spreads, in the end, to the whole farmyard population. A wonderful, wild, simple but subtle tale, outstandingly illustrated.

*A Rainbow of My Own   Don Freeman   (World's Work) Out of print.

Red is Best   Kathy Stinson, illus. Robin Baird Lewis   (Oxford paperback)

Red is certainly the key colour in this eye-catching book. A bright red frame rings the cover picture, and bright red endpapers lead into a book featuring red clothes of every description, page after page. The text is simple but lively; three is an age for fussiness about clothes and footwear, and the small girl pictured has a mind of her own.

*Robert the Rose Horse   Joan Heilbroner   (HarperCollins Beginner Book)

Ruby

Ruby to the Rescue   both by Maggie Glen   (Red Fox paperback)

Most literary bears – at least in picture books – are done unto; but Ruby *does*! Equipped in error during her manufacture (the machinist was dozing) with a leopard-skin front, non-matching ears and a crookedly attached nose, Ruby is marked with an 'S' (for 'second') and dumped in a box with other malformed toys, for disposal. Resignation is the prevailing emotion in the ranks of this sad mob – but Ruby changes all that!

In the second book, she goes to school with Susie, her young (triumphantly acquired) owner and once again discovers oppression – in the playhouse. One can feel Ruby spitting on her paws ... These big, squarish books, with their bold, good-humoured pictures of realistic – if irregular – bears and very natural children, strike a note for justice, and are funny as well.

Sally's Secret   Shirley Hughes   (Red Fox paperback)

All children like making houses, and Sally is no exception. The secret little house she constructs in the bushes is an enchanting place; but only when Rose comes to share it with her is Sally really happy. The pictures tell the story in warm, bright colour and careful detail.

Scruff   Gerald Rose   (Bodley Head)

The front cover of this cheerful saga of doggy irresponsibility sets the tone: Scruff himself poses perkily, rose between his teeth. Scruff and Grandma go shopping. Everywhere, people clutch their noses. 'Pooh! What an awful smell!' Grandma and Scruff speculate, without conclusion. No doubt at all is entertained by Tim and Debbie when the mystified pair arrive home. 'Well I never!' said Grandma. Scruff is duly scrubbed, and rinsed and brushed . . . The pictures are hearty in Gerald Rose's best tradition, generous in both number and colour, with that humorous comment on proceedings which is always, in this artist's work, set at child level.

The Shepherd Boy   Kim Lewis   (Walker/Walker paperback)

James is the son of a shepherd, and longs to join his father on the hills. 'You'll have to wait until you are a little older,' his father says. But meanwhile, James, often with his mother at hand (and always clutching his toy lamb), can watch the lambs being born and fed, the sheep shorn and dipped and finally sold at the market. By this time a whole year has gone by, and another Christmas comes around – with a cap and a crook for James under the tree, and best of all, his own sheepdog puppy in the barn! The illustrations are compellingly beautiful and often breathtaking. Wide landscape pages show in detail the work in shed, pasture and yard through the seasons. Family life is warmly lived, and James is a real little boy.

The Shopping Basket   John Burningham   (Cape/Red Fox paperback)

On the first page red-headed, bespectacled Steven is besought by a rather frayed-looking Mum to 'Pop down to the shop . . . and buy six eggs, five bananas, four apples, three oranges for the baby, two doughnuts and a packet of crisps . . .' The mission is simply accomplished, but more than usual difficulties attach to the journey home. In turn, a bear, a monkey, a kangaroo, a goat, a pig and an elephant confront Steven and

demand the eggs, the bananas ... Cleverly, Steven contrives
to part with only one of each commodity, and hurry on home
– to a mother who asks 'How could it have taken so long?' The
illustrations are vintage Burningham, and include diagram-
style pictures of the items bought, depleted at each encounter.
Good fun and counting practice.

The Sick Cow H. E. Todd, illus. Val Biro (Puffin paperback)
A genuinely funny story about a cow who says everything
except MOO! Efforts to cure her have bizarre results (she
merely switches to MEEOW! and Quack Quack!) but the cow
specialist from Vienna has the – not very medical – answer.
The pictures are admirable: realistic colourful and full of
detail.

Simpkin Quentin Blake (Cape)
Umpteen adjectives describe Simpkin – a typical Blake character whose cheerful if dotty individuality bursts from the pages:

> *Simpkin WARM and Simpkin Chilly*
> *Simpkin SENSIBLE and SILLY . . .*

Figures only, against a white background, offer an opportunity
to wallow in Blake's genius for depicting not only action, but
emotion, in line.

The Snowman Raymond Briggs (Puffin paperback)
My disapproval of textless books has had to be shelved in the face
of *The Snowman*. The story is told in explicit, step-by-step detail
in lovely, shadowy pictures; the snowman himself becomes an
unforgettable character, the boy who goes adventuring with
him, oneself when young. An enduring book, eloquent in its
silence.

The Snowy Day Ezra Jack Keats (Puffin paperback)
This is a simple and satisfying book about a small boy who
wakes up one morning to find that snow covers everything he
can see from his window. After breakfast he dons his snowsuit
and runs outside to play. His activities are described simply
and precisely; it is the illustrations, a combination of collage
and vivid colour, which give the book its true individuality.
Twenty-five years old this year, *The Snowy Day* is a likely

candidate for classic status. (The same engaging Peter stars in *Peter's Chair*.)

'Stand Back,' said the Elephant, 'I'm Going to Sneeze!'   Patricia Thomas, illus. Wallace Tripp   (Puffin paperback)

Not a new idea – but certainly an innovative treatment of an old one. The elephant's friends, being warned of the impending explosion, beg him to control his urge to sneeze, each animal describing past experiences of the catastrophe in graphic detail and expressive language. The text is presented in rhyming, but often non-scanning, verse which somehow matches the theme. The pictures are vigorously humorous, but convey a sensation of 'real' animals rather than caricatures. The whole lends itself admirably to *performance* – of either parent or teacher – and could well be dramatized on the spot.

The Story of Little Quack   Betty Gibson, illus. Kady MacDonald Denton   (Puffin)

Jackie lives in the country and is lonely until his mother gives him a duck of his own. Life changes for the better as Little Quack and Jackie explore the farm together. Then Little Quack disappears; yes, she has sought out her own kind on a neighbouring farm. Brought home, she soon disappears again. But this time, she is merely raising a family of ten fluffy ducklings in the brook at the far end of the pasture! Jackie brings the family home, fills up the old tub in the yard with water – and duck, boy and ducklings all have a swim. Not an original theme perhaps, but sensitively treated and splendidly illustrated in a style which has real virtuosity. (Just-three-year-old Emily fell in love with this story.)

* *The Three Bears and 15 Other Stories*   Anne Rockwell   (Puffin paperback)

* *The Three Little Pigs and Other Bedtime Stories*   Charlotte Voake   (Walker Books)

Two Terrible Frights   Jim Aylesworth, illus. Eileen Christelow   (Picture Puffin)

In an old farmhouse, a little girl mouse in the basement is thinking about a bedtime snack. At exactly the same time a little human girl upstairs has the same thought. Both are apprehensive about going into the dark kitchen, but both mothers encourage them, with foreseeable results. A gentle, satisfying story with an unobtrusive message built in: often, the very thing *you* fear is frightened of *you*! The illustrations have just the right degree of mild humour, and are aptly engineered in quiet colour.

Wake Up Mr B!　Penny Dale　(Walker Books)

One brief line of text per page details Rosie's doings on the day she '... woke up very early'. A brief sortie into other people's bedrooms (and finally, the kitchen) reveals that only Mr B, the family Airedale, is prepared to wake up. The vigorous activities which follow ensure that by the time the rest of the family arise, both Rosie and Mr B are asleep in the dog's large basket: an enchanting sight. *All* the pictures in this lovely book are enchanting, and would tell the story without words. But the words turn it into a *real* book!

Watch the Baby, Daisy　Ronda and David Armitage　(Scholastic)

Watching the baby means more than merely observing, as Daisy realizes after several near catastrophes. Fortunately, Mum is understanding, and even admits that she is the one who must shoulder responsibility for baby Amy's safety. Warm family relationships, sunny illustrations – and a disguised but telling message.

We're Going on a Bear Hunt　Michael Rosen, illus. Helen Oxenbury (Walker/Walker paperback and 'mini')

This prize-winning book is at its best in its extra large, hard-covered form, though its paperback and appealing 'mini' editions do bring it within all families' budgets. There is just something indefinably, expansively magic about the huge double spreads of the original! The story is based on a tradi-tional children's action rhyme, and is told in repetitive stanzas:

> *We're going on a bear hunt.*
> *We're going to catch a big one ...*
> *We're not scared ...*

An increasingly weary-looking father, with four energetic children, in turn force their way through long grass, water,

mud and other obstacles, with wonderful onomatopoeiac effects. (Swishy swashy! Squelch squerch! Hoo woo!) Their
meeting with THE BEAR puts the whole exciting expedition
into chaotic reverse, the gigantic though benevolent-looking
animal in lumbering pursuit. Words are inadequate to describe
the pictures. Helen Oxenbury's children invoke all that one
knows or may have forgotten about childhood, and children's
interaction with their world. A classic surely.

*What Do People Do All Day? Richard Scarry (HarperCollins)
When I Was a Baby Catherine Anhott (Little Mammoth paperback)

A cheerful little girl (whose mother is *not* pregnant!) asks about
her own arrival and babyhood and is given homely details,
with pictures to match. Mother and father are both in evidence
and the conclusion, 'I'm not a baby any more. Now I'm three
I'm big', is satisfying and reassuring.

When We Were Very Young A. A. Milne (Methuen/Methuen paperback)

This is the first Christopher Robin and Pooh Bear poetry
book, and should be available for all three-year-olds. You will
have your favourites among the poems, and may want to defer
using some until four or five, But a proportion of these verses
are so three-ish that they should not be missed.

Where's My Teddy? Jez Alborough (Walker Books)

The idea is novel, the illustrations sublime . . . one just has to
ignore the contrivance, in parts, of the rhyming text. Eddy is
hunting for his teddy (called Freddy) in a majestically depicted
forest. A huge bear has the same problem, and of course, their
paths cross. The miniature edition is enchanting.

Where the Wild Things Are Maurice Sendak (Bodley Head/Lion
paperback)

About Max, who sails off 'through night and day and in and
out of weeks and almost over a year to where the wild things
are'. There is no better example than this, among picture
books, of the power of the best words used in the best way, to
enchant; or of the right illustrations to support and sustain.
Sendak's monsters might be said to have started a monster

fashion; but they are themselves unique. Lumbering, benign, ferocious but friendly, they accept Max's domination. Theirs is a dream-world from which he departs when home calls. Max's participation in their 'wild rumpus' (which lasts for three un-worded pages) is one of the highlights of modern picture-book art. An unforgettable book; a rare experience.

Whistle for Willie   Ezra Jack Keats   (Puffin paperback)

Peter cannot whistle when this story starts, and can, when it ends. His dog Willie is as pleased as everyone else, when his master's persistent practice is rewarded with success. Arresting colour and sure design complement an appealing story to produce an outstanding book. (The same little boy is the subject of *The Snowy Day* and *Peter's Chair*, page 130.)

Wilberforce Goes on a Picnic   (also *Wilberforce Goes Shopping, Wilberforce Goes to a Party* and *Wilberforce Goes to Playgroup*)   Margaret Gordon (Viking Kestrel/Puffin paperback)

These are gently humorous stories about a sturdy little bear and his family. Domestic drama alternates with small adventures and predictable disasters, all depicted in cheerful colour. Bears are here to stay, it seems; Wilberforce is a welcome addition.

When I was Four . . .

6

When I was Four,
I was not much more

Understandable comment, in retrospect, but hardly true. The just-turned-four-year-old is much, much, 'more' than she has ever been before – on every front!

One might describe the four-year-old as 'launched'. She has cast off her three-year-old conformity and, like as not, her good manners and winning ways. She is entering a 'biff-bang' period which will exhaust you (but not her), shock the neighbours, and reduce you to frantically consider enrolling her full time at a playschool. Things get broken this year. Confrontations are unavoidable and understandable; the four-year-old is just as sure that she can look after herself as you are certain that she still needs supervision. You are both right, to a degree. She is bursting out all over, and neither you nor she has any real way of assessing where she is at any given time.

Four-year-olds express themselves volubly, and move about their world with ease, even agility. Every day seems to bring another accomplishment, another small ambition expressed or achieved. They make their way from buttons through zip fasteners to shoelaces; from spoon, through spoon and fork to knife and fork; from talking through singing to whistling. Their progress is so swift, so natural that it may be unnoticed by those around them, except in snatches. A member of the family who goes away for a few weeks may be astonished on their return by the youngster's progress.

No one else will have noticed. In fact, the four-year-old may be scolded for slopping milk on the tablecloth as she pours herself a drink when, only a week ago, she would not have attempted this feat at all. What is more, she will now watch and listen (within reason!) while you demonstrate a new skill. She half believes that it *is* a skill, and not just an adult privilege so far denied her.

Her imagination is on the move too, of course, and often runs ahead of her new understanding. Increased experience brings increased fear, and expanding self-awareness may reduce the extent to which children will demand immediate support from their nearest and dearest. This self-imposed deprivation may lead to loneliness. For the first time, children may begin to hide their feelings; deny them, even to themselves.

Four-year-olds are beginning to see things from viewpoints other than their own, although they will have no awareness of this developing capacity. They will use it unconsciously, however, to put themselves in other people's places, and this may lead to new apprehension ('If that could happen to that boy, it could happen to me!'). It is understandable that some parents feel that only 'happy' stories should be read at this time. It is reasonable to suspect that the inclusion of monsters which 'roar their terrible roars' and 'roll their terrible eyes', not to mention wolves who plot to gobble up whole families of unprotected young, will merely increase the youngster's own fear of catastrophe. Rest assured; it is clear that children harbour dark and formless fears whatever we say, do, or present to them. Adult silence on the subject can be just as disastrous as a refusal to recognize developing sexuality in adolescence.

Small children need to know that other people have fears too, that these are natural, and are common to all creatures. Human beings have always played out their fears instinctively. The earliest drama, dance and music arose from people's need to externalize their feelings about themselves and their world; to communicate and share their hopes, fears, and joys. We help small children to do this when we share stories with them, when we show them that people are not powerless, that purposeful action leads to predictable result, and that hurdles can be jumped, problems overcome. If we look carefully enough the whole purpose of fiction − of story − can be seen to be under way at this early stage.

The number of titles available for the over-fours is bewildering.

To find your way to those which should not be missed because they are classics, and yet be sure to include books of every type, can seem a daunting task. You should certainly, by now, be making regular trips to the library, usually with your child. Enlist the support of librarians, telling them when your child has enjoyed a book, and asking for further suggestions. Don't be put off if co-operation is not as forthcoming as you might hope; no human institution improves until the people for whom it is provided show that they expect it to give service. Your enthusiasm may well stimulate librarian interest, and feedback about success-ful titles for particular age groups will surely be appreciated. Don't hesitate to criticize the authorities if you feel that the children's section is under-supplied. One young woman I know earned the librarian's lifelong gratitude when she organized a group of parents to make representations to the council on the sorry understocking of the children's department!

You may feel that your brash, somewhat bossy four-year-old disturbs the peace of the library – and you may well be right. There was a time when librarians frowned on any interruption to the almost hallowed quiet of their surroundings, but this was before they realized that if children were obliged to act like elderly men and women in libraries, they just didn't come. The secret is to take them to libraries from birth, accepting that baby noises, and later toddlers' grabbing habits, are part of the human condition and must be accommodated by the race in general – meanwhile, yourself reducing your youngster's capacity to inter-fere with others by judicious and good-tempered supervision. If the worst comes to the worst, you can always pick her up, smile apologetically (but confidently) and make off. One of my daugh-ters was obliged to give up library visiting with her first child when she felt she could not face the inevitable tantrum again. Her toddler seemed to care nothing for taking books home, but shrieked with rage because she could not take one of the quaint little stools! After a search, we managed to buy one, and library visiting began again.

Increasingly, young children want to choose their *own* books, and this poses problems. All too often 'choice' is made impetuously, because the cover design appeals. Its contents may be quite unsuitable, or at best, hit-and-miss for the child's needs. To a certain extent, this problem is never solved, except by time; but it *is* a problem, especially if only one or two titles may be borrowed at a visit. Of course you welcome the youngster's increasing independence, and want to encourage initiative. But successful book provision is important too.

There is only one way in which you can lessen the chance of your child's choosing books which defeat this purpose: by interesting him or her in the *whole* book, in a natural way, instead of merely reading the story. Always, from this stage (or earlier, if the child is a really good listener) show the cover first. Run your hand appreciatively over it, and read the title and author, underlining the words as you do so. Then open the book to reveal the endpapers. In a picture book, these are usually coloured, and often decorated – and are repeated at the end of the book. Through your example, you can train your child to look in turn at endpapers and title-page, at which point you can again underline and read the title, author and publisher. You will be surprised at the interest he will find in this procedure, and how quickly he will pick up the expressions 'author', 'illustrator', 'endpapers', 'spine', 'publisher'. One of the scheme's chief benefits is that it can be used to help choose library books. The child will see the sense in examining the book well, if this has become entrenched as a habit. At all events, it will help the process of choice in the end – and his awareness of books and their unique qualities in the meantime.

One of my grandchildren, Oliver, became fascinated with endpapers when he was about five. He soon noticed that those at the end of the book sometimes varied from those at the front: slightly, in some cases, and dramatically in others. One day he asked me, 'Why aren't the front endpapers called "startpapers"?' For freshness of vision, give me young children any day!

Along with library visits must go visits to bookshops. In fact, a research programme in England established that children who come from families where books are *owned* are the best readers of all. (I don't need a scientist to tell me such an elementary fact, but I am pleased nonetheless.) Unfortunately, many adults never enter bookshops. It does seem as if the habit must start early if it is to endure. You may feel that even more problems will present themselves in a bookshop, where the bookseller must keep his stock in attractive condition for the ultimate buyer. Here again, early visiting is the key. Children soon learn that libraries and bookshops are different – and that the most 'different' bookshop advantage is that you don't have to return the book *ever*, once bought. Modern paperback publishing has brought many excellent titles within the means of average families; you needn't fear that a good bookshop will stock only expensive books. But do make sure that your child has the pleasure of owning a beautiful hard-covered edition of a much-loved book from time to time – possibly a title from the library which has been enjoyed.

A well-produced book is a thing of beauty. Learning to love such a book for its physical qualities as well as its contents is part of the process of becoming a 'real' reader – a person whose life is enriched by the sight and feel and smell of books.

If your child doesn't have her own bookcase by four, I would urge you to provide one. Simple sets of shelves can be made from planks (cut to length by a timber dealer) supported by bricks or concrete blocks. These have the advantage of being easy to move, and reassemble or extend, as the collection grows. If the youngster's very own shelves are right next to her bed, she will quickly see the point of reaching for a book when she wakes up. If only as a means of ensuring family peace in the morning, this makes sense!

Four-year-old scope is limited only by capacity, which in turn is the product of experience, temperament and innate intelligence. The range of scope is very wide, and it is easy to draw hasty conclusions about the reasons for differences. It is not difficult to understand the varying capacities of those children at each extreme of the scale; at this early level, when the child's experience of books naturally involves the mediation of a concerned family adult, it is easy to explain the bookish child's tastes and accomplishments. Similarly, at the other extreme, it is all too simple to recognize the tragic waste of human potential which has already taken place.

What about those in between? There are differences, and they must be recognized. It should not be assumed that all children can be transformed into committed readers of imaginative fiction, any more than that they can be turned into gymnasts or carpenters at will. Children inherit wide and diverse sets of characteristics, which, interacting with environment and body chemistry, determine the sort of people they become. Two and two never make four in human development; at best, three or five.

It is essential for children's best progress to accept them as they are. Some children at four will listen endlessly, their eyes glazed, their whole being so involved in the story that the real world around them does not exist. Others will listen only if the subject is one of their favourite topics, and then only in short bursts. They may keep interrupting and, jumping about – almost as if physical involvement is *their* way, and has to be practised simultaneously if the experience is to be successful. One might almost say that for *these* children, story-sessions, in whatever form they can take them, are even more necessary than for the others. Left to themselves, they might never tap the vital source that is there, in books. And reading is *different* from gymnastics and carpentry, or any other skill. At its very least, it is a tool. (Think how much has been written about gymnastics and carpentry.) At its best, it rescues readers from dependence on their own limited experience and thought, introduces them to other people, other times and other places, helps them to see shades of meaning and to discern relationships. No child should be lightly dropped from the ranks of potential readers – and the so-called 'practical' child runs this risk. Tragically, this type-casting of children draws its greatest support from the children themselves. Adult attitudes are all too easily sensed and absorbed so that many children cast themselves, early in life, as 'physical' types who will naturally kick balls, bang nails, sew cloth, *instead* of reading.

Why not all of these things? In a world in which identification of 'isms' is assuming astonishing proportions, this particular form of stereotyping (typism?) seems to go undetected. As it is universal in application and life-denying in effect, it is time we looked at it. It is *surely* one of the great dividers, taking in both sexes and all races.

And so to the books themselves.

Four-year-olds will continue to relish old favourites, meanwhile enjoying longer and more complex stories. As their own maturity increases, they will absorb more of the undertones of some stories, using their developing sensitivity to 'see' things which once flowed over and around them. For several years, their needs will hardly change, requiring for their satisfaction stories of increasing depth and detail, but similar topic and type. The essential need for illustration will be reduced slightly, but still remain important. Only the need for 'easy reading' books will vary the scene, and the timing of this phenomenon is, usually, in the hands of the educational authorities of the country in which they live.

Fortunate children of this age group – children whose introduction to books was successfully accomplished years before, and whose progress has been smooth and satisfying – will be ready, now, for some of the classics: Babar, Little Tim, the simplest of the Grimm and Andersen fairy stories and a whole host of titles, old and new, which will stir their imagination, expand their experience of people and things, make them laugh, and make them wonder.

A handsome new anthology will be welcomed as birthday or Christmas present by the four-year-old; such a book as *Tomie de Paola's Favourite Nursery Tales*. Seventeen stories, nine fables from Aesop and four poems (two Stevenson, one Longfellow and Lear's 'The Owl and the Pussy-cat'), all illustrated in de Paola's clear-lined, almost luminous style, make together a superlative book for a family, or lucky single child. Every page is framed; each is more than generously endowed with illustrations in rich but soft colour. This big, satisfying book might well be provided a year earlier; but a proportion of the tales, as well as the fables, are more suitable for five-year-old listeners, and the book will last, once acquired.

Rather than extend this chapter and the next to a tedious length (and because there is such a wealth of diverse and wonderful material available at this stage) I have used the final Book List to provide details of many of these titles. You will notice that I have combined the four and five-year-old Lists into one. As I have mentioned in earlier chapters, it is actually *impossible* to divide titles exactly according to children's ages – and hopeless to try, at this stage. Remember that this List and the others throughout the book constitute an essential part of the whole. Correctly used – and with reference to the instructions for obtaining books given in the Introduction – the 'Books to Use' sections should rescue you from that 'Where do I go from here?' confusion which I remember so well from my own early parenthood.

Without exception, and regardless of other fascinations, four-year-olds have a taste for realism. What other people are doing, how it all works . . . fours and over want to know. It would be very boring if this garnering of fact and deepening of insight could be accomplished only through books about people. Fortunately, heroes and heroines can be animals, vehicles, houses – there is no restriction.

An agreeable number of modern picture books do, however, present the small child against a recognizable family background, immersed in the typical concerns of everyday life. *Dogger* by Shirley Hughes concerns the loss and subsequent restoration of a much-loved cuddly toy called Dogger. The small hero, Dave, is independent and sturdy, inclined to seriousness, and rather overshadowed by his older sister Bella. His family is splendid. They all see Dogger's loss as a real tragedy, Dave's mute grief as the anguish it is. Shirley Hughes draws children's outsides in a way which leaves no doubt about her knowledge of their insides. Her stories are as sure-footed as her illustrations are perceptive. In *Moving Molly*, a small girl's loneliness after the family moves house is resolved in the only possible way when she finally, triumphantly, makes friends. These are not small concerns; they are universal. The youngster who meets them in picture and print is involved in human apprehension and its joyful resolution.

There are now five books devoted to the life and times of Katie Morag McColl, and they are all well worth searching out. The stories, simple in themselves, concern the trials, triumphs and everyday concerns of a small Scottish girl. Ordinary enough, you might say; and certainly, Katie Morag's affairs are hardly sensational. It is the setting that makes the difference, and the characters whom this able author-artist – Mairi Hedderwick – has created and brought to life. For Katie Morag and her family live on the Isle of Struay off the north-west coast of Scotland, and the reader takes up residence with them in no uncertain terms, from the first page.

To begin with, there are the endpapers, identical in each of the books. In turn, they show the small island settlement in the full light of busy, clamorous day and indolent, quiet night. Both wide, landscape illustrations, in delicate watercolour, are planned in chart-like detail to reveal the small harbour, ringed with buildings and other features which the reader, with the characters, will come to know: the 'Shop and Post Office' which is Katie Morag's home, the jetty whose role is central to island affairs, the five cottages, with their varied occupants, the long road round to the five farms on the opposite shore, the last of which belongs to Katie Morag's 'Grannie Island'. The illustrations in each book adhere scrupulously to the original. The characters are easily recognized, and panoramic background views reveal earth, sea and sky in different moods but identical detail. Novelty is introduced in the age-old way of islands, by the arrival of visitors: Granma Mainland, who bodes fair to be a drawback but in the end becomes (unwittingly) an asset; the five 'big boy cousins' who create such chaos but finally settle down, aided and abetted in all their moods by their eager 'small girl cousin'. The clutter and paraphernalia of indoor and outdoor life in a vigorous working community are here in glorious plenty – as are warm hearts, strong personalities (most of them female, for good measure) and the smells and sensations of life lived close to soil and sea. (These books are available in paperback; but do lose something in the conversion. Try to own at least one hardback, for the 'map' alone.)

Parents often ask me for a book about active, assertive girls and women, and the Katie Morag stories certainly fill this bill. Fortunately, there are many more such available – though I insist that choice should be made on a wide, rather than narrow set of criteria. A book is not a good book because of its subject. It is a good book if its subject is incidental to its real strengths, which must number a plot which has pace and shape, characters who come alive, satisfactory resolution of action and (always present in the books which go on from generation to generation) a certain quality which I can only describe as virtuosity.

Some of these qualities are present in *Phoebe and the Hot Water Bottles*, by Terry Furchgott and Linda Dawson. Phoebe is a small girl whose father, an ageing chemist who cares for her alone, can never see beyond hot water bottles as birthday and Christmas presents. Phoebe ends up with a whole fleet (157!) which she tends with love, nurses in sickness, educates, and takes to the pantomime for a treat. Phoebe is real. She has strength, a finely tuned understanding of her weary Dad's limitations, and real resource in emergency. She runs her own show, does Phoebe, and her book has style. (One of my grandchildren, when consulted about her hopes in the Christmas present stakes one December, said without faltering, 'One hundred and fifty-seven hot water bottles!')

Every now and then a book appears which seems to have an almost breathtaking number of successful ingredients. Such a book is *The Lighthouse Keeper's Lunch* by Ronda and David Armitage. Lighthouses – particularly set, as this one is, in a panorama of blue sky and smooth sea, with a line reaching to a house on the cliff down which a basket of delicious food comes each day – can hardly fail. Mrs Grinling's battle to divert the seagulls from their dastardly habit of purloining the lunch is funny in the extreme. The language has individuality, without any dreary intention to teach, and the illustrations are colourful and detailed.

The Lighthouse Keeper's Catastrophe, appearing years after the original story, is more than a mere sequel: it is a splendidly original tale in its own right. It all begins when Mr Grinling, exasperated with Hamish the cat who has just polished off the fish his master and mistress have spent the morning catching, locks both cat and, carelessly, *keys* in the lighthouse. Thereafter mishap builds on mischance to produce calamity. The ultimate solution hearkens back hilariously to the line-and-pulley bur-lesque of the first book. The absurdly bumbling lighthouse keeper and his resourceful never-say-die wife – not to mention the incorrigible Hamish – contrive to create astonishing chaos in an apparently idyllic situation, to the certain joy of young reader-viewers and their elders.

The Lighthouse Keeper's Rescue finds Mr Grinling growing inevitably older. 'Sometimes he could hear his bones creaking as he climbed the lighthouse stairs.' Disastrously, he starts to fall asleep in unsuitable situations; catastrophically, his shortcomings are discovered by the inspector of lighthouses ... Mr and Mrs Grinling will have to leave the little cottage on the cliffs! But when a gigantic whale casts itself on the beach and is saved only by the energy and enterprise of Mr Grinling – and the rescue is shown on television – a compromise is found: Mr Grinling will be given an assistant! Sam, the assistant, proves his value in more ways than one in the last saga of Grinling misadventure, *The Lighthouse Keeper's Picnic*. Now that he is enjoying semi-retirement, Mr Grinling's disasters change in nature, but not extent ...

It is common these days to hear people bemoaning modern youngsters' alleged 'lack of respect' for older people. Understandable, really; gone are the days when children could count on a resident – or at least close – granny or grandpa to forgive them their sins, lend an ear, and provide an occasional refuge. Getting to know the ageing, warm-hearted Grinlings, smiling at Mr Grinling's bumbling ways and his wife's organizing skills, provides useful insight into old age, with its mixed pleasures and problems. No amount of instruction could be half as effective.

Ronda and David Armitage have perfected a divided-page, almost comic-strip technique to vary the traditional whole-page treatments of their picture books, and this is seen again to advantage in *Don't Forget Matilda!*, a story about a family of koalas. Matilda is the sturdy, forceful small daughter whose father looks after her while her mother works. Father is genial and efficient, but both he and Matilda are inclined to forget things. The pages of this splendid book are crammed without being cluttered. 'Learning points' abound, again, without over-earnest intention. Family relationships are warm ('Perhaps a little something would take away the ache,' suggested Father) – but realistic ('Well, you'll just have to walk.'). Attention is guaranteed; action and humour abound. This koala family is a welcome change from badgers and bears, but is certainly in the same warm and woolly tradition.

Rosemary Wells has achieved fame through her stories of family life as lived by children, whom she depicts as small furry animals. But there is nothing cute about Wells's characters. These are real children, with all of childhood's self-absorption: cruel and kind by turns, devastatingly honest (especially about one another's shortcomings) devious, competitive and occasionally aggressive. That the books are funny – sometimes quietly, sometimes hilariously – is a bonus for parent and child alike. Wells's messages are certainly there, but she never preaches; and her text is nicely balanced with pictures which often seem to say it all, anyway. In *Morris's Disappearing Bag*, Morris, the youngest of four squat rabbit-children, is at first overjoyed with the bear he receives for Christmas. Later, especially by comparison with Victor's hockey outfit, Rosie's beauty kit and Betty's chemistry set, and the fun these exciting things engender for his siblings, the bear starts to pall. Then Morris notices a present left unclaimed under the tree. His rise to a position of power and envy in the family is meteoric; dream fulfilment on a huge scale!

Why koalas or rabbits or mice or badgers – or bears – instead of humans? Matilda and Morris and Nora and Benjamin, in their separate small persons, embody all small children. Perhaps their animal forms allow them to *be* all small children in a way human form would not? Or maybe children, who like small furry animals, just enjoy identifying with them; the 'moral' is perhaps blurred at the edges, the point taken more painlessly. Minarik's *Little Bear* has this same quality in his dealings with his family. He is all children, perhaps because of, rather than despite, his furry coat and clumsy bear paws. Certainly, these books seem to teach less obviously than some with real-child characters.

There are three books about Titch, and at first sight they may seem suitable for the twos and threes. No harm will be done, certainly, by acquiring one or all at an early stage, but the consideration of size and status is a strong four-year-old preoccupation, and Titch speaks loudly to this older group. Pat Hutchins both wrote and illustrated the books and her text is brief, to the point of sparseness. What it does not say is as significant as what it does.

> *Titch was little.*
> *His sister Mary was a bit bigger.*
> *And his brother Pete was a lot bigger.*
> *Pete had a great big bike.*
> *Mary had a big bike.*
> *And Titch had a little tricycle . . .*

The illustrations, brightly coloured, are seen against a plain white background. On all but one double spread, only the children and the objects mentioned are depicted. The middle spread demonstrates this gifted artist's flair for design, with green hill, yellow buildings and darker green trees creating a perfect setting for the kites which wheel in the sky above; and for the children on either side, Pete and Mary holding tight to their kite strings, and Titch clutching his pinwheel.

Titch himself is an uncompromisingly steadfast little figure, always bringing up the rear, never complaining. He has his moment of reward and glory when the seed he plants grows, and grows and *grows*. On the last page he allows himself a smug little smirk, while older brother and sister exclaim in wonder. In the second book, *You'll Soon Grow into Them, Titch*, the small protagonist is seen first demonstrating that his own clothes are too small for him – and then establishing that cast-offs from higher up the family are certainly a bit too big. Mum and Dad agree that '. . . Titch should have some new clothes' and Dad takes him shopping. The observant viewer may just notice Mum's knitting – and her considerable girth – throughout; Titch gives his outgrown apparel to the new baby with a histrionic flourish. 'He'll soon grow into them,' said Titch.

The third title, *Tidy Titch*, will amuse parents even more than children, I suspect. How many of us have not suffered from the squirrel-like acquisitiveness of the young? Over-four independence needs plenty of this red-blooded stuff to grow on.

In its less arrogant moments, it needs reassurance, too. Confirmation of parental love which is unconditional and total, not to be withdrawn now that babyhood is being left behind, manners are becoming brash, contours harshening. *Little Gorilla* by Ruth Bornstein speaks to any child who wonders in his innermost heart about his place in the world. It is, in a deep sense, about love and acceptance.

> *Once there was a little gorilla, and everybody loved him.*
> *His mother loved him.*
> *His father loved him.*
> *His grandma and grandpa and his aunts and uncles loved him.*
> *Even when he was only one day old, everybody loved Little Gorilla . . .*

Inevitably, Little Gorilla grows.

> *And one day, Little Gorilla was BIG!*

Here, thinks the small listener, comes the crunch. But

> *. . . everybody came, and everybody sang*
> *'Happy Birthday Little Gorilla!'*
> *And everybody still loved him.*

Certainly simple enough in both word and picture for two- and three-year-olds; but speaking most directly to the 'launched' over-four, making his way in the world with his heart in his mouth.

As a picture book this has true virtuosity. Little Gorilla himself avoids both the smart alecky and the sentimentalized monkey image. He is engaging but not coy, mischievous but not slick. The book itself is beautifully designed; its impact is immediate and eloquent. Against a soft green background, Little Gorilla, his family and friends come alive as characters of good humour and diverse temperament. The reaction of Giraffe, Elephant and other animals who suffer (cheerfully or resignedly) from Little Gorilla's ebullience is inferred, not stated. This is a perfect picture book.

By the same token, Pat Hutchins's *Happy Birthday, Sam* touches on a four-year-old concern: the frustration of *feeling* old enough to dress yourself, but of not being tall enough to reach your clothes hanging in the wardrobe – or the taps, when you know you can brush your own teeth . . . The neat resolution of Sam's problem is inspirational. Grandpa's present proves to be a sturdy little chair which allows Sam to service himself completely, and to sail his new boat in the sink.

'It's the nicest boat ever,' he said, 'and the nicest little chair.'

This title, also, is so triumphantly simple in both text, and bold, brisk picture, that you may mistake it for a two-year-old book. But it is a four-year-old book in all its fibres. One knows without being told that it was written by an informed and feeling parent for *her* 'turning' four-year-old.

The need for a short – or longer – stay in hospital is quite common among young children, and parents may feel that a book on the subject will help. Certainly, such books are available, but they tend to date, as hospitals and practices change, and there is very wide divergence in practices anyway; somehow, the pictured people and paraphernalia are never quite what one encounters. I have never been sure that this serious, factual preparation for the experience offers the reassurance parents are hoping to provide; and this doubt extends to other situations, from facing a new baby in the family to moving house, starting school, or whatever experience supposedly threatens the child's security. A story which is set against the relevant background is certainly likely to provide more enjoyment than a sober statement of procedure.

Of course, a booklet written to prepare small prospective patients for entry to a *particular* hospital is a different matter, and can be invaluable. I was asked recently to launch such a booklet at the new Children's Hospital (innovatively christened *The Starship*) in my own city of Auckland, and was delighted to find it well and simply written, with coloured photographs which reflected the text superbly. Somehow contriving to promote confidence without misrepresenting the less attractive aspects of illness, this is a splendid publication. If your child is due to enter hospital, you might ask if such a booklet exists − or even suggest to the management that one be produced.

One of my grandchildren spent many months of her first four years in hospital. *Crocodile Medicine*, by Marjorie-Ann Watts, a dead-pan story about a crocodile patient who disrupts hospital routine but enchants a small fellow patient, had her total, enraptured attention when I produced it for her. This title is now out of print, but a splendid successor, *Crocodile Teeth*, would have received equally joyful approval, I am confident.

Between its cheerfully colourful covers, the same crocodile, obviously now a staple feature of the ward, is seen to be in some distress, copious tears pouring over a swollen cheek. 'Toothache!' diagnoses the doctor; and Julie has the job of persuading − compelling − the great cowardly creature to submit to the kindly but firm ministrations of the dentist. Two for the price of one here! What to expect at the dentist emerges in the most explicit way as Crocodile loses a decayed tooth and has a filling. There is so much to look at, and it is all depicted with such precision, colour and clarity in the well-designed double-spread illustrations, that a child either in or out of hospital could not fail to be charmed.

And of course, blissfully, there is Madeline, whose midnight dash through the streets of Paris to the hospital has been so dramatically documented by Ludwig Bemelmans. Later, she is visited by the other eleven little girls who live with her 'in an old house in Paris that was covered in vines . . .' at which stage Madeline steals the show, as usual.

> *But the biggest surprise by far,*
> *on her stomach was a scar!*

Many years ago, visiting American friends gave our children their own copy of this notable book. It slipped immediately into all our hearts; and on to our tongues, too, for its compelling, exuberant verse was soon in daily use among us.

> *And afraid of a disaster,*
> *Miss Clavel ran fast and faster!*

The book itself seemed quite wonderfully, extravagantly, large to our children, accustomed as they were to post-war New Zealand austerity. And the exotic fly-away pictures were savoured as wonders from another world, as indeed they were. I have never forgotten the family's return from a regular Friday-night library visit a few years later. All of them seemed to fall through the door at once, shouting – from the twelve-year-old down – 'Mum! – *There's another Madeline!*' Their father reported that the fuss in the library had drawn disapproving looks from unencumbered adults selecting their weekend reading, but that Miss Fisher – *our* librarian, always on the side of the kids – had beamed. The new book was *Madeline's Rescue*, and there she was again, reckless, intrepid child, risking life and limb *and* Miss Clavel's sanity in the very shadow of the Eiffel Tower and the bridges over the Seine. (A priceless bonus, this artist's genius for bringing the sights and sounds of London and Paris alive.) Between 1952 and 1962, five more Madeline books were published in London.

Only two titles (*Madeline* and *Madeline in London*) are currently in print, but there is every hope that others will reappear. As an antidote to over-seriousness and the dull realism with which all too many modern adults would beleaguer children, *Madeline* is unalloyed treasure. The wonderful doggerel verses, outrageously flouting all rules of scansion, grammar and good taste, lodge in the mind:

> *Poor Miss Clavel, how would she feel*
> *If she knew that on top of the Ferris wheel,*
> *In weather that turned from bad to rotten,*
> *Pepito and Madeline had been forgotten?*

> *As a diet there is nothing worse*
> *Than green apples and roses for an old horse.*
> *'Dear lady' said Miss Clavel 'we beg your pardon.*
> *It seems our horse has eaten up your garden.'*

and

> *It serves you right you horrid brat*
> *For what you did to that poor cat!*

Incomparable stuff for the deserving young.

Librarians and booksellers are constantly asked for books on 'problem' subjects; and one of these is dying. It is my belief, formed over many years of reading and reviewing children's books, that the oblique approach is the best one here; and that animals as characters allow a child to participate in grief, as it were, at one remove from the raw pain of human loss.

For the oldest children in the group under discussion, *Badger's Parting Gifts*, by Susan Varley, offers a version of death in old age, its acceptance by those bereaved, and an assurance of the normality of their grief. The setting of this sensitive yet down-to-earth story has a *Wind in the Willows* flavour; the animals, Mole, Frog, Fox and Rabbit, live as neighbours in a woodland setting, all of them profiting from old Badger's kindness and wisdom. When he dies – which he does willingly – they are initially devastated. 'All the animals had loved Badger, and everyone was very sad. Mole especially felt lost, alone and desperately unhappy.'

Winter intervenes and the animals must cope with their sorrow as the snow covers their homes. With the approach of spring, visiting begins again, and they find themselves increasingly talking about Badger and the way he had helped all of them to learn individual skills. 'He had given them each a parting gift to treasure always. Using these gifts they would be able to help each other.'

The illustrations in this original book have a quality which is haunting; there is at once cosy domestic warmth and the beauty and harshness of nature, the inevitability of the seasons somehow echoing and reinforcing the certainties of birth, life and death.

I'll Always Love You, by Hans Wilhelm, is ostensibly about the death of a pet; but it is also about life, and how it can be lived richly. A boy tells us about 'Elfie – the best dog in the whole world', of how he and she grew up together . . . 'but Elfie grew much faster than I did' . . . and of how Elfie died when he was still a boy and she was an old dog. We see his love for Elfie in action; they are just as boisterous as one expects boy and dog to be, and the boy tells the dog every night 'I'll always love you,' and believes that she understands. There is humour, as well as pathos in the picture of the youngster toiling upstairs bearing the elderly Elfie; and the family grief, as they bury the loved old dog together, is expressive, but not sentimental. The boy's good sense is revealed as he refuses a new puppy. 'Someday I'll have another dog, or a kitten, or a goldfish. But whatever it is, I'll tell it every night: "I'll always love you."' This simple story demonstrates, superbly, the capacity of a good piece of fiction to suggest to readers of any age, useful ways of coping with unavoidable loss, and of enjoying those we love, be they people or animals.

It's no use asking me for a book to help a child face, or come to terms with, the death of a parent. I can only suggest that all books which are good, honest, loving books have a capacity to help people understand that life is shadow as well as light, sorrow as well as laughter, and that we all have to come to terms with it in our own way. Human scars heal in the end in a climate of love, goodwill and good humour. Don't waste time looking for a particular book in an emergency; the best book will be the one that diverts, amuses, engrosses, stirs the imagination and warms the heart. Such a book may well create a climate in which emotion can be expressed, and this is infinitely more important than 'understanding'. How can anyone, adult or child, 'understand' the death of another loved person?

However, there are many occasions in a child's life when a book may help him to accept or adjust to a particular situation. It is understandable that parents should be eager to find and use these books as need arises, but essential that they should be good books in their own right; not merely a book about new babies, going to playschool, the doctor, the dentist, the barber or whatever. *A Brother for Momoko* was so exactly right for my eldest grandchild when she stayed with me at three-and-a-half while her baby brother was born, that the experience of reading it to her was breathtaking. One felt Nicola experiencing that book with her eyes, her ears, her whole body. It was somehow, instantly, part of her. Such an experience must remain with a child always, however 'forgotten' the book. Iwasaki's sensed-rather-than-seen knowledge of, and feeling for, a tiny girl who just turned into a big sister is delicately but strongly transmitted, both by word and illustration, in this superb book.

> *He is tiny and soft and warm.*
> *And he is my very own brother.*

Regrettably, *A Brother for Momoko* is out of print as I write. I do not want to believe that it is gone for ever, and so have left it intact rather than allow it to become a casualty of this revision. (You will note that I have done this with some other dearly loved titles.) The library may be able to help, meanwhile.

Solo parents are commonplace in picture books these days; Phoebe and her elderly Dad have their counterpart in Alex and his youngish Mum, about whom Mary Dickinson has written five books. These are brisk, cheerful stories with an urban setting which is graphically portrayed in bold colour by Charlotte Firmin. Relationships are democratic. Alex and his Mum bicker and laugh together, and come out on top. Mum must certainly be acceptable to the feminists among us; she builds Alex a bed on stilts when he runs out of floor space in his tiny room. *Alex's Bed* is the first story. The other titles are listed at the end of this chapter.

If you have been reading to your child since babyhood, you will certainly notice by now how much he or she has learned about people, their relationships and interaction, from books. This is, of course, a lifetime phenomenon; novels which present real characters – men and women with all of humankind's diverse characteristics – will continue to nourish and sustain anyone lucky enough to have acquired the reading habit, to the end of life. Phoebe and her father, Alex and his Mum, and Titch and his family unobtrusively engender learning about the human condition in a way those books which set out to 'teach' never succeed in doing.

Children, as well as adults, find a 'series' satisfying in more ways than one. To begin with, 'another' story about the same people or place has a familiar, comforting aura before you even start to read it; and if you liked *one*, there is some certainty that the others in the series will be your cup of tea, too. Shirley Hughes has capitalized on this very human reaction in her Tales of Trotter Street. In the first book, *Angel Mae*, small Mae is obliged to perform in the school Christmas play while her mother is off having their new baby. Falling off a chair on the stage doesn't help her confidence – but Dad's appearance in the back of the hall at the last minute (with NEWS!) makes everything all right again.

In *The Big Concrete Lorry* the Pattersons at number twenty-six are short of space, and decide to build their own extension. When the concrete is delivered a day early, all the neighbours (including Mae's dad and Sanjit Lal and *his* dad) lend a hand to shovel, wheel, cart and carry the fast-setting stuff to the building site at the back of the house. 'Everyone laboured and struggled and fell over one another's feet . . .' This is a rousing story with universal appeal; and 'the small concrete hill' which sets unofficially outside the Patterson's front door, but '. . . was great for sitting on and for racing toy cars down', will have all young listeners yearning for just such a fortunate accident.

Wheels sees Carlos so envious of his friend Billy's new bike that he just can't be generous. Then Marco, Carlos's big brother, makes him a go-cart as a birthday surprise – and Carlos and Billy soar to fame in the local 'Non-Bicycle Race'. The Tales of Trotter Street are full of natural children and adults, all pursuing their everyday lives in their own individual ways. The families are culturally diverse, with the usual modern range of structure: Carlos and Marco's mother is bringing up her boys alone, and old Mrs Dean (Mrs *Mean*, on occasion, to the children) in *The Snow Lady* lives by herself and is grumpy and critical – but the overall tone is warm, the people themselves real – and the pictures wonderfully expressive. Children grow, in the face of stories like these.

And this is the time for poetry: no need, now, to confine yourself to nursery rhymes, with infusions of simple jingle and traditional rhyming story. All these will continue to have a place – but every manner of verse may now be tried. Owning a 'big' collection of poetry makes good sense, but poses a problem: which one?

My all time favourite, Louis Untermeyer's *Golden Treasury of Poetry*, is once again unavailable, but will surely reappear. First published in the United States of America in 1959 by Golden

Press and taken up almost at once – in time for my children – by Collins, in England, this handsome book served our family faithfully.

The Walker Book of Poetry for Children is one of the best 'big' collections available at the moment, and can certainly be acquired with assurance. Very comprehensive (containing 572 poems, the catalogue tells us), this almost dazing collection has the supreme advantage of Arnold Lobel's illustrations in full colour, with line drawings. Even a small child will browse happily through such a treasure house, increasingly finding favourites. Jack Prelutsky, the compiler, is himself a poet, and his choice has been sure-footed – as it has also in *The Walker Book of Read-Aloud Rhymes*. In this shorter collection, he has kept his eye firmly on the very youngest child and included only rhythmical verses with accessible content. He has paid attention to length, too. Nursery rhymes, with their short, pithy stanzas and long survival record, are surely the prototypes in this field. I would suggest using only a few of the poems at a time, with the emphasis strongly on repetition. For the well-remembered poem is the one which gives pleasure for years – even for life – and too wide a range may restrict the possibility of easy recall. So choose the poems that you like best, and concentrate on, say, six at a time for a reading session, repeating those your child obviously enjoys. Don't hesitate to note titles and page numbers of favourites in the front of the anthology – in pencil, if you feel badly about writing in books. (I have never been a purist in this field; one's own books are such intimate possessions that personal notes and comments seem to grace rather than deface them.)

Almost as I write, a new collection aimed directly at the age-group under discussion has appeared. Called simply *Poems for the Very Young* and compiled by Michael Rosen, this handsome book is worthy of inclusion in any family library (and would make a spectacular grandparently present!). Michael Rosen must have an open line to the threes, fours and fives; there is a splendid vitality about his choices and agreeable consistency in levels throughout the book. In his Introduction, Rosen says, 'Of all the ways of using words, poetry is surely the most physical, and is a particularly appropriate kind of literature to give to children. So the core of this collection is a playful use of words and sounds.' This quality is certainly present in abundance, and the choice of Bob Graham as illustrator is inspired. Graham's work has buoyancy and elegance, and is always affectionately funny.

But don't feel that any one collection will do! I will use Rosen's *Poems for the Very Young* constantly, now that I have found it, but will still need other books for other poems – particularly some old favourites ('Someone came knocking . . .' springs to mind). And wit and nonsense should be tempered with mystery and wonder, even at this early stage.

Because the child responds so quickly and spontaneously to humorous verse, you may be tempted to favour the funny examples over the more serious, and this would be a shame. Such lines as the following, from 'The Night Will Never Stay' by Eleanor Farjeon, will start to show a child how simple words can be combined in a way which makes them special. Children will not know that their senses are being prodded and their imaginations activated, but they will know that the experience is enjoyable.

> *The night will never stay,*
> *The night will still go by,*
> *Though with a million stars*
> *You pin it to the sky;*
> *Though you bind it with the blowing wind*
> *And buckle it with the moon,*
> *The night will slip away,*
> *Like sorrow or a tune.*

All children wonder about the mystery of night: its inevitability, its beauty, its secrecy. Known words which spring to mind, unspoken, in the face of this mystery give not only pleasure but form to the enigma. Security has more than one source in childhood. Access to language which defines and satisfies can be part of it.

The ordinary events and features of the natural world have fortunately received inspired attention from some of the best poets for children, and on these subjects, their work cannot date.

'April Rain Song' by Langston Hughes will spring to mind – and perhaps tongue – at bedtime:

> *The rain plays a little sleep song on our roof at night –*
> *And I love the rain*

and be complemented during a rainy day by Marchette Chute's cheerful and contrasting 'Spring Rain':

> *My hair is wet my feet are wet,*
> *I couldn't be much wetter*
> *I fell into a river once*
> *But this is even better.*

Rainbows are as magical to children today as they must have been a million years ago. Walter de la Mare caught this wonder in his lines from 'Rainbow':

> *I saw the lovely arch*
> *Of Rainbow span the sky.*
> *The gold sun burning*
> *As the rain swept by.*

The marvel and awe of a child's first encounter with the combined wonders of rainbow, sun and rain may well remain with him or her for life, if words and experience have fused.

And please do not take too seriously my warning about the blandishments of funny verse. Easiest of all to learn, it will lighten day or night, for any age. Families will have their favourites. Understandably perhaps, Spike Milligan's 'Granny' –

> *Through every nook and every cranny*
> *The wind blew in on poor old Granny . . .*

– has a firm place in my own family. Its last verse lends itself to a crescendo build-up:

> *It blew on man; it blew on beast.*
> *It blew on nun; it blew on priest.*
> *It blew the wig off Auntie Fanny –*
> *But most of all it blew on Granny!*

And why should Ian Serraillier's racy, little-known gem go unused among the world's young?

> *Aunt was on the garden seat*
> *Enjoying a wee nap and*
> *Along came a fox! teeth*
> *Closed with a snap and*
> *He's running to the woods with her*
> *A-dangle and a-flap and –*
> *Run, uncle, run*
> *And see what has happened.*

(which becomes 'hap – *and*'!) in the best renditions.

It is in the nature of children's poetry to be repeated and repeated, and this is a good argument for owning at least one 'big' anthology. Children take great pleasure in knowing poems by heart, and learn them easily if they hear them often. Poetry is a natural extension of nursery rhyme. Lilt and rhythm are instinctive to childhood and can be enhanced, given form and expression, by familiarity with a wide range of poetry.

> *What shall I call*
> *My dear little dormouse?*
> *His eyes are small,*
> *But his tail is e-nor-mouse.*

('The Christening' by A. A. Milne)

> *I found him lying near the tree; I folded*
> *up his wings.*
> *Oh, little bird, you never heard*
> *The song the summer sings.*

('For a Bird' by Myra Cohn Livingston)

> *Spin a coin, spin a coin,*
> *All fall down;*
> *Queen Nefertiti*
> *Stalks through the town . . .*

(Author unknown)

Wonder enters and stays with such poetry stored in the memory.

One of my children (the first Anthony) was fascinated when he was four by Robert Louis Stevenson's poem 'Where Go the Boats?' (Even the title stirs the spirit!)

> *Dark brown is the river,*
> *Golden is the sand,*
> *It flows along forever,*
> *With trees on either hand*
>
> *
>
> *Green leaves a-floating,*
> *Castles of the foam,*
> *Boats of mine a-boating —*
> *Where will all come home?*

This poem was Anthony's favourite; he was obviously carried away on the tide of the image it evoked for him.

> *Away down the river,*
> *A hundred miles or more,*
> *Other little children*
> *Shall bring my boats ashore.*

Hardly surprising that sailing later became one of this child's passions.

Don't neglect to point out to your child how different on the page different poems *look*. A familiar poem leaps at you from the page like an old friend. Long before he can read, your youngster will recognize the *shape* of a poem he loves, even in an unillustrated collection.

> *John had*
> *Great Big*
> *Waterproof*
> *Boots on;*
> *John had a*
> *Great Big*
> *Waterproof*
> *Hat;*

> *John had a*
> *Great Big*
> *Waterproof*
> *Mackintosh –*
> *And that*
> *(Said John)*
> *Is*
> *That.*

A. A. Milne's poem 'Happiness', from *When We Were Very Young*, with its sturdy, stomping rhythm, sounds good, even without the book. But with the book – and an adult who will point to the words as they are said – the whole thing becomes a visual experience, as well as a listening treat.

Familiarity breeds affection in this field. Years ago in an old, much-loved volume, we had a copy of Rachel Field's 'General Store'.

> *Some day I'm going to have a store*
> *With a tinkly bell hung over the door,*
> *With real glass cases and counters wide*
> *And drawers all spilly with things inside . . .*

Somehow, we contrived to lose this anthology. When one of the family mentioned the poem later, I said, 'Between us, we *must* know it by heart,' and we found that we did. But it was not the same. We needed to *see* it, its solid, all-of-a-piece bulk sitting on the left side of the detailed, black-and-white line picture.

> *It will be my store and I will say:*
> *What can I do for you today?*

Met again, in a new collection several years later, it was greeted with cries of joyful recognition. Here was an old friend; but a slightly changed, because displaced, friend. The old, lost copy was never supplanted in our hearts.

It is advisable to read poetry alone, rehearsing its rhythms and absorbing its sense, before offering it to the young. There is nothing more enjoyable than reading aloud material which you know and love yourself, and this is particularly true of poetry. The child's enjoyment will reflect yours (a well-known phenomenon in any sphere); and enjoyment that is mutual is the most intense enjoyment of all.

The Young Puffin Book of Verse should be in every child's home, with another copy in the family car for emergencies. This paperback collection contains an astonishing number of the best poems every written for children of four to eight – including 'Some day I'm going to have a store . . .' On no account face life without it!

And for real, mad fun, do lay in a copy of *Inky Pinky Ponky*, subtitled *Children's Playground Rhymes* and collected by Michael Rosen and Susanna Steele. Dan Jones has brought the inspired anthology to wild life with pictures of indescribable innovation. This is one collection which, once known, would be unimaginable without its pictures (And the rhymes are scrumptiously subversive!)

I have spent what may seem to be a disproportionate time on poetry at the expense of stories for this age group. This is because I feel strongly about the child's need to experience language which is vital, resourceful, exhilarating and harmonious, language which provides the human ear with a pointed and precise pleasure which is not available from any other source, language which is crucial to the development of intelligence and self-expression.

Our society is becoming increasingly dependent on the visual image. Television selects what we will look at; advertisements are designed so that non-readers will still get the point. Sound is often loud, strident and undifferentiated. The precise, searching, illuminating impact of good and true words is in danger of being lost against the blaring and glaring background of the modern child's world. Parents are not to blame for this, and many of them, through no fault of their own, have no real 'feeling' for the sort of language which will help their children to develop into sensitive, confident, articulate women and men. I believe that the best books, from birth, will do as much for parents as for children in this area, and at the same time keep them in touch with one another. And this is the most important thing of all.

Now is the time to introduce the occasional story without pictures. In fact, I feel that the fourth birthday might well be marked by the acquisition of a collection for this purpose. Have you ever told a child a story which you invented as you went along – and felt her close attention to the words, almost *seen* the picture she was building up in her mind? This is what happens – what *must* happen – when, later, children read to themselves. They must carry the image in their minds, modifying it, building on it, taking the action a step further ... What better time to start giving practice than now? I will say more about this topic in the next chapter, but feel strongly that the practice should be established in the year between four and five. You will find suggested titles in the Book List, and might, perhaps, read ahead to my remarks on the subject. Four- and five-year-olds have much in common, and are travelling at their own pace through the same landscape. There is simply no sharp division between them – or any other of the age-groups under discussion.

There is something very special about a child's fifth birthday. Parents feel that *real* childhood is about to begin, and commonly communicate this idea to their children. Even the number '5' itself is special. After all, it is half of '10', the basis of our decimal counting system. (This sensation persists through life; '45' feels like a more certain landmark than '43' or '46'.)

Some near-fives are already noting the conventions of printed text. Many can write their own names and recognize simple numbers. Some print-passionate children ask, constantly, about written signs and symbols. These are the youngsters who 'drive us mad with their questions!' Others are sublimely uninterested in deciphering written material of any sort – and may later take in all they need in great gobbling gulps. The majority makes steady, less spectacular progress on the road to literacy (and many of these excel in the end), while a few experience difficulties and may need extra help. This is not the time for comparisons.

One thing is certain: nourishing children's minds is infinitely more important than evaluating their progress – which we cannot do with any reliability, anyway. Some of the most creative children are the least conforming, the most divergent. Some children love to perform, and want to impress adults; others are intent on their own concerns – which may not often converge with ours! Relying on books, in all *their* diversity and richness, to cater for this varied group makes good sense.

When I was Five . . .

7

When I was Five,
I was just alive

. . . Emerging, undeniably from the long apprenticeship of infancy and toddlerhood; launched, but with still a way to go! Five-year-olds are enjoyable people. Their belief in adults as fountains of love, wisdom and support is flattering, and their needs are easy to meet. They like to be acceptable, in the main, and this means a reduction of that risk-anything insubordination which seemed to characterize their behaviour in the preceding year. Of course, five-year-olds are also as different, one from the other, as are fifteen-year-olds or forty-five-year-olds. But, like the members of these other age groups, they have much in common.

Five-year-olds are at the crossroads. At home, particularly if there are one or more younger children, they seem large, competent and bossy. Their joy in their own apparent strength bubbles over into wild action; they play indefatigably, indoors and out, devising games which reflect their entire repertoire of experience, both first- and secondhand: from shopkeeper through doctors and nurses to Superman, all in a single afternoon. Sometimes, they seem drunk with the sheer joy of being alive.

Wise parents of five-year-olds postpone plans for home redecoration which include fragile, handmade ornaments and pastel furnishings, unless their home is large enough to provide an 'out-of-bounds to children' section. (Shades of the Victorian parlour!)

This is seldom possible in the average modern house, and has its limitations as a policy, anyway. Furniture can be stout and functional and still attractive, and prohibitions few but sensible. Of course, there must be limits; but if their infringement (inevitable, occasionally) leads to real damage or disaster, there will always be tension in the family. Children must have scope for imaginative games, if their minds, bodies and spirits are to be nourished. By this provision for creative play during childhood, we encourage their development into competent and responsible adults.

School as a hurdle must not be underestimated in the life of the five-year-old. Pre-school groups are for fun; school is in deadly earnest. We may make light of it, but the message is received. For better or worse, school-starters enter a huge, bureaucratic organization which will seem to possess them for an unimaginable period of time. (Remember that five-year-olds find it impossible to imagine next week.) Requirements are made of them, inexorably, whether they value or understand these demands or not – or want to be thrust out from the comfortable security of their homes, into this strange, new, dazing environment, anyway. Some of the most original children are the least conforming. Other children naturally prefer a degree of order and peace. To these children, the jungle of the large school playground must seem like a nightmare, full of roaring noise and violent action.

In this setting, the 'big' five-year-old is very small indeed, and may feel even smaller. For five-year-old competence is only skin deep. Obliged for the first time in their lives to keep track of personal possessions, five-year-olds need constant servicing from adults. 'Where is your jersey (shoes, school lunch, handkerchief, book, bus fare, raincoat)?' and other reasonable demands, bounce endlessly off the bemused school-starter. Understanding of cause and effect is minimal at this stage, and likely to be reduced by the sheer trauma of new demands and circumstances.

But appearances must be kept up in public, and this means that home and family must take up the slack. The phenomenon of the well-behaved school-attender (aged five) who collapses into an ungovernable passion on arrival home is well known to experienced parents. Language in the service of reason avails us little, here. We must treat this exhausted, over-stimulated, confused and despairing human being as a two-year-old, gather her up and find some way of establishing home base as a warm and accepting haven all over again.

Don't imagine that this is easy, or that what works for one

child will necessarily work for another. The art is to help the child to learn to cope with her own reaction to stress; a lifetime problem for all of us, actually. We expect a lot of these small, inexperienced people.

Some parents resort to television as a pacifier at this stage. Certainly, its capacity to remove human attention from the real scene of action, without itself making any intellectual demands, is impressive. But do we want to produce a human being who switches on the television set when the going gets tough? What about helping children to accept their own and other people's reaction to life as it is, the opportunity to start developing strategies for coping with reality? This is what we all need, and I don't believe that it is advanced by the use of the flickering screen as a mindless comfort.

The habit of an after-school story session, once the pattern is set, will become a strength; something for both the child and the parent to look forward to. This is an age when all children love individual parental attention.

Certainly, differences in temperament play their part in establishing needs. For some people, life will always be more difficult than for others. But for most, the sixth year of life has particular trials. Allowances must be made.

And the passage of time does help. Five-year-olds *want* to be acceptable, and are now prey to painful embarrassment when things get out of hand. Their growing understanding of the way things *should* be done is in strong contrast to their capacity for accomplishment.

They still need shelter from possible failure and unwelcome limelight, and look to us, their family, for this protection. Our support must be total. We expect a lot from our children; temporary adjustment of our own lifestyle is more than justified in their cause.

Nor should we be lulled into a belief that problems solved will *stay* solved, in the early years. Almost all children, at some stage during their first year at school, are swamped, suddenly, by the realization that their lives have been taken over by 'the system'; that their range of choices has narrowed drastically, if not dried up utterly. Resentment, if not open revolt, may result – and is as common in the confident as in the apprehensive child. (The cheerful, outgoing youngster *expects* to have some say in his own destiny, and may be outraged to discover that this is a vain hope!)

Extra support is needed in the face of such reaction. More attention at home, small after-school treats and an occasional day off will help. Evidence is required that people really do care, and are prepared to support. Accompanying, rather than dispatching the child to school for a time may help, and avoiding recriminations certainly will. It is easy to slip into panicky verbal reaction – we are all thrown off our perches when our apparently stable offspring show signs of rebellion. 'Don't be silly – you're a big girl now, and you *like* school!' 'Look at Peter!' (who started last week, and is bathed in new-found glory). 'He's much younger than you and *he* isn't making a fuss!'

The whole of life – our own, as well as our children's – is a complicated and messy business, at best. We never progress in any field, but that we slip back a few notches in another. Some days we know we are operating below par. We suspect that we would be better tomorrow, if we were able to walk on the hills today ... but we have been brought up to believe that work, however unrewarding, is good for us, and we press on.

We must, at all costs, avoid conditioning our children for a world which is ceasing to exist. We cannot know what lies ahead for them, but we can be sure of one thing. Qualities of originality, flexibility and good humour have always helped human beings to lead good lives, even in difficult times, and we must try to believe that they always will. Any other course has us defeated at the outset. We must, and *can* fortify and equip our children by our love and concern for them, and by the example we give them of our own energetic involvement in the affairs of our immediate world.

And books will help us to do this, immeasurably.

Five-year-olds are ready for a wide range of books. While continuing to love picture books (as indeed they will, throughout this whole period and beyond), they will listen, increasingly, to stories without pictures, or with very few.

Learning to listen – 'to make the pictures in your own head', as one of my children described the process – must be seen as an important skill for the five-year-old. Evidence exists that, in our over-graphic world, many children lag in this capacity, with serious results at a later stage. Recent research reveals that students of seventeen and eighteen years of age commonly have listening difficulties which have nothing to do with deafness; they merely cannot construct mental concepts from heard, or read, language, without the help of pictures or diagrams. This is, of course, a serious handicap, for the ear surpasses all other organs as an implement of effective learning.

If you find this hard to believe, think of the plight of totally deaf children. Because they find it so hard to learn to speak and to read, the majority of deaf children have limited chances of reaching their full intellectual potential. By contrast, blind children, their ears alert to the language around them and with braille books at their disposal, may keep pace with their normally equipped contemporaries, and even, helped by the development of compensatory senses, outstrip them intellectually.

Blindness is a tragic disability; but it does not compare with deafness in its capacity to limit or distort the growth of mind and personality. When one considers that the students described above were *not* deaf, but merely incapable of using their physically perfect senses of hearing, through the influences of the environment which the modern world provides for them, there is certainly cause for alarm.

There can be no doubt that the capacity to listen – responsively and imaginatively – is one which we must help children to develop. Just as certainly, recourse to books, as sources of material which will induce this sort of listening, is not only sensible, but imperative.

Ideally, the five-year-old child has been listening to stories without pictures for at least a year. If this has not been the case, then I would suggest a special effort, perhaps in the proportion of one story without illustrations, to two picture books. If the child seems reluctant to make the change, I would give practice in listening to a *told* story, rather than a tale from a book. You need not feel unequipped for this task. Every time we say to a friend, 'Guess what happened yesterday!' we are launching into a story-telling venture – and most of us do it well!

Some people are born storytellers. Usually, the art comes so easily that they neither recognize nor value it. They just love telling anyone who will listen about things which have happened to themselves, or to other people. Their reward comes in the response of their listeners: rapt and goggle-eyed attention, as like as not.

Family life provides a rich source of such tales, which, like the best traditional stories, grow in the telling. (The time our year-old baby was seen to be wearing her upturned bowl of porridge as a hat . . . the famous day on which our four-year-old, shrouded to his ankles in a cardboard box, walked over the edge of the terrace and bowled down the hill . . . No one, least of all the central figure in the drama, has ever tired of hearing about these and other homely catastrophes. All families have them, surely! Your material is there and waiting.)

The next step is, of course, to produce a book without pictures; and it helps to explain the process to the young listener, in simple terms. I recall the following example, which fell into my lap some years ago. A small grandson and his father were lying on the beach. David was reading to Oliver, holding the book (*The Adventures of Sam Pig*, by Alison Uttley) at arm's length, using it as a shield from the sun. 'Bring it closer! I can't *see*!' said Oliver, with the bossiness of the five-year-old to his nearest and dearest. David pointed out that, since there was not a picture in sight, Oliver might as well lie back, close his eyes and make the pictures in his head. Oliver complied with this suggestion, and after a short while said, 'I'm doing it, Dad! It works!'

The fortunate chance of three grandchildren born within three weeks (now all aged fifteen) presented an excellent opportunity for (unobtrusive!) comparison of their interaction with books from birth, and the year they all started school was particularly fascinating. Notes made at the time reveal wide differences, and yet they were all from 'bookish' families. Christopher, when listening to an unillustrated story, would gaze into the distance, his eyes reflecting the mood of the story. Hannah also gazed dreamily at nothing in particular but would return to the book abruptly at intervals, asking 'Where are we up to?' A finger pointing satisfied her. Oliver, their cousin, consistently looked at the book, as if meaning might emerge spontaneously.

What was going on in each very different child's mind? Were they reflecting on the process by which the reading adult converts print into sensible language, or did they believe that some sort of magic was at work? Their comments indicated that they believed that reading was something that occurred. 'You can read when you're six,' said Christopher. (Oliver earlier made this same prediction about his ability to tie his shoelaces, using five as the key age. Sure enough, in the week after his fifth birthday, he was seen to be practising resolutely – with swift success, which did not seem to surprise him at all.)

We cannot know, with any certainty, what is going on in a child's mind, but it is a field of inquiry in which the parent can rival the expert. The opportunity to develop awareness, to observe children closely and sensitively, to relate what happens one day to what emerges as an utterance, or an action, the next day – or the next month – is the parent's priceless preserve. Insights, revelations, and mysteries come thick and fast at those parents who listen, look and reflect. (Child-watching beats bird-watching hands down, and you need never crawl out at dawn and risk a wet and muddy stomach . . . well, not often.)

What sort of stories will best nourish this burgeoning personality, then?

Almost all children, however inexperienced as listeners, will attend to realistic stories. Children of one's own age having fun, getting into trouble and bouncing back – here is drama indeed. And no one tells stories of everyday family life better than Astrid Lindgren.

The ups and downs and doings of small Lotta Marten, as recounted by slightly older Maria, with older-still Jonas, playing his mostly responsible part, make wonderful reading in *Lotta Leaves Home* and *The Mischievous Martens*. For good measure, their father sets an example of good-humoured parenthood which all fathers might use as a yardstick.

'Once when he came home,' [*says Maria*], *'we hid behind the coat rack and were very quiet, and Daddy said to Mother, "Where's all the noise around here? Are my children ill?"*
'Then we jumped out from behind the coats, laughing.
'"You mustn't frighten me like that," Daddy said. "There has to be a lot of crashing and banging when I come home, otherwise I get worried."'

The Marten children visit the dentist (where Lotta refuses to open her mouth), foist themselves upon kindly old Mrs Berg next door (where Lotta unravels the old lady's knitting and Jonas wins a leaning-out-of-the-window competition by falling right out) and go by train to stay with grandparents. Astrid Lindgren understands childhood profoundly; the three children's behaviour and escapades are always based solidly in child-nature. Many of their apparently funny remarks reveal keen perceptiveness, a quality often present in the comments of young children, if adults are prepared to listen. (When Lotta's cousin, Thomas, who is also staying at Grandmother's house, is afraid to sleep without the light on, his mother points out that at home he is never afraid of the dark. Lotta explains, 'At home it's his own dark, Aunt Katie. He isn't used to Grandmother's dark . . .')

Teddy Robinson must be met at five, if he has not been encountered earlier. He is a 'nice, big, comfortable, friendly teddy bear', who belongs to a little girl called Deborah. Things certainly *happen* to Teddy Robinson, but they are always visited upon him; never does he take action. Throughout his long catalogue of mishap, calamity, reversal, and modest victory, he remains an extension of his small owner, an owner whose spirit and imagination do nicely for the two of them, fortunately. You can *count* on Teddy Robinson, just as he counts on Deborah.

Teddy Robinson's creator, his namesake Joan Robinson, is also responsible for the existence of Mary-Mary, a figure of classic proportion. Mary-Mary is a clear thinker and an honest practitioner. Here she is, making a cake, 'a nice raw cake', as she describes it, having decided that she prefers her cakes raw. This is, of course, an unofficial activity; but then Mary-Mary's doings invariably owe more to originality than to protocol. Two eggs in succession have just landed on the floor.

'Oh, well, eggs will be eggs, I suppose,' said Mary-Mary. 'It's no use getting annoyed because they're slippery. If I can't get the eggs to the cake, I shall have to take the cake to the eggs.'

So she did. She turned the bowl upside down and mixed the whole lot together on the floor. It was not so good as a bowl, because there was nothing to keep the mixture from spreading, but Mary-Mary walked round and round, pushing it in from the edges with the wooden spoon. It made the floor rather slippery so she had to be careful where she trod.

Mary-Mary's long-suffering family are models of calm resignation.

'My goodness!' said Martyn (confronted by Mary-Mary's cake-making efforts) and he went away to tell Miriam.

'You really are a nuisance, Mary-Mary,' said Miriam, when she came in. 'Why can't you do something nice and clean and quiet like everyone else?'

Mary-Mary's ventures, however outrageous, are always rewarded, quite unfairly, with success. She has a spectacular quality which is seen in bold relief against the serenely ordered backdrop of her everyday life. She appropriates – from the dustbin – a disreputable handbag, which, in the face of family threat of disposal, she keeps buried in the sandpit. As necessary, she digs it up. The author's own black-and-white illustrations for both Teddy Robinson and Mary-Mary are lively and pertinent. At the time of writing, *Mary-Mary* is out of print, but one hopes it will return. Meanwhile, ask at the library.

You may notice that the titles I have suggested so far in this 'pictureless' category (though all have scattered black-and-white line drawings) have been in print for a long time. I can only say that this is *proof* of their popularity with the young. Publishing is, of necessity, a merciless business; the fact that certain books keep reappearing indicates their tested worth – and I have included several more 'modern' collections in List 5 on page 196.

Perhaps the oldest of all is *Milly-Molly-Mandy*, a virtual veteran in the field. First appearing more than sixty years ago, Milly-Molly-Mandy should not be missed by the modern young. There is honesty, energy and engaging detail in these tales of small child activities. Against a nostalgically evoked background, which has much to offer in its sheer freedom from modern pace and stress, the small heroine and her friends Billy Blunt, Little Friend Susan and Miss Muggin's niece Jilly make their purposeful way through village and field, exploiting to the full the resources of their idyllic environment. Even the characters' names fascinate the five-year-old. (Their influence was clearly present some years ago in my eldest grandchild's list of her best friends: 'Heather-Next-Door, Simon-Down-the-Road and Bruce-Over-the-Bridge.') Lotta, Teddy Robinson, Mary-Mary and Milly-Molly-Mandy – and several others, such as Abigail, Tom, (from *Tom's Saturday Trousers*) and Peter Potts the Plumber, whose exploits are related in books listed at the end of this chapter – all have one chapter devoted to each of their adventures, a useful arrangement for reader and listener alike. Five-year-olds are not known for their patience, and a tale which starts and ends at a sitting may provide a more satisfying experience than an instalment.

Julia Eccleshare, a modern authority on children's literature, has edited a series of storybooks which any family might collect with profit for read-aloud sessions. The *Collins Book of Stories for 4 Year Olds*, and its companion volume for *5 Year Olds* are both characterized by a very wide and diverse range of tales. There are modern stories both realistic and fantastic, traditional tales, and stories from other countries. What they all have in common is their immediate impact; not one story in either of these collections failed to snatch the total attention of the children to whom I read it, immediately; though I must confess that I never managed to read one story *only*, at a sitting, during this experiment! The six-year-old collection would be accessible to many of the best listeners in this group – and it is good to know that Julia Eccleshare has also edited collections for seven- and eight-year-olds in the same series.

Some five-year-olds will have met Sara and Stephen Corrin's *Stories for the Under-Fives*, and will now appreciate *Stories for Five-Year-Olds*. These are well-chosen anthologies, which dip into many of the established favourites (including several mentioned above) and also include lively retellings of traditional tales. Children love to meet well-known characters out of context; an isolated Teddy Robinson story will be welcomed as an old friend by the initiated, and serve to whet the appetite of newer readers. Never reject a collection because it has an already familiar story in it. You will be surprised at the reception your child will give to an old friend. And take note that *Stories for Five-Year-Olds* is the only current source of an incomparable story called 'The Little Boy and His House' by Stephen Bone and Mary Adshead – a story which, in its original picture-book version, I was obliged to read aloud so often to a five-year-old son that I finally knew it by heart!

Both Eccleshare and the Corrins have produced other collections with self-explanatory titles (*More Stories for Five-Year-Olds*, and such). There is certainly no dearth of good stories, once you start looking. Experience will help you develop a sure feel for what *your* child will enjoy.

Some five-year-olds of course, particularly the practised listeners, are ready for stories which proceed through whole books, each chapter dependent on what has gone before. Occasionally, our children surprise us.

Years ago I was looking for a ten-year-old son whose turn it was to dry the dishes, when our four-year-old said, 'Perhaps he's gone off to Narnia.' Somebody laughed, and she said indignantly, 'Well, there could be a magic wardrobe in our house. *There could be!*' Obviously, C. S. Lewis's book *The Lion, the Witch and the Wardrobe*, at that time being read aloud to brothers of eight and ten, was making more sense than one might have imagined to their smallest sister.

Folk and fairy tales provide a fertile field in the search for stories which will capture and keep the attention of the five-and-overs. During this century, psychologists and others have attempted to explain the existence of myths and legends, folk and fairy tales, in terms which relate to the origins, growth and aspirations of humankind. There is little doubt that our fascination for such stories arises, in part at least, from their universality. We see our world, with all its truth and ugliness, its compassion and its violence, its wisdom and its stupidity, reflected in the myths and legends of every culture; and we see ourselves in the queens and the scullery maids, the princes and the woodcutters who people the folk and fairy tales.

The work of the scholars who study the old tales in the hope of uncovering evidence of their 'meaning' makes fascinating reading, and is available for those who are truly interested. But it need not concern us overmuch here. It is enough to know that the magic words 'Once upon a time . . .' will hold 'children from play, and old men from the chimney corner' as successfully today as ever they did in the dim past. And we can demonstrate this to ourselves any time we choose.

The Fairy Tale Treasury, its thirty-two stories selected by Virginia Haviland and illustrated by Raymond Briggs, is probably the most beautifully produced collection available for young children today. Its large, picture-book format makes it especially suitable for reading to a group of children, or as a present to a family. Raymond Briggs's pictures, in alternate double spreads of brilliant colour and black and white, are humorous or dramatic, friendly or frightening, as demanded by the flavour of the story. The retellings are consistently sound; Virginia Haviland has in some cases used existing versions of the tales from approved sources, and in others, retold the stories herself. This is an outstanding book, which can be owned and used for years, with confidence and pleasure.

Don't be put off by the term 'fairy tales'. You will find no gossamer-winged, namby-pamby creatures in these robust stories. In fact, with the exception of the odd evil old woman or two (as, for example, the bad fairy whose pique at being excluded from the party led to the Sleeping Beauty's difficulties), you will find no fairies at all. Rather ogres, giants, wolves, bears, goblins and trolls make trouble for a succession of millers, queens, peasants and princes, with a generous sprinkling of third sons and spirited daughters. Your concern will be to preserve your five-year-old from the worst excesses of their hair-raising interactions!

I suggest treading warily, until you have established your child's resilience. But you may well be surprised. Psychologists tell us that all children have fears and fantasies which eclipse the contents of the most horrific tales, and that bringing these terrors out into the light of day to be shared (however scarily) with others, serves to reduce tension as well as to entertain. Certain it is that children love to hear these tales repeated, over and over again. One of my five-year-old grandchildren currently 'collects' versions of *Hansel and Gretel*; he can never hear this story too often. Why? No one knows, but most of us can recall our own similar fixation with a story or book, or have seen evidence of it in our children.

Sadly, many parents reject the old fairy tales as unsuitable for modern children. Boys are reported (by mothers, in particular) as being 'only interested in space and cars'. A little probing usually reveals that these children have never actually *heard Jack and the Beanstalk* or *Rumpelstiltskin* read aloud by their own parents. Their acquaintance with these and other stories has been hit-and-miss, to say the least. Exposure to a well-told version soon gives the lie to parental belief about child preference! It is safe to say that no stories are more certain to succeed with children than the old, time-tested ones.

A word about 'versions'. Because copyright restrictions do not apply to the work of the Brothers Grimm and Hans Andersen, or to the many stories whose source is unknown, such material is often published in cheaply produced 'mass market' editions. Usually, these books have garish and trite illustrations, and one cannot count on the text to have that simple and pleasing flow which is the hallmark of the genuine fairy tale. Such books (along with comics and some of the 'series' paperbacks) do little harm, if children are exposed, also, to the 'real thing'. In fact, children start quite early to discern differences of quality, unconsciously preferring the best, if we help them to develop a sensitive palate for language – without divulging our intention, which might put them off entirely! It is as well, however, to get value for money when actually *buying* a book, and several easy rules of thumb will ensure this.

Make sure, to begin with, that the publisher has invoked the services of an editor, or collector, and that the sources of the tales, wherever possible, are given. This information will be printed on the title page, and possibly on the flap of the dust-jacket, or on the back cover. This is your guarantee that someone has taken care over this book. The price may be a little higher than that of the 'mass market' edition, but the worth will be there, if the editor has done his or her job responsibly. The name of a reputable publisher, again on the title page, and also on the spine, is an additional assurance of quality. You will soon start to recognize these once you are interested, and librarians and book-sellers will certainly advise you, if consulted.

There have always been differences of opinion about the age at which children should be introduced to fairy stories. Often, of course, the decision is taken out of parental hands; the child hears a potentially frightening story read aloud by an adult at play-group, or in a friend's house, or in his own, where it was intended for an older child. Often, also, the young child surprises his parents by remaining undisturbed. There are as many reactions as there are children, in this field.

The arousal of fear, however, is not the only factor to be considered. Some of the best stories have complex and extended plots that make demands on both concentration and understand-ing which five- and six-year-olds may not be able to meet. It is hardly surprising that, in the face of such stories, they emerge believing that they 'don't like fairy stories'. The tragedy in this case lies not only in the child's present loss. There is a wealth of traditional material available for readers – and listeners – not merely of seven and eight, but of eleven and twelve and over, if the door is not closed by the use of over-difficult stories at an early stage.

(My youngest child kept me reading aloud to her until she was over thirteen – and, immersed as she was at other times in novels and text books, her choice for these sessions was always a fairy tale. And a son of fourteen, whose haversack I was reorganizing for a school camp, proved to have packed, as his weekend reading, the third volume of *The Lord of the Rings*, an indescribably sexy-looking paperback – and Andrew Lang's old *Blue Fairy Book*!)

A point which is sometimes overlooked by those who fear to present fairy tales in which violent or frightening events occur is that, from a very early age, children seem to understand that such stories are at one remove from real life. Five-year-olds might well be expected to be terrified by a film which showed two modern children purposely abandoned by their parents in a forest, and shortly confronted by a wicked old woman who proposes to cook and eat them. However, the 'Once upon a time' formula seems to act as a buffer (even if the magic words are not actually uttered). How do children recognize the formula?

The secret lies, I think, in the unconscious identification of form. The typical, time-honoured opening (There was once . . . Once upon a time . . . Once, in a country far away . . .) is followed by the immediate introduction of characters, who just as quickly become involved in action.

In a cottage near a large wood there once dwelt a poor woodcutter, with his wife and two children by his former marriage, – a little boy called Hansel and a girl named Gretel. The woodcutter was very poor, and once, when there was a great famine, he could not procure even his daily bread. One night as he lay in his bed, tossing and turning with worry, he sighed and said to his wife,

'What will become of us? How can we feed our children when we have no more than we can eat ourselves?'

'Listen to me, my husband,' she answered. 'We will lead them away, quite early in the morning, into the thickest part of the wood . . .'

Place and time are not specified, and only Hansel and Gretel are named. The characters are prototypes, the stepmother cruel but strong, the father kind but weak. The children, seemingly helpless, prove to be resourceful and brave – the girl especially so. She it is who persuades the witch (totally evil) to put her head into the oven which is being heated to cook Hansel, thereby allowing Gretel to give her '. . . a push that sent her headlong into the flames . . .'

It almost seems that children enter into a contract. 'Terrify us temporarily, but let us know, by the flavour and framework of the story, that all will be well in the end. Keep it all a bit removed from modern life, and make the good people good, and the bad people bad, so that we know where we are.' (It is significant, I think, that few children notice the weakness of the father in *Hansel and Gretel*. He loves his children, so he is good. Ambivalence towards a character is out of the question.)

Picture books tumble thick and fast from the presses of publishers, and there is wealth to be uncovered by the discerning eye. Those five-year-olds who are lucky enough to encounter this deluge are fortunate indeed. But some of the best books are still the oldest. No five-year-old (or six or seven-year-old) should be denied the joy of Edward Ardizzone's work.

The twelve titles which document the astounding exploits of Tim, Lucy, Charlotte, Ginger and their friends will (like the Arthur Ransome titles for an older age group) keep moving in and out of print, for as far ahead as the mind can grasp, I suspect. For they are classics in the making. (The first, *Little Tim and the Brave Sea Captain*, was published in 1936 and has appeared on every reliable 'best books' list ever since.)

However, I see disturbing evidence that these incomparable stories are constantly passed over by adults in favour of more 'modern', often crude and spiritless, picture books. Anyone who reads aloud often, and perceptively, to small children knows that while bright colour may initially attract, it is the story which renders the experience memorable, or otherwise. Ardizzone's stories, reflected and extended by illustrations which uniquely complement their spirit, transport the child reader to another place and time; to a world in which children are not helpless and subservient, but capable and independent; a world in which dangers must be faced and reversals accepted, before one can hope to return safely to home and hearth.

In his more 'domestic' tales, Ardizzone's work has the same realistic flavour. However improbable (and *Diana and Her Rhinoceros* must surely be the least likely tale ever told) one *believes* in these stories. Within their own framework they have honesty and integrity. Diana does not consider deserting her rhinoceros, whom she loves with clear but undescribed devotion, any more than Sarah and Simon (in *Sarah and Simon and No Red Paint*) would swerve from the course of helping their penniless father buy the paints he needs to finish his masterpiece, and repulse the wolf from the family door. And Johnny the Clockmaker, resolute in the face of impatience and derision, stands staunchly beside Little Tim and Lucy, each of them involved in concerns which *matter*. Children do not deserve triviality or triteness in their books, and recognize quality almost unconsciously, given the opportunity. Books which have stood the test of time – as have the Little Tim tales, de Brunhoff's Babar the Little Elephant stories and Virginia Lee Burton's incomparable pair, *The Little House* and *Mike Mulligan and His Steam Shovel* – must be seen as classics in the making, their omission from our children's lives a grievous loss.

The shared enjoyment of such a book as *Miss Rumphius*, by Barbara Cooney, can be a richly rewarding experience for both reader and listener, combining as it does illustrations which have both elegance and sparkling beauty, and language which is rich yet unpretentious.

In the evening Alice sat on her grandfather's knee and listened to his stories of faraway places. When he had finished, Alice would say,

'When I grow up, I too will go to faraway places, and when I grow old, I too will live beside the sea.'

'That is all very well, little Alice,' said her grandfather, 'but there is a third thing you must do.'

'What is that?' asked Alice.

'You must do something to make the world more beautiful,' said her grandfather.

'All right,' said Alice. But she did not know what that could be.

In the meanwhile Alice got up and washed her face and ate porridge for breakfast. She went to school and came home and did her homework.

The speech of children whose literary bread and butter, taken daily, consists of stories such as this one, reflects the colour and drama of their experience. They are equipped, not only for the prime tasks of expressing themselves and forging relationships with others, but, in a practical sense, for mastering the arts of reading and writing. They are favoured children.

It is natural that parents will want their children to learn about life in other countries; and disappointing when documentary-type books do not hold their interest. What is needed is a steady supply of picture books which succeed in involving the child through the force of their story, their creation of characters who come alive, the relevance of theme to children's lives everywhere. Such a book is *Not So Fast, Songololo*, and I venture to suggest that any child who comes to know and love this book will have little trouble identifying with black South Africans, regardless of the politics of their elders.

Shepherd is any small child, anywhere, pleased to be accompanying his Granny to town because, as his Mama says, 'He is a big boy now.' Gogo, his grandmother, is old '. . . but her face shines like new school shoes. Her hands are large and used to hard work, but when they touch, they are gentle.' Gogo understands the ways and dreams of small boys, and knows that Shepherd's sneakers (his 'tackies') are old and secondhand. Somehow, money that might have provided Gogo with new shoes (hers are like '. . . worn-out tyres on an old car') is used instead to buy Shepherd a pair of new red-and-white tackies. 'Shepherd feels so happy that it hurts him just to sit still.'

Nothing is said in this well-favoured book about Gogo's tiredness throughout the long journey by bus and on foot, though Niki Daly's picture of the old woman dozing, hands in lap, in the bus terminus while 'Songololo' (his grandmother's pet name for him) sits, knees under chin, gloating over his new shoes, conveys a wealth of fact, as well as feeling. There is a radiance about *Not So Fast, Songololo* which will be felt by all who experience it, young or old.

As I write, South Africa and the world are celebrating the near-miraculous achievement of democracy in that troubled country. Problems still abound, and true progress in living standards for black citizens may be slow to come. But our children, favoured beyond measure by comparison, will do well to be reminded of the terrible oppression practised by one race against another over almost half a century in South Africa. That country is now the concern of the world – but will continue to seem remote and unreal to our children, unless we can bring its people alive for them. Books which do this are rare; but *Not So Fast, Songololo* is one.

A modern confusion over the role of Christianity in children's lives needs facing, and resolving. Parents who are not themselves religious, and wish their children to come to their own conclusions as they grow up, are often reluctant to introduce any stories which have Christian associations. It is a great shame if this reluctance deprives children of the rousing (often bloodthirsty) Old Testament tales. In the early years, it is the story of the Nativity which is most likely to be omitted from listening experience.

Christmas is an important festival in all children's lives, regardless of its implications; and the Nativity story is one of the most simple and yet awe-inspiring ever told. There is something universally satisfying in the thought of a child who was destined for lasting glory beginning his life in a lowly barn, the child of humble parents. Regard it as a legend, a folk-myth if you will, but don't spurn it any more than you would any other legend, because you fear indoctrination.

I would go further, and make certain that all young children grew to know and love the most beautiful version of all, that from the Gospel of St Luke:

And she brought forth her firstborn son, and wrapped him in swaddling clothes, and laid him in a manger; because there was no room for them in the inn . . .

Why should modern children be shielded from exposure to these pure, easily absorbed, time-worn phrases?

But Mary kept all these things, and pondered them in her heart.

Reducing language to the flat, graded-vocabulary utterances of many modern retellings certainly makes sure that children will not ponder these things in *their* hearts! Why this deprivation, when such a splendid heritage has been forged for them by earlier generations?

Two major requirements of Nativity retellings are dignity and simplicity. Fortunately, there are several versions which fulfil these conditions, and provide infinitely more, while avoiding mention of the divine element in the story. Astrid Lindgren's *Christmas in the Stable*, with Harald Wiberg's moving, luminous illustrations, permits of any, or no interpretation. The child's parents, and the shepherds, wear modern clothing; and the kings do not appear at all. And yet the book has a pervading peace and wonder about it that is irresistible. It was produced in time for my youngest children's pleasure and is still well loved in our family.

But for total, uncompromising involvement in the glory (angels and all), the earthiness, the fear, the incomparable detail (what other baby ever received frankincense, myrrh, and gold?), Felix Hoffmann's version has no peer. The *Story of Christmas* begins with the Angel Gabriel announcing, and ends with Herod raging, and the holy family escaping. Every step of the story is made memorable by the formal and yet infinitely personal pictures. The baby himself is a Botticelli cherub; his parents dazed by his special role but resolute in their acceptance of it. This, for me, is the best Christmas book ever produced.

As I revise *Babies Need Books*, Hoffmann's incomparable 'Christmas' book is out of print. Its inclusion in this chapter is rendered even more important by this fact. In the Preface to the second edition of *Babies Need Books* I quoted Geoffrey Trease's wise words on the subject of 'out-of-print' books: 'If "out of print" came to mean "unmentionable", many a good book would never be rescued from the limbo into which it had temporarily fallen.'

I still hold fast to this belief, and have, indeed, seen many such a book resurface after years of out-of-print obscurity. Clearly, keeping a fine book alive in people's memories is worth while, and sometimes pays off.

One cannot fail to notice how every fashion among reforming adults is taken up by aspiring authors for the young and used as an 'improving' theme in a book on the subject. Predictably, we have seen a plethora (almost a plague!) of picture books lamenting the disappearance of forests and various animal species, the pollution of the environment and the evils of civilization. Sometimes, the services of a superior artist has been enlisted to support the text of an indifferent writer. All too often, the result is a boring 'bandwagon' production which disappoints on all counts. Unless a story is good in its own right, regardless of its apparent moral or ethical value (or its 'political correctness' – odious phrase!), it will not engage the sympathies of the young.

By contrast with a growing number of tedious tracts which pose as picture books, John Burningham's *Oi! Get Off Our Train!* succeeds because it is rooted in fantasy and laced with fun. A small boy's game of trains is interrupted by his mothers demand that he '. . . get into bed immediately'. Not surprisingly, he dreams of driving a train – a furious, fire-belching monster which is boarded by successive animals, all of which have problems of survival and are ultimately allowed to join the boisterous company. There is nothing serious about this story, and nothing furtively didactic, either; and Burningham's illustrations are, as ever, buoyant and yet sensitive. But the conservation message is there. The fact that it comes in on the wings of a real story – revealed almost entirely in the pictures – ensures not only its enjoyment, but its power to influence attitudes.

A trend which one can only applaud wholeheartedly is that which depicts more children of different race and colour pursuing their lives between the covers of picture books. Ezra Jack Keats led the field in America with *The Snowy Day* and *Whistle for Willie* in the early sixties, both titles (and later, others), successfully crossing the Atlantic a few years later.

My Brother Sean, by Petronella Breinburg, with Errol Lloyd's vivid pictures, made a lasting impact in England in 1973. In our family this book is remembered as a favourite of our granddaughter Cushla, who, at nearly three, kissed Sean's 'howling little face' at every reading, and beamed with relief when he finally 'smiled a teeny-weeny smile'.

The last twenty years have seen a steady growth in the number of such multi-racial books, at every level from board books to young adult novels. At 'early-novel' stage, Leon Rosselson's *Rosa's Singing Grandfather* and its sequel *Rosa's Grandfather Sings Again* stand out for their warm, sensitive treatment of relationships in a family which includes both black and white skins – and Ann Cameron's stories about Julian and his family are notable.

Of course, in this field, as in any other, standards must apply. No book should be accepted simply because it includes children with dark skins – or contains any other desirable feature, however worthy. Children deserve the best, and the best does not include shabbily disguised tracts, on any subject. Fortunately, good authors and artists are increasingly addressing this multi-cultural need. The books are there, for the finding.

'And "early readers"?' I can hear some parents ask. 'What of these? Surely five-year-olds, rising six, should be starting to read themselves?' I can hardly leave this book without touching on the subject, certainly.

It is my firm belief that a certain sort of 'early reader' has turned more children off reading – *real* reading – than it has ever drawn into the circle. I do not believe that we should worry about a young child's performance on textbooks, or lists of words. In fact, I believe that irreparable harm is done to some children at this stage by our insistence on such performance. This is a time when children's minds and imaginations are flowering and burgeoning in all directions at once, when they tend to ignore something quite 'simple' which we try to teach them, meanwhile mastering something much 'harder', smoothly, so that we may not even notice – or appreciate the accomplishment, if we do.

And only the strongest and most perceptive of us can leave well alone, at this stage! Learning as the result of *being taught* seems more valuable somehow. Success ought to involve effort, and if that effort is enforced by those in authority, so much the better. Our puritanical streak is just below the surface when it comes to education.

Ideally we can leave 'graded material' to the schools, in the early stages (and hope that they keep it to an absolute minimum!).

Nourishing children's minds is what matters – and what graded reader ever did this? Fortunately, there are several series of 'easy to read' books which contrive to combine some spirit with simplicity, and these may prove useful once a child is anxious to practise new-found fluency. But even these stories are greatly inferior, in imaginative and descriptive content, to the best picture books (and should *never* be used for reading aloud!).

As six draws near, schools – and parents – usually start to look for 'real progress' in the acquisition of reading skills. If they are dissatisfied with what they see, they sometimes start to apply pressure, achieving, all too often, quite the opposite result from that intended. Parents should be alert to this period as a 'danger spot'; a time when their children's cheerful expectation of becoming readers may falter.

Nothing works as well in this situation as good-humoured nonchalance about the whole topic – with a downturn in attention to the mechanical skills, and an upturn in attention to *real* books: books which will lift the spirit and set the imagination flowing. Good books to look at, listen to and become part of: herein lies the cure for apprehension and self-doubt!

I can hear readers asking all sorts of questions: What about sexism in children's books? Shouldn't we reject all books which show girls pursuing traditional girls' roles, boys doing all the exciting, extending things? Thousands of successful parents through the ages have taken no such drastic precautions, and have, none the less, raised vigorous, independent and self-accepting daughters – and sons. If books are good books, they engender true thought and feeling and so allow children to think clearly, to feel deeply. These children will make necessary changes in their own lives and, ultimately, in the wider world. Of course we should reject those books which subtly and insidiously convey stereotyped attitudes; but these books are likely to be poor books in any case.

The best books reflect the best thought of their times. I believe that the best modern books will help us to raise children whose minds are free from unworthy prejudice, children who can love, and laugh, and get on with the business of living. I believe also that the best modern authors are conscious of the need to avoid stereotyping; that the campaigns which concerned people have conducted over the last few decades have borne fruit, and that we have, already, a growing body of good books which reflect their influence.

During the years that have elapsed since this book was first published, considerable progress has been made in the world towards a more liberal way of looking at certain crucial issues: women's rights, the evils of racism, the desperate need for international cooperation in the interests of sheer survival. But accomplishment lags far behind expressed attitude and intention, and little seems to change. Our children are born into a world in which violence, drug abuse, prejudice and inequality are rampant. The hopes of the last century's reformers that education would banish social evils have not been realized.

What recourse does the 'ordinary' parent have, in the face of these conditions? I believe that there is a way. We increase our own satisfaction, our own sense of worth, if we find ways of fortifying our children; equipping them to face a life which, despite its evident perils, still offers the age-old satisfactions of work to be done, things to laugh at, people to love and causes to fight for.

Children are the world's only true resource. Certainly, if we cease to produce children, the world as we know it will cease to exist. Real change must be made in the lives of children, if it is to endure, for the world's hope lies with the next generation. This is an area in which parents need not feel ineffective. In fact, parents have enormous power.

This may sound sweeping and idealistic, but, like most truths, is actually simple. 'The hand that rocks the cradle' indeed 'rules the world' – though the owner of that hand should not be exclusively female, must not be constantly overtired, undervalued, deprived of companionship and support. Parents must be helped to see that their job is the most important of all, in every society; for it is.

What has this to do with books? A great deal. Through the agency of good books, lovingly shared, children can be immeasurably ably strengthened to face their lives. Every little bit helps, in this field, and books are not 'little bits'. A good book is huge in its implication, vast in its potential, limitless in its capacity to inspire, nourish and sustain.

Five, rising six, is a good age: calmer and more assured than the year before, with less need for aggressive assertion, greater capacity for realistic self-assessment. The here-and-now satisfies this age group. Its members, attempting in the main only what is possible, are inclined to achieve, in a steady if unspectacular way. Troublesome times may lie ahead as horizons, beyond six, roll back and back. For the time being, the world is controllable because confined; success is achievable, problems surmountable.

Fortunate nearly-six-year-olds use language which is rich and resourceful to explain themselves to others, to meet their own needs, and to investigate their environments. Their imagination is active, their sense of humour at the ready for laughter, their sympathy available, their love overflowing. Language, laughter and love is the prescription; and each of these will have been fed, constantly and surely, by their contact with books, and with adults who have cared for them and have been prepared to use all the means at their disposal to help them to see the world squarely, and to use its resources wisely. With conviction, and with good reason, the six-year-old announces:

> *But now I am Six I'm as clever as clever.*
> *So I think I'll be Six now for ever and ever.*

Book List 5

Books to Use between Four and Six

As mentioned in Chapter 6, I have assembled one (rather long) list only, for the four- to six-year-olds. It cannot be said too often that it is impossible to divide books according to age groups, in any but the most arbitrary way; and at this stage of their lives, children vary widely. And of course, many of the titles in the list will appeal to both younger and older children, as well as the four-to-sixes. I have personally used all the books listed with young children, and found them successful. (You can tell, from my comments, which ones brought the house down.)

You will find a mixture of picture books and 'storybooks' (usually of smaller size, with much more text and fewer pictures) in the following pages. But every single book is meant to be read aloud; it is the value of *sharing* stories that I have tried to stress in *this* book. A healthy mixture of both types and all possible categories is the recipe for success from now on. I have done my best to include a wide range: traditional tales, everyday stories, poetry, funny stories, books for special situations, and many more.

I hope you will enjoy them all, and keep a weather eye out for books of your own choice as well, to use with this burgeoning age group.

* *About Teddy Robinson*
* *Dear Teddy Robinson*
* *Keeping Up With Teddy Robinson*
* *Teddy Robinson Himself* all by Joan G. Robinson (Puffin paperback)
* *The Adventures of Milly-Molly-Mandy* (omnibus edition)
* *Milly-Molly-Mandy Stories*

*Further Doings of Milly-Molly-Mandy
*More of Milly-Molly-Mandy
*Milly-Molly-Mandy Again all by Joyce Lankester Brinsley (Puffin paperback)
Alex's Bed
Alex and Roy
Alex and the Baby
Alex's Outing
New Clothes for Alex all by Mary Dickinson, illus. Charlotte Firmin (Scholastic)
Alfie Gives a Hand Shirley Hughes (Bodley Head/Lion paperback)
All the Better to See You With Margaret Wild, illus. Pat Reynolds (Little Ark)

Here is a book about a childhood disability without the faintest taint of intention to teach, preach or castigate. In fact, it is a rousing, thoroughly successful story in which the main character, Kate, undergoes a transformation when it is realized that she has always been short-sighted. The illustrations contribute greatly to the book's success. Each landscape double spread has warmth, charm and beauty; detail, colour and clarity combine to make this a book which will be read and reread. The story is triumphant, and will give any bespectacled small child a boost. The two I read it to bewailed their own lack of glasses and, after several readings, took turns wearing mine.

All Join In Quentin Blake (Red Fox paperback)

This wonderful book contains seven poems spread across thirteen landscape openings and will gladden the hearts of the young. The poems share a theme: the chaotic possibilities when a mob of like-minded, diabolical children addresses itself to the ruination of everyone else's peace. Blake's words exactly match the dotty exuberance of his sketchy, vibrant pictures. 'When Bernard kicks the dustbin it really makes a din. But the very best of all is when we ALL JOIN IN!' (This is no passing kick; the dustbin is on its side, the fiendish Bernard on his back inside it, legs flailing.) Blake's inimitable pictures will be scanned, searched and savoured. His genius lies in his capacity to address a universal audience without malice, ridicule or condescension – but with an anarchic slant which speaks directly to the over-controlled young.

Alpaca   Rosemary Billam, illus. Vanessa Julian-Ottie   (Lion paperback)

This is the story of a well-loved and worn toy rabbit who is passed over for a new pink doll and a stuffed owl at Ellen's sixth birthday party. Alpaca's hurt is great, but fortunately the desertion is temporary. When Ellen's friend Mary offers to swap him for one of her toys, 'Ellen didn't need time to think ... "I wouldn't swap Alpaca for anything. He's always been my best friend. I can make him better."' And together the two little girls do just that, using Ellen's nursing kit. The illustrations are wonderful in their fascinating, detailed coverage of the action. They have an exuberant warmth which appeals immediately. Alpaca himself is utterly engaging. A sequel, *Alpaca in the Park*, sees him lost and found – and keeps up the standard.

*Angel Mae   Shirley Hughes   (Walker/Walker paperback)

Angelo   Quentin Blake   (Cape/Picture Lion)

Angelo belongs to a long-ago family of wandering players; a happy family who enjoy their art and their way of life. Angelina by contrast, lives with an old, mean, rich uncle, is badly treated and quite unloved. Her deliverance is portrayed energetically by both text and picture, against an authentic Old Italian background. A warm, humorous book.

Aunt Nina and Her Nephews and Nieces   Franz Brandenberg, illus. Aliki   (Puffin paperback)

A landscape-shaped book full of the sun and fun of a summer day. On her cat's birthday, Aunt Nina, who has neither children nor husband (one sees her, purposefully writing, in a book-lined study), invites her three nephews and three nieces to come to a party. They spend the day in glorious, inventive play, in basement, attic and in between – ostensibly searching for Fluffy, but in fact demonstrating to the modern child that staying at home can sometimes be 'better than the zoo ... better than the theatre ...' The birthday cat is found at last, complete with six brand-new kittens – necessitating a visit to the children's families from Aunt Nina, in due course, bulging basket in hand. *Aunt Nina's Visit* has the energetic six and their co-operative aunt *and* the kittens producing a riotous puppet show, and *Aunt Nina, Goodnight* reveals the endlessly patient aunt pushed to surely intolerable lengths – without any loss of good humour. Enjoyment of all three books may be tinged with envy, but will certainly be whole-hearted.

Avocado Baby John Burningham   (Cape/Red Fox paperback)

Most children over four will recognize this story for the ridiculous spoof that it is, and love it despite – or because of – this quality of farce. Everyone likes the idea of an elixir which will transform the ugly into the beautiful, the weak into the strong, the dull into the brilliant. Here, it is the honest avocado pear that not only rescues Mr and Mrs Hargrave's baby from puny ill-health, but transforms it into a super-baby, able to pursue a burglar with a broom brandished on high, hurl a pair of bullies into the pond . . . Burningham's deadpan pictures are part of the secret, but not all. Vicarious satisfaction in the triumph of the unlikely? At all events, it works.

*Badger's Parting Gifts Susan Varley   (Anderson Press/Harper paperback)

A Balloon for Grandad Nigel Gray, illus. Jane Ray   (Orchard/Oliver & Boyd paperback)

The catastrophe of a lost balloon is here turned into a triumph. Sam, a small boy of mixed English-Arab descent, is devastated when his red and silver gas-filled balloon escapes from his house and is snatched by the wind. His resourceful father, however, invents a journey for it: '. . .high, high over the sparkling blue-green sea where silver fish leap from the waves; high over the hot yellow sand of the desert . . .' to Grandad Abdulla, who is 'looking after his goats and tending his date trees, on an island in a river, far, far away'. This illustrator is renowned for her beautiful cards, and here provides pictures of stunning beauty, which are totally at one with the eloquent, assured text. Love and understanding between the boy and his father permeate the story. This is an outstanding book.

Benny's Visit Linda M. Jennings, illus. Krystyna Turska   (Macmillan paperback)

Benny, the ultimate in scruffy barge dogs, trades love-in-reduced-circumstances for what he believes will be superior comfort with a wealthy family, only to find that constant washing, discipline and confinement in no way compensate for freedom; not to mention the loss of Tom, his disreputable but faithful old master. The story is funny and heartwarming, but the illustrations turn this book into a work of art. Scrupulously observed details of Victorian house, garden barge, riverside, adults (both the upstairs and downstairs variety) and children combine to produce a book of real beauty (with, as a bonus, a humorous insight into the priggish snobbery of an earlier age).

* *The Big Concrete Lorry* Shirley Hughes (Walker/Walker paperback)

Blossom Comes Home James Herriott, illus. Ruth Brown (Pan, Piper)

To date, eight stories from the famous vet's saga of animal and human life in an English rural setting have been adapted as picture book texts. Here, a farmer sadly faces the fact that he must part with his old cow, Blossom. Blossom is just as certain that they belong together, and her evasive action is both riotous and successful. These are wonderful tales, gently funny and wholly engrossing. Both Ruth Brown's and Peter Barrett's pictures are impressive in themselves and totally complementary. These are beautiful books, which will be read, reread and treasured.

Other titles: *Bonny's Big Day*, *The Christmas Day Kitten*, *The Market Square Dog*, *Moses the Kitten*, *Only One Woof*, *Oscar, Cat-About-Town* and *Smudge's Day Out* (all Pan, Piper)

The Boy Who Was Followed Home Margaret Mahy, illus. Steven Kellog (Puffin Paperback)

Robert is an ordinary little boy to whom an extraordinary thing happens: first one, then two, and ultimately forty-three hippopotami follow him home from school. The pictures make no attempt to be funny; they merely illustrate the text and are detailed, earnest and hilarious. All is well, in the end, Robert thinks . . . (How wrong he is is revealed on the last page.) A great joy, this book.

* *A Brother for Momoko* Chihiro Iwasaki (Bodley Head)

Brown Bear's Wedding   (Hamish Hamilton/Puffin paperback)
White Bear's Secret   both by Martine Beck, illus. Marie H. Henry
(Puffin paperback)

> Bears who live in a fairy-tale chalet in a romantic alpine
> landscape, fall in love, marry and produce a child . . . ? All too
> sickly-sweet for words, you may be forgiven for thinking. You
> may just be won over by the illustrations, which complement
> the artless but by no means dull narrative and show sturdy,
> humorous, real people (bears withal) pursuing the simple life,
> helping one another in times of hardship, enjoying themselves
> skating, skiing and making merry in the good old-fashioned
> way. Perhaps we, and our children need more of this. Cer-
> tainly, the children I read it to enjoyed both books. If your
> taste is for rustic interiors and enchanting wintry landscapes
> you will fall captive, too. The illustrations are earthily
> beautiful.

Burglar Bill   Janet and Allan Ahlberg   (Heinemann/Mammoth
paperback)

> A rousing story of a cheerful, warm-hearted burglar who steals
> a 'nice big brown box with little holes in it'. When it proves to
> contain a baby, Bill is in a quandary – until he is burgled by
> Burglar Betty who is, of course, the baby's mother. A rollicking
> romp of a book with considerable text – but such fun that the
> average five-year-old will love it. The pictures strike exactly
> the right note – and Betty and Bill marry, reform and return
> all their joint loot.

Cannonball Simp   John Burningham   (Red Fox paperback)

> First published in 1966, and loved by my youngest children,
> and now grandchildren, Simp is 'what most people would call
> an ugly little dog . . .' who is dumped by an uncaring owner.
> But Simp has spirit, and personality, and *ideas*. Animal activists
> may protest at her ultimate attainment of fame in a circus, but
> the young revel in her triumph (and over-earnestness has no
> place in the assessment of such a piece of tongue-in-cheek fun.)
> Like *Harquin* (see below), also by Burningham, Simp has a
> place in literary history.

Captain Pugwash
Pugwash Aloft
Pugwash and the Sea Monster
Pugwash and the Buried Treasure
Pugwash and the Ghost Ship
Pugwash in the Pacific   all by John Ryan   (Bodley Head/Puffin paperback)

> Pugwash is a pirate who thinks himself 'the bravest, most handsome pirate on the seven seas'. The reality is very different. Pugwash is actually bumbling, faint-hearted – and rather lovable. The rogue of the piece, Cut-throat Jake, is certainly villainous but fortunately also incompetent. In fact, the only character in the whole series who has any sense at all is Tom, Pugwash's small cabin boy, who knows how to 'work the compass, sail the ship and make the tea'. First published in 1957, Captain Pugwash cannot, and will not date. Both text and pictures are rousing, ridiculous – and fun.

*Christmas in the Stable Astrid Lindgren, illus. Harald Wiberg (Hodder & Stoughton/Knight paperback)
*The Collins Book of Stories for 4 Year Olds
*The Collins Book of Stories for 5 Year Olds
*More Stories for 5 Year Olds   all by Julia Eccleshare   (Lion paperback)

Come Away from the Water, Shirley   John Burningham   (Red Fox paperback)

> First published in the late seventies, this was one of the first books to present two dimensions simultaneously: the actual and the imagined, side by side. The most ordinary family in the world go to the beach on a bleak day. 'Of course it's far too cold for swimming, Shirley.' But Shirley's imagination is far from ordinary. To the accompaniment of her parents' dreary catalogue of prohibitions, she embarks upon a rousing adventure with a gang of rascally pirates. There is much to look at, and more to think about, in Burningham's evocative illustrations.

*Crocodile Teeth Marjorie-Ann Watts (Deutsch)
A Dark Dark Tale Ruth Brown (Andersen Press/Scholastic paperback)

Once upon a time there was a dark, dark moor.
On the moor there was a dark, dark wood.
In the wood there was a dark, dark house . . .

Everyone must know the old, spine-tingling tale. Here, one is led through house, hall and passage, up stairs and through curtain, all depicted in the best tradition of Gothic horror, to a dark, dark corner of a dark, dark cupboard to a dark, dark box . . .in which an utterly engaging little mouse has made her home: a spick and span, shipshape little dwelling from which she peers in terror at our graceless intrusion. A masterpiece, this matchlessly illustrated book, and one which will encourage by-heart performance after several sessions.

Days with Frog and Toad
Frog and Toad all Year
Frog and Toad are Friends
Frog and Toad Together   all by Arnold Lobel   (Mammoth paperback)
Like Minarik's *Little Bear* (see below), good-natured Frog and apprehensive Toad have defied their inclusion in a series of 'readers' I can read to become famous figures in the literature of the young. The interaction of two fond but different characters has never been better demonstrated; the author has an extraordinary talent for evoking personality in a pair of small, cold-blooded creatures without abandoning their essentially animal natures. His illustrations capture homely interior, leafy countryside and quality of relationship equally, and make of these books small gems.

Dear Daddy . . .   Philippe Dupasquier   (Andersen Press/Puffin paperback)
The bottom two-thirds of each double spread in this appealing book depicts the same house and garden through the course of a year. Outside and in, a small girl, her mother and her baby brother pursue their lives as the seasons pass, and the children grow. The top one-third of each opening shows the 'Daddy' of the title conducting *his* life as able seaman aboard a freighter in faraway places; you can find him easily in the panoramic pictures. His hair is as red as his small daughter's. The detail

in both home and distant scenes is comprehensive but never dazing; it invites scrutiny and speculation. The little girl's letter is simple and touching: 'Please come back quickly. Love from Sophie.' Daddy, meanwhile, is on his way home. Ultimately the bus drops him outside the house, and Sophie is off her bike and running!

* *Diana and Her Rhinoceros* Edward Ardizzone (Red Fox paperback)

Do You Dare?   Paul and Emma Rogers, illus. Sonia Holleyman (Orchard)

A brief, rhyming text with pictures which are boisterously dramatic, offers a chance to speculate on one's own courage – and to relish the inevitable tingling of the spine attendant upon cuddling a ghost, hugging a (gargantuan!) bug, snuggling up close to an (elephantine!) slimy slug, and other excessive challenges. Brief, but fun; and youngsters straining to snap parental ties do have personal doubts.

Do You Know What Grandad Did?   Brian Smith, illus. Rachel Pank (Orchard Books)

Grandpa and three children welcome Mum home from work, the young vying with one another to regale her with Grandpa's delicious doings in her absence. Everything from letting them swing on the front gate (and taking a turn himself), teaching them a rhyme from his own childhood ('He says it isn't really rude!') and buying them some wonderful bubble-gum ('. . . the sort we aren't allowed!'). Love and good cheer invade these splendid pictures; would that all children had such a grandpa!

Doctor De Soto William Steig (Andersen Press)

Once the reader adjusts to the fact that a dentist who happens also to be a mouse might be unwise enough to agree, however reluctantly, to treat a fox with toothache, the potential for humour of a bone-chilling kind is obvious. William Steig explores it to the full. The tone is one of earnest dignity; Doctor and Mrs De Soto are the soul of dental decorum and the fox struggles with himself, as the temptation to betray his benefactors becomes irresistible. The doctor and his tidy little wife are a perfect pair, and more than a match for their transparently avaricious patient.

*Dogger   Shirley Hughes   (Bodley Head/Red Fox paperback)

Don't Forget the Bacon!   Pat Hutchins   (Bodley Head/Puffin paperback)

> The boy in this story sets out to buy for his mother 'Six farm eggs, a cake for tea, a pound of pears . . .' and is sternly instructed not to forget the bacon. His desperate attempts to remember the list have overtones of those party games in which whispered messages become more and more garbled. Much of the fun is in the pictures, which have this artist's characteristic bright yellows and blues and clear outline. The minimal text lends a deceptive air of simplicity; recognizing the likeness in sound between 'six farm eggs', 'six clothes pegs' and 'six fat legs' is essential to understanding as the muddle increases. If the reader's performance gives emphasis to the separate ideas, five-year-olds will enjoy the joke, and soon 'read' the book themselves.

**Don't Forget, Matilda!*   Ronda and David Armitage   (Deutsch)

The Doorbell Rang   Pat Hutchins   (Bodley Head/Puffin paperback)

> One could read this cheerful story to three-year-olds with certain success. But fives and sixes will appreciate the need to divide the cookies Ma has made into increasingly small servings as more and more visitors arrive – and may even attempt the computation necessitated by the influx, themselves. Sam, Victoria and Ma manage impressively welcoming smiles (though their expressions do grow a little bleak as the cavalcade proceeds). In the nick of time, there is Grandma at the door with a gargantuan tray of cookies. 'And no one makes cookies like Grandma!' Colour is brilliant, and extra touches are there for the searching: a few – finally dozens – of muddy footprints on the black-and-white tiled floor, the family cat engrossed in the goings-on, a bike, dolls' pram and skateboard in turn parked in the corner. Warmth, fun – and a little instruction on the side. Excellent stuff!

The Dragon of an Ordinary Family   Margaret Mahy, illus. Helen Oxenbury   (Mammoth paperback)

> A rollicking yarn about the acquisition by an ordinary family of a pet dragon. An engrossing experience, for which the illustrations must be held half responsible.

Duckat   Gaelyn Gordon, illus. Chris Gaskin   (Scholastic)

The interaction of Mabel, and a duck which is determined to prove it is a cat, is described with style and illustrated with grace. The theme is hardly original, but the treatment certainly is.

Early in the Morning: A Collection of New Poems   Charles Causley, illus. Michael Foreman, music by Anthony Castro   (Puffin paperback)

This is a signal book, I feel. Most of the poems are in the time-honoured tradition of the nursery rhyme, while others stop you in your tracks with their substratum of seriousness. But then, were not most nursery rhymes and playground jingles sober in intent originally, however rousing and farcical they now seem? Here, then, are forty new nursery rhymes, embellished with vigorous and feeling pictures by Michael Foreman. Twenty of the poems have been set to music: a bonus for school use perhaps, but inclined to confuse the nature and purpose of the book. (It could be such a rousing, browsing book for the small child lucky enough to acquire it.) No matter: these are poems which will last, to appear in other people's anthologies, and in many cases no doubt, to become picture books in their own right.

Edmond Went Far Away   Martin Bax, illus. Michael Foreman (Walker paperback)

There is considerable text in this peaceful story of a small boy's 'expedition', but bookwise children will love the detail. Edmond lives on a farm, and decides to explore his world. He says goodbye in turn to his friends the ducks, the pigs, the cows and the old horse, and sets off. Just as he reaches a point from which his house is no longer visible (and a potentially dangerous lake) he is joined by his father, equipped with sleeping bags, food and camping equipment. Together, they row on the lake and sleep under the stars. Michael Foreman's pictures, in the lovely colours of summer, are a joy.

Emily's Own Elephant   Philippa Pearce, illus. John Lawrence   (Walker paperback)

Emily lives with middle-class parents (of the shabby, country-dwelling kind) in peaceful surroundings. The acquisition of an elephant – a real elephant – and the subsequent disruption of family life are documented in this famous author's flowing prose with wonderful understatement. John Lawrence's quiet but evocative illustrations reflect the text exactly.

The Enormous Crocodile   Roald Dahl, illus. Quentin Blake   (Puffin paperback)

You probably need to be rising six before you are amused, rather than shocked, by a crocodile who announces casually to his friends, 'For my lunch today . . . I would like a nice juicy little child.' Of course, the Enormous Crocodile has never actually managed to *catch* a child yet, but he is sure that this will be the day! The other jungle animals are equally certain that they will be able to foil his dastardly intentions, and they prove, of course, to be right. Quentin Blake's talent for the ridiculous but believable has produced wonderful pictures of the boastful but inept crocodile passing in turn as a coconut tree, a roundabout animal at a fair and a see-saw in a school playground – all to no avail; it is he who comes to grief in the end. In fact, he is 'sizzled up like a sausage!' (Just what the barbarous young would prescribe!) Plenty of text, but the suspense assures avid attention.

*The Fairy Tale Treasury   Virginia Haviland, illus. Raymond Briggs   (Hamish Hamilton)

Farmer Bungle Forgets   Dick King-Smith, illus. Martin Honeysett (Walker Books)

Mrs Bungle's exasperation at her husband's forgetfulness is understandable; but one's sympathy is inclined to be reserved for the bumbling and confused farmer. After all, the unfortunate consequences of his innocent stupidity always seem to rebound on *him* . . . The illustrations complement the text nicely, and there's a cunning twist at the end.

First Poems   compiled Julia Eccleshare, illus. Selina Young   (Orchard Books)

A wide-ranging collection which will give good service from about four to eight, selectively used. (Some four-year-olds may find the fate of Jim, Who Ran Away from his Nurse and was

Eaten by a Lion, nightmarish rather than funny; the mock-earnest tone of Belloc's verse demands a sophisticated response which may not yet be developed.) But the mixture of old favourites and newer poems is agreeable – and the illustrations are well executed and nicely positioned. A generous book, with an attractive cover – and a dust jacket!

A Fish Out of Water Helen Palmer, illus. P. D. Eastman (Harper-Collins, Beginner Books)

This is an absolutely believable story which rushes along at breakneck speed. A small boy tells the tale: how he was warned by Mr Carp at the pet shop not to overfeed his new fish.

> *So much and no more!*
> *Never more than a spot,*
> *Or something may happen!*
> *You never know what.*

Predictably, he ignores this good advice. As you might expect also, the results are spectacular. Otto grows and grows and GROWS! He outgrows his little bowl, a succession of ever greater kitchen utensils, the family bath, the cellar, the local pool . . . ! Police and Fire Brigade, both magnificently co-operative, work frantically against rapidly increasing odds. The little boy himself is splendid and undaunted, and finally comes up with a solution. The illustrations, in racy cartoon style, could not be bettered. A quarter of a century old already, with its glory intact, *A Fish Out of Water* is likely to endure.

The Fisherman and His Wife Mark Southgate (Andersen Press)

This is a simply told, brightly illustrated version of the age-old story. A fisherman catches a fish which offers him a reward for sparing its life. The man is happy with the gold coin he receives, but his wife demands bigger and bigger rewards until finally she overreaches herself – and they find themselves back in their original 'dirty old hut'. The moral is strong; but the action, and the repetitive text, will appeal to children. The book itself is well produced, with endpapers which themselves tell a story.

Five Minutes' Peace Jill Murphy (Walker/Walker paperback)

Three-year-olds would certainly enjoy this good-humoured tale of domestic chaos arising from Mrs Large's bid for 'five minutes' peace', but the over-fours will go further towards appreciating its nuances. The Large family are elephants and Mrs Large is not one to mince words or pull punches. 'Because I want five minutes' peace from *you* lot', is her answer, when her children demand to know why she is decamping to the bathroom with her breakfast on a tray. One might expect Lester, Laura and the little one to be forceful by nature and enterprising in action, and so they prove to be. The pictures are beautifully planned and executed; they are simultaneously funny and sympathetic, the characters so true to *human* life that one marvels at their elephantine reality. (Jill Murphy *must* have small children of her own, to be able to appreciate and convey Mrs Large's desperate enjoyment of 'three minutes and forty-five seconds of peace'!)

Floss Kim Lewis (Walker Books)

Floss is a border collie who lives in the city and loves playing with the children in the park – until she is taken to the country where she is to be trained as a sheepdog. But the farmer has two children, and the children have a ball . . . Floss finds it hard to separate her old and new roles, until the farmer decides on a compromise. The rural landscapes are breathtakingly beautiful, the people and animals depicted with assured sympathy and skill.

Flossie and the Fox Patricia C. McKlissack, illus. Rachel Isadora (Puffin paperback)

The illustrations for this story are so outstanding that one might be forgiven for buying the book on their account alone. But the story of Flossie and her battle of wills with the crafty and conceited fox has its own integrity; and the richness of the Black language of the American South is no impediment to either reading aloud, or understanding. This is a superbly produced book which, with its fable-like tale and superlative pictures, should endure. For near-sixes, rather than just-fours.

Fourteen Rats and a Rat-Catcher Tamasin Cole and James Cressey (A. & C. Black)

An exercise in viewpoints: upstairs, a nice old lady plans to rid her house of the nasty rats in the cellar. In the cellar, a nice rat family would be happy, were it not for the nasty old lady living above them ... The illustrations, framed in chocolate-brown borders (with the text similarly framed below) are outstanding. Rich colour and excellent design combine with a funny, tongue-in-cheek tale to create an assuredly successful book.

Frog and the Birdsong   Max Velthuijs   (Andersen Press/Red Fox paperback)

Frog finds a blackbird in a clearing, lying quietly on the ground. He goes to find Big, who is picking apples. Duck and Hare join them. There is no doubt about it: the blackbird is dead. 'Everything dies,' says Hare. Together, they bury the bird, covering the grave with 'a beautiful stone'. It is very quiet – until they take up their game again, and another bird sings. A gentle tale which affirms ongoing life. The pictures, in this artist's favourite rich greens and browns, are clear and expressive.

The Goose that Laid the Golden Egg   Geoffrey Patterson   (Macmillan paperback)

This book is unusual, and immediately attractive. The use of an earthy brown as page colour seems appropriate to the old tale, which is here given a country setting. The goose is seen as the pet of an old peasant couple, and this makes its destruction at their hands more immediately distressing than the bird's brisk dispatch in the original fable. Perhaps the story is none the worse for this; greed is as rampant today as it ever was. The illustrations have life and colour, and the book is beautifully produced.

Gorilla   Anthony Browne   (Julia McRae/Mammoth paperback)

This immediately attractive book is a satisfying experience, whether or not the point is taken: that a child who longs for her solo parent's companionship and attention can create fantasy situations to meet her need if the real thing is not forthcoming. Here, Hannah's overworked and abstracted father comes up trumps in the end. The last picture in which both are seen from behind, the toy gorilla dangling from Hannah's hand, on their way to the zoo, is heartwarming. 'She was very happy.'

The Great Man-Eating Shark   Margaret Mahy, illus. Jonathan Allen   (Dent/Puffin paperback)

A rather sophisticated 'message' (if you deceive others often enough, your own trick may backfire on you!) does not prevent the young from enjoying this whacky tale of Norvin, who disguises himself as a shark to ensure an uncrowded swim in the bay. Naturally, a *real* shark surfaces; but the author is not quite unkind enough to allow Norvin to be eaten! The pictures strike the right note of crude humour.

Gumdrop: The Adventures of a Vintage Car   Val Biro   (Hodder & Stoughton/Puffin and Knight paperbacks)

Gumdrop is a real car, who belongs to the author. He is an Austin Clifton Twelve-Four, and was made in 1926. (There are enchanting diagrams of his innards on the endpapers.) Between covers he is given colourful life and real style by Val Biro's jaunty and copious illustrations. Gumdrop has a capacity for trouble which is irresistible; and if you like him, you may search out a very large number of titles, both hard-covered and paperback (near enough to twenty, at my last reckoning), though at any given time some are out of print. Libraries, however, usually have a supply – and *The Bumper Gumdrop Omnibus* is a wonderful family present, but not available as I write.

Hannah's Helpers   Emilie Boon   (Doubleday)

A story which combines reality and fantasy in the best possible way. Hannah wakes up one morning and decides that she had better clean up the house, before her parents and the baby wake up. She phones her friends for help, and a carful arrives 'with a bang and a beep and a roar and a squeak'. That they happen to be a horse and a sheep and a pig and sundry other farmyard animals is never mentioned, but their successful house cleaning help is pictured in all its cheerful thoroughness. Emilie Boon's art is, as usual, a model of clarity, colour and deft design. Three-year-olds love house-cleaning *and* animals;

and they just may notice the bevy of 'friends', in their reduced sizes, sitting on Hannah's toy shelf in the final picture!

Happy Birthday, Sam   Pat Hutchins   (Bodley Head/Puffin paperback)

Harquin the Fox Who Went Down to the Valley   John Burningham   (Red Fox paperback)

First published in 1967 and well on the way to classic status, *Harquin* is essential reading for five-year-olds. It is the swaggering tale of an insubordinate fox cub who does not obey his parents' orders to keep away from the valley where '. . . the huntsmen will see you and follow you back here . . .' (Like Peter Rabbit, whose father had been 'put in a pie by Mrs McGregor', Harquin had an uncle who had been 'caught by the huntsmen'!) But Harquin is clever as well as daring, and vanquishes the hunt, irascible squire and all, efficiently and spectacularly. (The double spread depicting the red-coated, black-booted gentry being hurled from their mounts into the slimy marsh must be one of the most magnificent in all picture book history.)

Helpers   Shirley Hughes   (Bodley Head/Red Fox paperback)

George is a teenage babysitter; clearly known and loved by Mick, Jenny and the baby, Sue, clearly determined to cope, and just as clearly defeated by the children's children-ness and the consequent impossibility of changing anything or reforming anyone. He and they are warm, accepting, loving – and natural. As is Mum, when she returns. George is exhausted . . . but cheerful still. Shirley Hughes creates children who live, breathe, exasperate and delight. A joy of a book.

Hiawatha's Childhood   H. W. Longfellow, illus. Errol Le Cain   (Puffin paperback)

Fifty or more years ago, most children learned these particular verses from the long story-poem 'Hiawatha' by heart. Thirty years ago, they used to spring to my tongue when I needed an off-the-cuff offering – and the short lullaby of old Nokomis was always sung to a tune whose origin had been long lost, even in those days.

Ewa-yea! my little owlet!
Who is this that lights the wigwam?
With his great eyes lights the wigwam?
Ewa-yea! my little owlet!

Errol Le Cain has given the haunting extract inspired treatment. All pages are drenched in the rich deep browns, reds and greens that one associates with the Canadian woods-and-lake landscape, the text set handsomely in edged frames within the greater, totem-embellished borders of the pages. Its certain appeal to adults does not mask the fact that this is a book for children. Hiawatha himself is engagingly small-boyish, Nokomis grandmotherly, the whole warm and joyful.

Horton Hatches the Egg
Horton Hears a Who
The Lorax
The Sleep Book
The Sneetches
Yertle the Turtle   all by Dr Seuss   (HarperCollins – various editions)
These fine books, all by Dr Seuss himself, were originally published in larger format than the regular Beginner Books, but have now joined the mainstream list. The incomparable 'doctor' had a matchless talent for producing rhyming texts which were not only wildly original, but actually revealed his own caring concern for people and the world's woes. Words and pictures blend into one hilarious whole in these stories, and there are memorable lines which will pass into the family vernacular ('A person's a person no matter how small!' from *Horton Hears a Who*, in my own family's case.) Another title, *The Butter Battle Book*, a wicked exposé of the stupidity of war, is currently out of print – but, with the indomitability of all Beginner Books, will surely resurface, given time.

A House is a House for Me   Mary Ann Hoberman, illus. Betty Fraser   (Puffin paperback)
A mind-boggling list of houses, realistic and fanciful, turns this wordy book into a read-aloud marathon! Impossible to imagine how much information and how many ideas proceed from

book to brain and imagination, during the listening. The rhyming, four-line stanzas induce learning by heart, and the illustrations are copious, detailed and varied. In fact, there seems to be something more to look at and think about at each reading. Not for the faint-winded; but a feast for the hardy, both reader and listener.

I Hope You Know ... Gina Wilson, illus. Alison Gatley (Hutchinson)

This book is ostensibly about a dog and a boy, but it is actually about relationships, and the meeting of needs. The cover shows a large, long-haired dog rolling on its back in that 'here I am, love me' attitude which dog owners know so well, while a young boy obliges with a fond rub and a private smile. Inside, the dog gives instructions, which the boy faithfully obeys ('When I pull at my lead ... run like the wind'). Each short caption is accompanied by an illustration of such sensitive beauty that the book would be worth buying for these alone. The last page, with the dog in her basket for the night, and the boy leaning on the door post ('... and I hope you know I'm your best friend forever') is utterly right.

*I'll Always Love You Hans Wilhelm (Knight paperback)

I'm Coming to Get You! Tony Ross (Andersen/Puffin paperback)

The 'loathsome' monster of this story makes its way by space-ship, destroying all 'the gentle banana people', their 'tiny peaceful planet' and sundry small stars on its way to Earth. Here it seeks out little Tommy Brown (located by radar screen) and already a little scared of monsters. Tommy has had a chilling story for bedtime entertainment, gone to sleep and risen to face a new day by the time the monster arrives – and proves to be approximately one-third as tall as Tommy's shoe! A nice twist; and Tony Ross's vivid pictures have spirit and humour.

Imagine Alison Lester (Viking Kestrel/Puffin paperback)

'Imagine if we were deep in the jungle ... or out in the country, or crossing the ice-cap, or surrounded by monsters ...' Alternate panoramic spreads invite one to imagine, and then provide breathtaking vistas of the named locations with, for good measure, a host of relevant nouns in the narrow band outside the frame which rings the picture (humpback whale, narwhal, arctic dolphin . . .), and the challenge, one senses, to hunt and find. This is a startlingly good book: imaginative, informative, full of fun, and quite simply, beautiful.

*Inky Pinky Ponky Michael Rosen and Susanna Steele (Lion paperback)

Jam Margaret Mahy, illus. Helen Craig (Mammoth paperback)
With a wife who is a scientist and three lively children to care for, Mr Castle prides himself on being 'an excellent house father'. His daily round, described in Margaret Mahy's individual style, is energetic indeed; and he certainly does not intend to let the fast-ripening plums go to waste! Plum jam sets the tone – or perhaps the flavour – of the Castles' life for one whole year, by which time . . . Warm-hearted and funny with overtones of lunacy; in short, vintage Mahy. The pictures are detailed, with touches which extend the text without taking over.

Jeremiah in the Dark Woods Janet and Allan Ahlberg (Puffin paperback)
'Once upon a time there were three bears, seven dwarfs, five gorillas, a frog prince, some sleeping beauties, a wolf, a dinosaur, a Mad Hatter, a steamboat, four firemen on a fire engine, a crocodile with a clock in it, a considerable number of giant beanstalks – and a little boy named Jeremiah Obadiah Jackanory Jones.' Pause, but only for breath. My generation would have described this as a ripsnorting yarn, and no better description springs to pen. Extensive colour at every second opening, with irresistible black and white in between. Tongue-in-cheek nonsense, which positively romps along. Missing *Jeremiah* at five constitutes deprivation.

John Brown, Rose and the Midnight Cat Jenny Wagner, illus. Ron Brooks (Viking/Puffin paperback)
Domestic devotion between John Brown, a gloriously huge and shaggy dog, and Rose, whose 'husband died a long time ago', is undisturbed until 'the midnight cat' appears in the garden. Rose wants to take him in; John Brown is obstructive.

The illustrations are striking; soft, night-time colours reflect the mood faithfully. The domestic interior is scrupulously detailed, the outdoor scenes authentic to the missing fence post. An unusual, important book with an unobtrusive but certain message.

John Patrick Norman McHennessy – The Boy Who Was Always Late John Burningham   (Cape/Red Fox paperback)

A tongue-in-cheek, repetitive tale in which the always-late hero ultimately has the satisfaction of seeing his (understandably) exasperated schoolmaster get his come-uppance. Farcical, but with an underlying message for those who are prepared to see. As usual, Burningham's artwork delights.

The Jolly Postman Janet and Allan Ahlberg   (Heinemann)

It is impossible to resist the charm of this book-with-additions – no matter how strong your preference for 'straight' books may be (and I thought mine was inviolable). A cheerful postman sets out on his delivery round. Each second page thereafter is an envelope containing a communication (letter, card, invitation – even a tiny book) of astonishing originality. From *Goldilocks* to *The Three Bears*, a letter of apology, with nice touches. '*Mummy says I am a bad girl. I hardly eat any porij when she cooks it . . . Daddy says he will mend the littel chair . . .*' From *Hobgoblin Supplies Ltd* to *The Occupier, Gingerbread Bungalow, The Woods*, a brochure offering *Little Bag Pie Mix*, '*The Complete Book of Foul Curses*' and a '*matching tie and sock set for the Wizard in your life*'. Design, colour and settings all reflect the standards we are accustomed to, in the work of this splendid author-and-artist team. A sequel, *The Jolly Christmas Postman* is equally innovative. Either of these compact, sturdy little volumes would make a wonderful gift for a special occasion.

The Julian Stories Ann Cameron, illus. Ann Strugnell   (Gollancz/Fontana Lions paperback)

There are six stories in this attractively produced book, and each strikes a singular note. This is not just another collection of simple 'at home' stories. To begin with, Dad features rather more strongly than Mum; and Dad has style, imagination and a natural flair for fun. In the first story, he is making a special pudding for the boys' mother, who is out shopping. While he is taking a nap, the boys try the tiniest taste . . . with predictable results. But there is nothing predictable about their father's response to this outrage! In another story Julian, who relates the stories, inadvisedly tells his little brother Huey that a catalogue is 'a big book full of pictures of hundreds and hundreds of cats. And when you open it up, all the cats jump out and start running around.' Their father's ingenuity is strained to the utmost to cope with Huey's disappointment when the catalogue arrives, but cope he does, with an originality born of long practice. These are good, well-rounded stories, beautifully illustrated in black-and-white by Ann Strugnell. But it is the narrative itself which sets them apart. Ann Cameron uses language assuredly to create characters one can believe in. Her children are children, direct and enterprising. Their conversation is credible, their behaviour utterly believable but never stereotyped.

*_Katie Morag Delivers the Mail_   (Bodley Head/Lion paperback/Red Fox paperback)
Katie Morag and the Two Grandmothers   (Oliver & Boyd/Bodley Head/Lion paperback)
Katie Morag and the Tiresome Ted   (Bodley Head)
Katie Morag and the Big Boy Cousins   (Bodley Head/Lion paperback)
Katie Morag and the New Pier   (Bodley Head/Lion paperback)   all by Mairi Hedderwick

A Kindle of Kittens   Rumer Godden, illus. Lynne Byrnes   (Macmillan paperback)

This is a picture book for the experienced listener, for the text is full and descriptive. The author's assurance with language guarantees attention; there is no bulk, no contrivance, and the narrative flows. She-cat has four kittens and makes sensible arrangements for their adoption and upbringing. The old town of Rye offers a perfect background for the story, which is unsentimental and yet eloquently tender. The pictures glow; they are at once robust and elegant.

The Lady With the Alligator Purse   Nadine Bernard Westcott   (Little Mammoth paperback)

The old rhyme is here given new life in a picture book of its own, and a new twist. The horror has been banished; Tiny Tim no longer expires 'with a bubble in his throat' but takes the day with a flourish. The old jauntiness is there, and the pictures are lively, funny and colourful.

* The Lighthouse Keeper's Lunch
The Lighthouse Keeper's Catastrophe
The Lighthouse Keeper's Rescue
The Lighthouse Keeper's Picnic　all by Ronda and David Armitage (Scholastic/Puffin paperback)

Lily and the Bears
Lily and the Present　Christine Ross　(Methuen)

Lily provides an admirable example for the young of both sexes; she is purposeful, innovative and likeable. In the first book she contrives to don her bear suit on a class visit to the zoo, is mistaken for the real animal, and locked up. In the second, Lily's determination to buy a present for her baby brother plunges her into unlikely and hilarious predicaments before she solves her own problem simply and appropriately. Christine Ross's skill with words equals her skill with pen and brush; in both titles, her stylish prose and expressive, meticulous pictures have produced outstanding books. (*Lily and the Present* was Children's Picture Book of the year in New Zealand in 1993.)

Little Bear
Little Bear's Friend
Little Bear's Visit
Father Bear Comes Home
A Kiss for Little Bear　Else Holmelund Minarik, illus. Maurice Sendak　(Mammoth paperback)

These enchanting stories are included in the *I Can Read* series, but are as unlike 'readers' as one could imagine. Sendak's illustrations are in classic mode, and the stories are worth telling. They are funny, warm-hearted, and varied in theme.

The Little Girl and the Tiny Doll　Edward and Aingelda Ardizzone　(Puffin paperback)

An exceptional book which defies description. Enough to say

that it has a proven capacity to fascinate which transcends its modest appearance; a singular quality which ensures rapt attention from the first page. A tiny doll is dropped into the deep-freeze in a grocer's shop by a child who 'did not care for dolls'. The doll is seen by another child, who undertakes her care at long range. Ardizzone's eye and ear for the concerns of the young are impeccable. Here is perfect pitch and true vision.

Little Gorilla Ruth Bornstein (World's Work) Out of print.

The Little House Virginia Lee Burton (Faber) Out of print.

Mike Mulligan and his Steam Shovel Virginia Lee Burton (Puffin paperback)

Impossible to think of these two superlative products of this century's picture-book art except together (they were both first published in the early forties).

The first tells the story of a humble little house which began her life ' . . . on a little hill, covered with daisies and apple trees growing around . . .' Through endless days, nights, seasons and years, the little house stays the same. But the countryside does not; gradually the landscape is transformed, as first roads, then buildings, then a subway, then an overhead railway surround and ultimately swamp her. Her deliverance is triumphant; she is discovered by 'the great-great-granddaughter of the man who built the house so well . . .' and towed away '. . . to a little hill, covered in daisies'. The detail is copious and meticulous, the whole a joy. (Out of print, but surely bound to resurface.)

Mike Mulligan and his steam shovel, Mary-Ann, win all hearts, on acquaintance. Mike cannot bear to discard Mary-Ann, despite her outdated and outworn condition. In the end, he doesn't have to. The story has tension, climax, warmth and imagination; its message concerns the capacity of goodness and courage to convert spite and greed to its own ranks. Young children ought not to miss it; the illustrations support and extend its impact

Little Tim and the Brave Sea Captain Edward Ardizzone (Puffin paperback), also *Tim All Alone, Tim and Charlotte, Tim in*

Danger, Tim's Friend Towser, Tim to the Lighthouse and *Tim and Ginger* (Oxford paperback)
The Little Train
The Little Fire Engine
The Little Horse Bus
The Little Steamroller   all by Graham Greene, illus. Edward Ardizzone (Viking/Puffin paperback)

These are the famous author's only children's books, and Ardizzone's illustrations complement the earnest but warm-hearted texts precisely. Old-fashioned machines were so much more exciting than the inscrutable modern variety. To begin with, they hissed, and puffed and snorted – or were drawn by unpredictable and highly diverse animals. Modern children should experience them vicariously, if no other way is available. And Greene tells a good yarn!

*Lotta Leaves Home
*Madeline
Madeline in London both by Ludwig Bemelmans (Scholastic)
Magic Beach Alison Lester (Viking Kestrel/Puffin paperback)

All the charm and virtuosity of *Imagine* (see above) and yet quite different. Wide landscape pictures again portray fascinating detail – alternately, children (as many as twelve) playing realistically at a beach ('. . . our beach, our magic beach . . .') and then embarking upon imagined games. Princesses, dragons, castles and moats mingle with pirates and treasure chests and sharks; Alison Lester's people, young and older, are spirited, engaging, and original, her backgrounds fresh and sparkling, always. An utterly satisfying book.

*Mary-Mary
*More Mary-Mary
*Madam Mary-Mary Joan G. Robinson (Harrap) All out of print.
A Million Chameleons James Young (Little, Brown)

> *A little chameleon all in vermilion*
> *Danced alone in a garden pavilion . . .*

begins this beguiling book. The engaging little fellow is joined, unaccountably but spectacularly, by a million others, who thereafter keep changing colour as they proceed through a series of locations (which are almost unrecognizable, being totally effaced by the vast mob). This is a wonderful colour nonsense book, but exercises the tongue, too. Only a very determined child would try any counting.

The Minpins   Roald Dahl, illus. Patrick Benson   (Cape/Puffin paperback)

Roald Dahl died in 1990, leaving this book as the last of a series of famous – if sometimes controversial – books for children. Despite its exciting theme and action, *The Minpins* is unlike many of Dahl's earlier books in that it completely lacks the crude humour which was inclined to shock certain (adult!) readers. Instead, the tone is almost Victorian, with lonely little Billy answering his mother's repeated question, 'What are you up to in there?' with a mild, 'I'm being good, Mummy.' This apparent virtue fortunately does not stop Billy from escaping maternal vigilance to explore the fearsome forest of Sin, and here he meets, and ultimately becomes the hero of, the Minpins, a race of engaging tiny people who live in miniature homes inside huge trees. The illustrations are lavishly beautiful, the whole a fitting memorial to Dahl's life. In particular, the last words in the book speak directly to near-six-year-olds with their burgeoning passion for independence: 'And above all, watch with glittering eyes the whole world around you because the greatest secrets are always hidden in the most unlikely places.

'Those who don't believe in magic will never find it.'

* The Mischievous Martens   both by Astrid Lindgren, illus. Ilon Wikland   (Mammoth paperback)

Miss McTaffety's Cats   Liz Underhill   (Cape)

An outstanding book which might be classed in the 'novelty' category, as many of its strong pages have cut-out windows which reveal tantalizing details of both indoors and out. However, the book is a thing of beauty as well, and the story is engrossing and heartwarming, without any intrusive sentimentality. Old Miss McTaffety lives alone in a splendid Edwardian house, 'in a street full of other big houses'. But all her friends have long ago moved away. She is lonely, and shy, until the day she makes a courageous sortie to Papa Luigi's Restaurant. The people, the cats, the architecture and the street scenes are magnificent, and yet the story appeals to children; and may even give them to think, about old age, loneliness and kindness.

Mog on Fox Night Judith Kerr   (HarperCollins)

The indulged but irresistible Mog here becomes involved with a family of foxes who follow her out of the snow, through her cat-flap and into the family kitchen. Predictable disorder results; but Mog continues to emerge unscathed, her reputation even (falsely!) enhanced! It is hard to put a finger on Mog's irrefutable, almost classic appeal. Suffice merely to acquire the latest instalment in her innocent adventures.

Morag and the Lamb Joan Lingard, illus. Patricia Casey   (Walker Books)

When Russell and his dog, Morag, go to stay in the country, they are cautioned that Morag must not 'worry the sheep'. 'Why should the sheep be worried about Morag?' wonders Russell. In the event, Morag saves a lamb which is tangled up in a bramble bush, by fetching Russell to help, and all is resolved; the farmer is reassured, and Russell receives an explanation. Wide country scenes in delicate colour, with realistic boy, dog and adults set the seal on an appealing story.

* *Morris's Disappearing Bag* Rosemary Wells   (Lion paperback)

* *Moving Molly* Shirley Hughes   (Julia MacRae/Red Fox paperback)

Mr Archimedes' Bath Pamela Allen   (Puffin paperback)

A tongue-in-cheek spoof on the theory of water displacement commonly attributed to the great mathematician of the third century BC. Here, the hilariously plump, pink Mr Archimedes shares his tub with a kangaroo, a goat and a wombat – and the water swamps the floor. His experimentation with the bemused animals makes for great fun and enables the artist to produce absurdly funny pictures – *and* provides an elementary lesson in science. The text is particularly clear and simple, the book beautifully designed.

My Naughty Little Sister Storybook   Dorothy Edwards, illus. Shirley Hughes   (Methuen)

> These tales of the misdeeds of a four-year-old girl (and her friend Bad Harry, a small male of equally demoniac bent) are ostensibly told by an older sister of seven or so, and range from the mildly amusing to the wildly hilarious. They are always, however, believable; we have all experienced the dismayed exasperation of the offending child's family – even if not quite so consistently! There is a feast ahead if the tales are enjoyed, as this is merely a selection – but a good place to start, as the pictures have been coloured to produce almost picture-book effect, and are in the well-known illustrator's inimitable style. The characters, young and old, come alive; the children are believable and the stories all possible (Several one-story picture books are also available, with more liberal pictures – and the black-and-white line illustrated collections are not beyond the best listeners of this age-group).

The Nickle Nackle Tree   Lynley Dodd   (Spindlewood/Puffin paperback)

> An unusual counting book in which original and spirited verse is complemented by elegant and sprightly pictures.

> > *Seven haughty Huffpuff birds with hoity-toity smiles,*
> > *Eight cheeky Chizzle birds in cheerful Chirpy piles.*

> The ultimate collapse of the overloaded Nickle Nackle Tree is predictable and amusing.

The Night Before Christmas   Clement Moore, illus. Tomie de Paola   (Oxford paperback)

> It is fitting that this long Christmas poem should receive the attentions of a superlative modern American illustrator, for the author was also American. First written in 1822 for his own children, and published the following year, this story-poem is given new life by de Paola's beautifully designed, vibrantly coloured pictures. A note in the book tells us that the artist used his own home in a small New Hampshire village as model, and that his borders were based on patchwork quilts

owned by his own family. Certainly, warmth, care and artistry have gone into the making of this book, with satisfying results.

Noisy Nora

Shy Charles both by Rosemary Wells (Lion paperback)

These titles seem to belong together; they share both child-directed humour and a sly insight which will appeal to adult readers, while not spoiling the fun. Nora is being ignored by her parents in favour of her sister and baby brother, she believes. Her response will strike a chord in all breasts. Charles's parents are puzzled and embarrassed − and ultimately exasperated − by his shyness. When his babysitter (to whom he will not speak) falls downstairs, Charles gets everything right: he rings for help, wraps Mrs Block in a blanket and administers cocoa. When congratulated, he creeps inside his mother's coat. Charles, we now know, is brave and resourceful − and shy. Nora's lot are mice, and Charles's rabbits. (Why not?) Astute Stuff!

*Not So Fast, Songololo Niki Daly (Puffin paperback)

The Nutshell Library Maurice Sendak (Collins)

Four enchanting little books in a slipcase. All children love miniature objects, and these tiny volumes are splendid books in their own right. There is a counting book, a cautionary tale, an alphabet and a book of months and seasons − all distinguished by Sendak's singular and pointed use of words, and his incomparably earthy, knowing illustrations. Out of print at the time of writing, these matchless little books must be kept alive in memory, for they will surely return in a more expansive day.

Oh, Abigail! Moira Millar, illus. Doreen Caldwell (Methuen/Mammoth paperback)

The keynote of Abigail's family is informality, of a warm and cheerful kind. The parents' mode of speech mirrors the mood of good-humoured exasperation which Abigail's behaviour understandably arouses. 'Well go on!' yelled Mum. 'Get it sorted out before I dump the lot in the bin!' The stories are entertaining, and Abigail, her brother Paul, and Mum and Dad all come alive as the spirited and caring lot that they are. Doreen Caldwell's black-and-white illustrations are exceptionally good;

detailed, but clear-lined, well designed and executed. A second volume, *Just Like Abigail*, carries on the tradition.

Old Bear
Little Bear Lost
Little Bear's Trousers
Jolly Tall
Jolly Snow all by Jane Hissey (Red Fox paperback)

Jane Hissey's *Bear* stories are cosy rather than literary, but their appeal to the young is undoubted. Her pictures have touching appeal which just avoids tipping over into sentimentality. Here are real toys as all children know them, having the sort of behind-the-scenes adventures that their young owners have always suspected they had. Two collections, *Old Bear and His Friends* and *Old Bear Tales*, with twelve and ten extra stories respectively, make very good presents – and are certainly handsome books.

Once Upon a Time Alan Garner, illus. Norman Messenger (Dorling Kindersley)

'Once upon a time, though it wasn't in your time, and it wasn't in my time, and it wasn't in anybody else's time . . .' is the full title of this lovely book. The back cover tells us that the author 'retrieved three stories from the timeless world of folktale . . .' to create it; but the tales have Garner's own masterly touch. The book itself is superbly produced, with fine paper, handsome cover and arresting endpapers. Messenger's illustrations are quietly perfect for the themes of the three stories.

One Moonlit Night Ronda and David Armitage (Deutsch/Puffin paperback)

Tony's Dad assures Sam and Tony that their first night sleeping in the tent in the garden will be great fun. The boys are not so sure, but are duly installed. Parents will be familiar with the ensuing upsets, and everyone will enjoy Dad's difficulties when his plan to provide the boys with support backfires on him. This is an assured and entertaining book from an author and artist who know from experience how family life proceeds. The colours are warm, the characters believable, and the text lively.

Owls and Pussy-cats: Nonsense Verse   by Edward Lear and Lewis Carroll, illus. Nicki Palin   (Oxford)

This is a lovely 'presentation' book comprising the most popular work from those two nineteenth-century masters of nonsense, Lear and Carroll. *Jabberwocky, The Owl and the Pussycat, The Walrus and the Carpenter, The Quangle Wangle's Hat, The Mock Turtle's Song* and thirteen more daft and dotty verses together provide a feast to be read aloud, and repeated and repeated until *known*, by children fortunate enough to own the collection. The illustrations are magnificent; the artist has used the style and spirit of the Victorian Age and the wonders of modern technique and reproduction to provide a glorious celebration of nonsense.

The Party in the Sky   Alison Catley   (Red Fox paperback)

Claire is turning six and is having a party. But she lives on the tenth floor of Beechwood Towers. How can you have an exciting party in a small flat? Fortunately, her parents are not only loving; they are inventive. The apartment is turned into a 'castle in the sky' – with Dad dressed up as a jester, dispensing fun and balloons. The realistic pictures have a glowing beauty which invites initial wonder and continued enjoyment.

The Patchwork Cat   William Mayne, illus. Nicola Bayley   (Cape/Julia MacRae/Red Fox/Puffin paperback)

Cat lovers of all ages might covet this book for its illustrations alone; they have a luminous beauty, and the cat herself almost springs from the page. Mayne's idiosyncratic use of words is engaging and will be taken up and repeated with relish by the young listener. 'Ah,' says the mother, 'we have done some snatchwork on your patchwork. We have thrown it out because it is so very dirty, and we shall buy a basket.' Tabby does not want a basket. She will 'do some angry scratchwork on it if it comes.' Her campaign to retrieve the beloved patchwork from the tip is triumphant. The basket idea is abandoned.

Peter Potts the Plumber   Margaret Ryan   (Puffin paperback)

Eight very short stories about a cheerful plumber and his diverse and agreeably daft customers, with large print and black-and-white illustrations on every page. Easy to read, easy to listen to.

Phewtus the Squirrel V. H. Drummond (Walker)

This book was first written and illustrated (in black and white) nearly fifty years ago. Reissued, its pictures coloured by its still active author-artist, it has lost none of the spirit and bounce which has always characterized V. H. Drummond's work. Its length and complexity offer some comment on the expected concentration of small children in pre-television days; Julian is clearly about three, and yet the text is substantial. Fortunately, it is full of incident, with unlikely twists which are related so seriously that one cannot doubt their veracity. The new publishers have, sensibly, used a large, clear print face, and every single page rejoices in its share of the expressive, elegant-but-sturdy pictures. The story of Phewtus's extraordinary adventures will certainly appeal to modern four-year-olds.

*Phoebe and the Hot Water Bottles Terry Furchgott and Linda Dawson (Deutsch)

*Poems for the Very Young   ed. Michael Rosen, illus. Bob Graham (Kingfisher)

Polly's Puffin Sarah Garland (Puffin)

Sarah Garland depicts the ordinary lives of recognizable parents and children against ordinary urban backgrounds superbly; but there is nothing ordinary about what happens to Polly's toy puffin. Her little brother Jim, who 'never stopped throwing things', is in true form one day in the teashop, and hurls the puffin into the hood of a duffle-coated gentleman who, abstracted and unaware, makes off before Polly can repossess her beloved friend. The pursuit is glorious, and takes in, among other places, a department store, a church and a library, before a quirky chance returns the puffin 'like magic'. Polly reflects that 'she might leave her puffin safely at home' in the future. Jim, meanwhile, is throwing his shoes away ... Rousing stuff, sympathetically handled; and some of the backgrounds have unexpected elegance.

The Quangle Wangle's Hat Edward Lear, illus. Helen Oxenbury (Mammoth paperback)

This outstanding book brings one of the most popular of Lear's poem-extravaganzas to spectacular, bursting life in picture book format. This is probably, with *The Owl and the Pussycat*, the best Lear of all.

A Quarrel of Koalas   Ronda and David Armitage   (Scholastic)
The same Matilda Elizabeth met earlier in *Don't Forget, Matilda*, this time grown older and in company with brother Harry and Mother. The koalas are on a shopping expedition; Matilda determined to choose her own new shoes, Harry just as determined to reject *any* new shoes. They behave so badly that Mother decides to show *them* up in public – and carries the day! Blackmail, certainly, but . . .

'What lovely children I've got!' says Mother, as a total metamorphosis is accomplished. Lovely rich colour throughout, with plenty of action.

A Quiet Night In   Jill Murphy   (Walker Books)
It's Dad's birthday, and the Large (elephant) parents have decided to have 'a quiet night in', the proposal being to hustle the children into bed and enjoy a special meal on trays in front of the fire. Things don't turn out quite as expected . . . but then they never do in these entertaining stories about the oh-so-human Larges! Clear colour and line enhance an original story.

Rhymes Around the Day   Jan Ormerod   (Viking Kestrel/Puffin paperback)
This is a satisfying collection of poetry for the young, presented in an individual way. A family comprising twin girls of perhaps four or five, and a small brother who reveals his engaging, messy two-ness at every opening, are seen throughout an entire day between early and late bedroom scenes. During the day they go shopping, dress up, eat a meal, and create domestic mayhem in ways that are familiar, ultimately welcoming Dad home to the cheerful chaos. The rhymes are supportive, rather than central to the action, the illustrations delicate and yet buoyant, and the children real.

The Rich Man and the Shoe-maker   La Fontaine, illus. Brian Wildsmith   (Oxford/Oxford paperback)
This book, and those listed below, are all retellings of fables from the French collector La Fontaine. Brian Wildsmith's rich, glowing colours have produced books of startling beauty.

Texts are simple to the point of sparseness; morals easily
divined. These are books to treasure.

Other titles: *The Hare and the Tortoise, The Lion and the Rat,
The Miller, The Boy and the Donkey, The North Wind and the Sun*

Schnitzel von Krumm's Basketwork   Lynley Dodd   (Spindlewood)

Here is one of Hairy Maclary's boisterous bunch, in a book of
his very own. The mournful little dachshund is deprived, by
his well-meaning family, of his smelly old outgrown basket,
and equipped with a handsome new model. Schnitzel von
Krumm's grief is exceeded only by his determination to effect
restitution of the comfortable old wreck. Uncluttered, expressive pictures and rhyming text are successful, yet again, in
producing an attractive book.

Scraps   Mark Foreman   (Pan Macmillan)

Mrs Kelly makes a shelf of toys to sell at the market: a sailor doll,
a kangaroo, a crocodile, an elephant, a monkey, several teddies –
and Scraps. All the toys look forward to being sold, and one by
one go off with new owners, except Scraps. He returns home
sadly with Mrs Kelly, to sit in lonely state on the shelf. But not for
long! The addition of a baby to the family – a baby who cries and
cries – means that Scraps is desperately needed! A warm-hearted
tale of loyalty and devotion, with bright, jaunty pictures – and a
pattern at the back to help you make your *own* 'scrap' doll.

The Scruffy Scruffy Dog   H. E. Todd, illus. Val Biro   (Carousel
paperback)

Everyone likes to witness the triumph of the underdog, and
here the victor really *is* a dog. Mind you, one could hardly call
him humble; Scruffy is as cheerful and confident in his 'underdog' role as he is in his hour of triumph. The story is genuinely
funny, and the brightly coloured, generous pictures totally
complementary. The social commentary is gentle ('Come along
Fifi darling,' said Lady Fitzherbert, 'hold up your paw and
shake hands with the nice man'), if a little stereotyped, the
story itself substantial.

The Sign on Rosie's Door   Maurice Sendak   (Bodley Head/Puffin
paperback)

There are four separate stories about the same group of children in this baffling book (Sendak bypasses adults when addressing children, which he likes most to do). You may think there is no child quite as strange as yours until you meet Rosie, Kathy, Lenny, Pudgy, Sal and Dolly. You will then recognize the uniqueness and the sameness of all children everywhere. This is probably the only book ever written which should be issued by 'the authorities' to all the five-year-olds in the world. You can't afford to let yours miss it.

Slinky Malinki   Lynley Dodd   (Mallinson Rendel/Spindlewood/ Puffin paperback)

> *Slinky Malinki*
> *was blacker than black*
> *a stalking and lurking*
> *adventurous cat . . .*

and stalk and lurk he does, for the purpose of raiding the neighbours' kitchens, halls and porches of edibles, wearables and assorted paraphernalia, valuable and otherwise. Of course, he gets his come-uppance, and, we are told, reforms:

> *When whispers of wickedness*
> *stirred in his head,*
> *he adjusted his whiskers and stayed*
> *home*
> *instead.*

Slinky Malinki, Open the Door   reveals the fallacy of his reformation, again in cheerful rhyme and expressive picture.

* *The Snow Lady*   Shirley Hughes   (Walker/Walker paperback)

Starting School   Janet and Allan Ahlberg   (Puffin paperback)

'Gavin and Errol and Sophie and Sushma and David and Kate and Robert and Alison are . . . starting school.' This detailed catalogue of their day-by-day doings, ups and downs and reactions, makes fascinating listening and looking – and will certainly both inform and fortify aspiring school-starters. Janet Ahlberg's pictures are, as always a mixture of earthy reality, careful observation and adroit craftsmanship – in a framework of heartwarming humour.

Stories for Under-Fives
More Stories for Under-Fives
Stories for Five-Year-Olds   all by Sara and Steven Corrin (eds.)   (Puffin paperback)

The Story About Ping   Marjorie Flack and Kurt Wiese   (Bodley Head/Julia MacRae/Red Fox/Puffin paperback)

> Ping is a duck of originality. His home is a boat on the Yangtze River to which he must return each night. But one night, he rebels. His subsequent adventures have become justly famous since his emergence in 1935. Text and pictures are well integrated in this sound and satisfying book.

The Story of Babar
Babar at Home
Babar and Father Christmas
Babar's Friend Zephir
Babar the King
Babar's Travels   all by Jean de Brunhoff   (Methuen)

> First published in France (1934 in England) and loved by generations since, Babar, the lumbering, wise and gentle elephant who becomes king of Celesteville featured in six wonderful books (and an ABC, now out of print) before his author's death in 1937. Laurent de Brunhoff, Jean's son, carried on the series, but never achieved his father's imaginative handling of character, background, or story. (My own 'precious' shelf houses a crumbling set of early 'Babars', with the original cursive script texts. One of them – *Babar and Father Christmas* – is inscribed in the name of Simon Butler. Underneath is written, in my handwriting, 'Bought on the 17th March 1961, because he did not have a Babar book' – and I recall this small son, four-and-a-half at the time, dictating the triumphant inscription after the whole family had returned from an expedition undertaken for the sole purpose of acquiring the book – and silencing the determined complainant.)

The Story of Christmas   Jane Ray   (Orchard Books)

> The biblical text, sensitively abridged, is here made memorable with pictures which glow, while they retell the old story with loving precision. A beautiful book, to treasure and hand on.

Sven's Bridge   Anita Lobel   (Julia MacRae Books)
   This satisfying book is nearly thirty years old, though only
   recently published in Britain. My family's old copy has had
   spells over the years of roosting in the living-room for months
   on end, someone – child or grandchild – requiring regular
   repeats. (It is there again as I write.) Set in an unspecified
   time when kings travelled about the countryside in their own
   boats, wearing their crowns and, in fits of pique, even requiring
   their crews to blow up inconveniently placed bridges, *Sven*
   cannot date. Anita Lobel's sturdy peasant characters are robust
   and believable. Sven himself has a quiet dignity; his calm
   kindness leads to the reinstatement of the bridge (after the
   king has learnt his lesson). The triumph of benevolence over
   violence is gently demonstrated, with no preaching. The detailed elegance of Lobel's work amply warrants the decades of
   loving perusal my family has given it. *Sven's Bridge* is a book to
   own, and to preserve for future generations.
Teddy Tales   Sally Grindley, illus. Peter Utton   (Orchard Books)
   Ten bears of different size, disposition and personality disport
   themselves cheerfully through this well-designed book. There
   are Curly Bear, Pocket Bear, Texan Ted and seven others, all
   depicted on the endpapers and each involved in a short self-
   contained story. The large, clear print will give extra service
   when the child begins to read alone; and the illustrations are
   generously scattered throughout.
Tell Me a Story
Tell Me Another Story
Time for a Story
More Stories to Tell   all by Eileen Colwell   (Puffin paperback)
   Four books which between them provide a wealth of usable
   tales in a short and simple form. Colwell is a renowned
   storyteller, and her stories have impact, pace and shape. These
   collections are fortunately available in inexpensive paperback
   editions. One in the car, one in the kitchen and one in the
   bedroom would solve all problems!
There's a Hole in My Bucket   illus. Nadine Bernard Westcott   (Little
Mammoth paperback)

The old cyclical verse which starts with the discovery of the hole in the bucket and proceeds, by way of innumerable instructions from the bossy Liza to the guileless Henry, to the proposition that the materials needed to mend the pail are useless without water, and Henry's plaintive reiteration: 'But there's a hole in my bucket, dear Liza, dear Liza . . .' Modern children should encounter the old rhymes, and this one comes equipped with hilarious pictures.

The Tiger-Skin Rug   Gerald Rose   (Puffin paperback)

A truly hilarious story about a dusty, moth-eaten old tiger who manages to pass himself off as a rug in the Rajah's palace. Highly original theme, well-rounded plot and lively, colourful pictures ensure its success with small readers and their parents. He's a *character*, this particular tiger!

Tilly's House   Faith Jaques   (Mammoth paperback)

An outstanding picture book on a subject which has perennnial appeal for the over-fours. House-or-hut building really enters the scene at this stage; and the appeal of dolls' houses is ageless. Tilly is an oppressed but spirited little kitchenmaid in a Victorian dolls' house, until her moment of rebellion arrives. A decision to find 'a place where I can be free and decide things for myself' launches her into an escape which is documented in detail in the meticulous and charming pictures. The home which Tilly subsequently sets up in the garden shed is evidence of her incomparable ingenuity, resourcefulness and industry. Teddy helps, but is bumbling by comparison. Tilly's achievements are direct reflections of her cosy maxims:

> *Where there's a will there's a way.*
> *Waste not, want not.*

A joy for all children lucky enough to meet it – as is the sequel, *Tilly's Rescue*, in which the indomitable Tilly embarks on a rescue mission when Edward, the bear, is lost.

The Tin Can Band and Other Poems   Margaret Mahy, illus. Honey de Lacy   (Puffin paperback)

Eleven poems from this modern master of nonsense, wonder,

hilarity and hope. Culled from earlier anthologies of story and poetry, the collection can be read aloud at a sitting – and repeated on demand. Mahy's inimitable capacity to invoke the imaginative on the one hand –

> *When I was but a little boy and played beneath a tree,*
> *Seven kings and seven queens there came to talk to me . . .*

and the everyday on the other –

> *'No!' says the granny, 'I'm right as rain*
> *And I'm going to go on till I get to Spain'*

reflects the nature of four-to-sevens precisely. I'd keep a few copies in hand for birthday presents. This is Everychild's stuff (and the pictures are wonderful).

Tiny Tim   Jill Bennett (ed.), illus. Helen Oxenbury   (Mammoth paperback)

Twenty well-chosen verses with vigorous, superbly appropriate pictures. Unlike many longer anthologies, this brief collection demands non-stop reading. There is no invitation to gloom or even introspection in the poems; even Charles Causley's 'I saw a jolly hunter' will be seen as funny by reason of its slapstick flavour, long before its message starts to emerge.

*Titch   (Bodley Head/Puffin paperback)

**You'll Soon Grow into Them, Titch*   (Bodley Head/Red Fox/Puffin paperback)

*Tidy Titch   all by Pat Hutchins   (Julia MacRae/Red Fox paperback)

Tom's Saturday Trousers   Harriet Graham   (Puffin paperback)

Tom is turning six and goes to school, but the ten tales in this excellent collection document his home, rather than school doings. The author evokes the true concerns of a small boy who has a baby sister, makes a snowman, behaves both well and badly, runs away when reprimanded . . . and is usually rescued by his Gran, when in trouble. The stories are engrossing, and will give admirable 'listening' practice.

*_Tomie de Paola's Favourite Nursery Tales_   Tomie de Paola (Methuen)

The Tomten   Astrid Lindgren, illus. Harald Wiberg   (Floris Books/ Viking)

> A book of unique quality. This is the story of a small Swedish troll, '. . . an old, old Tomten who has seen the snow of many hundreds of winters . . .' who lives at an old farm, deep in the forest. No one has ever seen him, but each night he plods from animal to animal, comforting them, and talking to them in tomten language, 'a silent little language a horse can understand'. Each whole-page picture almost demands to be framed and hung. The mood of the long Northern night shines from these sombre, glowing scenes; and the text is sheer poetry. To be a child is to wonder. How could this evocation of remote serenity _not_ bolster and fortify?

> _Winters come and summers go, year follows year, but as long as people live at the old farm in the forest, every night the Tomten will trip around between the houses on his small silent feet._

The Trouble with Jack   Shirley Hughes   (Corgi paperback)

> This engaging story is simple enough for a younger child – but the message is for a big sister. Jack (about two) almost wrecks Nancy's party, but, after the crisis is resolved, she reflects: 'The trouble with Jack . . . is that as he's my brother I've got to put up with him whatever he's like.' Shirley Hughes's children are, as usual, flesh and blood.

The Very Worst Monster   Pat Hutchins   (Bodley Head/Puffin paperback)

> _When Billy Monster was born, his pa said,_
> _'My son is going to grow up to be the Worst Monster in the World.'_
> _'No, he's not,' said Hazel, Billy's sister. 'I am.'_
> _But nobody heard Hazel._

> How Hazel contrives to establish the truth of her assertion, in brief text and energetic picture, makes a good book; and Hazel's clear affection for her monsterish little brother is warmly established.

* *The Walker Book of Poetry for Children*   Jack Prelutsky (ed.), illus. Arnold Lobel   (Walker)

* *The Walker Book of Read-Aloud Rhymes for the Very Young*   Jack Prelutsky (ed.), illus. Marc Brown   (Walker)

A Welcome for Annie   Helen Craig   (Walker paperback)

Alfred and Susie are firm friends: partners in crime, actually. When Annie and her family come to live next door to Alfred, he and Susie hatch a plot to 'welcome Annie'. Fortunately it backfires, and all is well in the end. The adults in the piece remain calm, if a little shocked, and Annie reveals herself as a worthy adversary and likely confederate. (Certainly a vigorous example to her sex.) That they are all pigs – drawn with feeling and skill which avoids exaggeration and reflects human reaction deliciously – is a measure of this author-artist's wit and capacity. The endpapers are a bonus.

What Do People Do All Day?   Richard Scarry   (HarperCollins)

They dig and cook and paint and drive and clean and build . . . and in this very large, colourful volume you can watch them doing it. Scarry's busy little animal-people provide fascinating entertainment for the young, either to enjoy alone, or with obliging adult on hand to help.

* *Wheels*   Shirley Hughes   (Walker/Walker paperback)

When Dad Did the Washing   Ronda and David Armitage   (Scholastic/ Puffin paperback)

Will strike a chord in many memories. Who can honestly claim never to have produced unexpected colour effects in the family wash? And why is it never an old, unimportant garment that suffers the full impact of the catastrophe? In this case, it is Mum's new white skirt (not to mention other people's socks, pants and T-shirts) which takes on a blushing pink hue – and Joss who is responsible. How could Dad know that, while he was busy with a caller, Joss would throw his own bright red track suit into the already loaded washer? Shock all around! But Mum's dismay quickly assumes that philosophical resignation that most mothers develop in time as the only possible response to the vicissitudes of family life, if survival is to be ensured. And she does 'look lovely' in the pink skirt, she is later assured by all! David and Ronda Armitage have together produced a believable, funny story with brilliantly complementary pictures. As a model of warm-hearted family life – in all its cheerful messiness – *When Dad Did the Washing* is a gem. That Dad is the homemaker while Mum goes out to work strikes a blow for role flexibility – and, for those of us who remember, Mum is surely that same Rosie Posie Hubble, 'the best loved of 'them all', who ran 'the only general store on Kotuku Island' (and, it would seem, still does!) in the Armitages' 1981 book, *Ice Creams for Rosie*. My family welcomed her back. We all expected her to be still calm in the face of disaster.

When I Was Little Marcia Williams (Walker Books)
This book will stand hours and hours of earnest scrutiny. It begins: 'When my granny comes to stay, she always says to me . . .' and proceeds, with marvellous predictability, to list Granny's rose-coloured recollections of a bygone childhood. Each opening reveals at least three, and as many as eighteen, framed pictures of fascinating complexity, yet brilliant clarity. Informative as well as entertaining for any age group, and certainly within reach of the near-sixes.

Where's the Baby? Pat Hutchins (Bodley Head/Red Fox paperback)
Grandmothers are noted for their rose-coloured-spectacle approach to small grandchildren, and Grandma Monster is determined to approve. Atrocity after atrocity is revealed, as the family searches anxiously for the baby. And then we find that the dear, innocent little fellow has put himself to bed, and is sleeping, like the cherub Grandma claims he is. 'What a lot he can do!' she purrs, monster-style. But more is in store . . . (My small listener-viewer was enraptured with the domestic chaos.) This sequel to *The Very Worst Monster* cannot fail: it has action, humour, suspense and colour.

Where's Julius? John Burningham (Cape)
A big book this, providing opportunity for regular inclusion of those colourful, large-canvas paintings which the artist does so well. There is sensitivity as well as exuberance in both story and picture. Julius is seen at the beginning and end of the book having meals with his parents. Between, he is never there

– he is '. . . riding a camel to the top of the tomb of Neffatuteum which is a pyramid near the Nile in Egypt . . .', '. . . watching the sunrise from the top of the Changa Benang mountains somewhere near Tibet . . .' or '. . . about to shoot the rapids on the Chiko Neeko River somewhere in Peru in South America.' His serious, ever-patient parents deliver the food they have cooked, diligently. (This, too, is carefully described.) A lovely, wordy, tongue-in-cheek book which will sustain innumerable read-aloud sessions.

The Whirlys and the West Wind   Christine Ross   (Methuen)

Mr and Mrs Whirly and their three children Flora, Jack and baby Rose are an ordinary family 'who were hardly ever surprised by anything . . .' A certain degree of surprise – even dismay – is evinced on the day that the Whirly parents are swept into the sky by the fierce west wind; but the children, on the whole, adjust to the lack – and can even see them, at times (with the telescope) flying across the sky. 'Sometimes from right to left and sometimes from left to right.' The illustrations are glorious. Scenes of (gradually lessening) chaos are nicely offset by the earnest, outrageous text – and the parents, reappearing at last, admit to having found the experience '. . . quite invigorating, really . . .' This author-artist knows what children are like. Try it out on one, and see for yourself!

The Whistling Piglet   Dick King-Smith, illus. Norman Johnson (Walker Books)

Out-of-line behaviour is always savoured by the young, who inevitably feel over-controlled. Henry, Mum pig's tenth piglet, who whistles beautifully, is a certain hero. All the young on the farm love him, from the farmer's little daughter to the calves and lambs and baby chicks. Their elders are not so sure. One tune especially has a spectacular effect:

> *Come follow, follow, follow,*
> *Follow, follow, follow me . . .*

The wide double spreads of all the young creatures on the farm leaping fences, hedges and gates to follow Henry 'To the greenwood, to the greenwood . . .' are enchanting. Such anarchy, in such ordered surroundings! A scrumptious tale.

The Wild Bears   John Richardson   (Red Fox paperback)

These bears are boisterous, rather than barbarous; almost any four-year-olds would jump at the chance of inclusion in their ranks. Jack Alabaster (lovely name!) goes out with his family for the day, enjoining his own two rather humourless teddy bears to 'Keep guard while we are gone'. But 'five wild teddy bears are hiding behind the potting shed . . . !' Jack's luckless bears do not prove to be up to the job. The invasion is in the best tradition of child bear mayhem – the bath overflows, honey slops on the furniture and floor, flowers are picked by the armful. All this is gloriously revealed in brilliant, double-page pictures of irresistible charm and vigour. When the family is heard returning, the subversive bunch flee; but 'the tiny little baby bear called Grub' is left behind! Anarchic four-year-olds will relish the uproar, but also the appealing baby bear's final restoration to his family.

Wilfrid Gordon McDonald Partridge   Mem Fox, illus. Julie Vivas (Puffin paperback)

This book speaks directly to adults, particularly those who will not see sixty again; but also to the four-and-overs, who see nothing strange in Wilfrid Gordon's search for old Miss Nancy's memory. There is unusual collusion between text and illustration here, and a true feeling for extreme old age, with its uncanny overtones of extreme youth. The result is an overriding flavour of poignancy and gentle humour. One cannot categorize such a book; but sharing it with the young is a joy.

Will There Be Polar Bears?   Julia Jarman, illus. Priscilla Lamont (Heinemann)

Sam and his family are going to stay with Great Aunt Addie 'up north', for Christmas. How will Father Christmas know he is not in his usual house? worries Sam; and surely Great Aunt Addie must be an Eskimo, if she lives 'way up north?' In the event, the old lady proves to be disappointingly ordinary; but things are not always what they seem. Priscilla Lamont's quiet but expressive pictures capture children, house, snow – and Great Aunt Addie – superbly.

The Witch in the Cherry Tree   Margaret Mahy, illus. Jenny Williams (Dent/Puffin paperback)

First published in 1974, and out of print when this book was last revised, the story of David, his mother, and a witch who happened to be '. . . whirling like a lonely cinder . . .' high above the city on the day David's mother was baking cakes, fully deserved to reappear. It would be hard to fear this particular witch. She thoroughly enjoys the burnt cakes that David throws her, and the bright cheerfulness of the pictures, with the witch's mumbled comments ('It's not much *fun* being a witch') maintain a tongue-in-cheek humour throughout. (And the recipe for Gingerbread Witches in the back really works.)

The Yellow House   Blake Morrison, illus. Helen Craig   (Walker Books)

An appealing, slightly eerie story about a little girl who climbs the gate into the garden of a deserted house, where there is 'a lawn, a goldfish pond . . . but never any people, never any children.' Who is the little boy 'in dungarees and a bobble hat' who invites her to play, then? He does look very like the garden gnome . . . Suitably sketchy pictures in muted colour strike the right note. A thoughtful, 'read-it-again' book.

The Young Puffin Book of Verse   Barbara Ireson (ed.)   (Puffin paperback)

Conclusion

I hope that this book has gone some way towards convincing you that books are important for your baby and child, and for babies and children everywhere. I hope also that I have conveyed my reasons to you for my belief in books, and given you a true picture of what I feel they can accomplish in the lives of young children.

A great deal is said and written these days about the need to speed up the learning process, to get children's minds ticking over at earlier and earlier ages. It can all sound very serious; quite out of touch with the joy, the bounce and the humour that is the real nature of childhood. Heaven forbid that I should have contributed to this over-sober view of a parent's role!

My hope for children is that they will learn to live richly and well; that each child will use her unique qualities to become a happy, contributing adult.

Every person in the world is unique, and every person is essentially alone. We cannot change this aloneness, but we can reduce its effects. Relationships are the key. We nourish our essential humanity when we make contact with one another.

Forging a close relationship with our own baby is easy. Babies are totally unstinting in their willingness to accept us as fountains of pleasure and support. We will be immeasurably enriched by their uncritical devotion, and they, by our love, in return. But we need things in common. No relationship can survive on a basis of mutual, unquestioning adoration.

For relationships, minds have to engage. Ideas are essential, and books constitute a superlative source of ideas. Books can be bridges between children and parents and children and the world.

There is one overriding requirement, however, if books are to work for children in this way. They have to be successful books, books which will make children sit up and take notice, laugh, and ask 'Why?' Books which will involve them deeply, and lift them out of the here-and-now to a place of wonder. 'Read it again' will always be the highest accolade. Such books exist. I hope that *this* book will help you to find some of them and identify others, and that your own developing relationship with your child will keep you reading them together.

Index

Discover more about our forthcoming books through Penguin's FREE newspaper...

Penguin Quarterly

It's packed with:

- exciting features
- author interviews
- previews & reviews
- books from your favourite films & TV series
- exclusive competitions & much, much more...

Write off for your free copy today to:
Dept JC
Penguin Books Ltd
FREEPOST
West Drayton
Middlesex
UB7 0BR
NO STAMP REQUIRED

READ MORE IN PENGUIN

In every corner of the world, on every subject under the sun, Penguin represents quality and variety – the very best in publishing today.

For complete information about books available from Penguin – including Puffins, Penguin Classics and Arkana – and how to order them, write to us at the appropriate address below. Please note that for copyright reasons the selection of books varies from country to country.

In the United Kingdom: Please write to *Dept. JC, Penguin Books Ltd, FREEPOST, West Drayton, Middlesex UB7 0BR.*

If you have any difficulty in obtaining a title, please send your order with the correct money, plus ten per cent for postage and packaging, to *PO Box No. 11, West Drayton, Middlesex UB7 0BR*

In the United States: Please write to *Consumer Sales, Penguin USA, P.O. Box 999, Dept. 17109, Bergenfield, New Jersey 07621-0120.* VISA and MasterCard holders call 1-800-253-6476 to order all Penguin titles

In Canada: Please write to *Penguin Books Canada Ltd, 10 Alcorn Avenue, Suite 300, Toronto, Ontario M4V 3B2*

In Australia: Please write to *Penguin Books Australia Ltd, P.O. Box 257, Ringwood, Victoria 3134*

In New Zealand: Please write to *Penguin Books (NZ) Ltd, Private Bag 102902, North Shore Mail Centre, Auckland 10*

In India: Please write to *Penguin Books India Pvt Ltd, 706 Eros Apartments, 56 Nehru Place, New Delhi 110 019*

In the Netherlands: Please write to *Penguin Books Netherlands bv, Postbus 3507, NL-1001 AH Amsterdam*

In Germany: Please write to *Penguin Books Deutschland GmbH, Metzlerstrasse 26, 60594 Frankfurt am Main*

In Spain: Please write to *Penguin Books S. A., Bravo Murillo 19, 1° B, 28015 Madrid*

In Italy: Please write to *Penguin Italia s.r.l., Via Felice Casati 20, I–20124 Milano*

In France: Please write to *Penguin France S. A., 17 rue Lejeune, F–31000 Toulouse*

In Japan: Please write to *Penguin Books Japan, Ishikiribashi Building, 2–5–4, Suido, Bunkyo-ku, Tokyo 112*

In Greece: Please write to *Penguin Hellas Ltd, Dimocritou 3, GR–106 71 Athens*

In South Africa: Please write to *Longman Penguin Southern Africa (Pty) Ltd, Private Bag X08, Bertsham 2013*

READ MORE IN PENGUIN

A SELECTION OF FICTION AND NON-FICTION

The Inn at the Edge of the World   Alice Thomas Ellis

Five fugitives from Christmas are lured by an advertisement to a remote Scottish island. 'With her warm, acerbic wit, Alice Thomas Ellis has the audacious gift of moving us by her manner of poking fun at human misery. She edges the supernatural with sensible restraint and conjures forth a story full of pleasure' – *Mail on Sunday*

Notes of a Native Son   James Baldwin

Richard Wright's *Native Son*, Hollywood's *Carmen Jones*, boyhood in Harlem, the death of his father, recovery and self-discovery as a black American in Paris – these are some of the themes of James Baldwin's early essays, which established him as among the greatest prose stylists of the century.

Florence: The Biography of a City   Christopher Hibbert

A celebration of an extraordinary metropolis, *Florence* explores the art, literature, archaeology and social history that have shaped Italy's famous city across the ages, and is also an indispensable guide through the streets of Florence today.

Shelley and His World   Claire Tomalin

'A vivid, amusing yet heartbreaking picture of Shelley emerges: poetry, politics, travel, friendships, love affairs, scandals, mysteries, children, visions – all gracefully combined' – *London Review of Books*

The Penguin Guide to Jazz on CD, LP and Cassette
Richard Cook and Brian Morton

'An incisive account of available recordings which cuts across the artificial boundaries by which jazz has been divided ... each page has a revelation; everybody will find their own' – *The Times*

READ MORE IN PENGUIN

A SELECTION OF FICTION AND NON-FICTION

Some Irish Loving Edna O'Brien

The Irish approach to love is a many-splendoured and ripened refinement of the senses, which includes the barbed cosiness of friendship, the fleetingness of sex and the drama of woe. Edna O'Brien reflects these varieties in her selection of poems, letters, plays and story excerpts.

Memories of the Ford Administration John Updike

'Updike is surely the finest chronicler of post-war American life, and what a sad, if sadly beautiful, chronicle he has made. At the centre of all is loss, loss of love, of opportunity, of time itself . . . one of the best things you are likely to read this year' – *Irish Times*

Cider With Rosie Laurie Lee

In telling the story of his early life in a remote Cotswold village, Laurie Lee gives us a loving and intimate portrait of a country childhood and an unforgettable record of an era and a community that have disappeared.

Visiting Mrs Nabokov Martin Amis

'Amis is as talented a journalist as he is a novelist, but these essays all manifest an unusual extra quality, one that is not unlike friendship. He makes an effort; he makes readers feel that they are the only person there' – *The Times*

Acts of Defiance Jack Ashley

Devastated when a minor operation in 1968 resulted in the total loss of his hearing, the Labour backbencher Jack Ashley, now Lord Ashley, had even announced his resignation to the press. What he went on to achieve is shown here in both a remarkable autobiography and a classic essay on the arts of politics and the possible.

Famous Trials Volumes 1–9

From matricide to mutilation, poisoning and cold-blooded murder, this classic series, now reissued in Penguin, contains nine volumes of gripping criminal investigations that made headlines in their day.

READ MORE IN PENGUIN

A SELECTION OF FICTION AND NON-FICTION

A Damsel in Distress   P. G. Wodehouse

There are some rather unusual things going on at Belpher Castle. For one thing, the Earl's sister is set on pairing off her stepson, Reggie, and niece, Lady Patricia. But the latter has her sights set elsewhere . . . Love, anarchy, Machiavellian plots, silly asses – perfect Wodehouse reading!

The Rapstone Chronicles   John Mortimer

The rise and rise of the odious arch-Tory Leslie Titmuss is charted here, from his days as an unpopular schoolboy to his success as the pragmatic and self-seeking Secretary of State. 'Beautifully written, witty and often very, very funny' – *Spectator*

Leonardo   Serge Bramly

'Bramly makes it possible for us better to understand Leonardo's greatness. He does this by fixing him in his time, and interpreting his life and work with an unfailing intelligence and sympathy. This is a very fine book' – *Daily Telegraph*

Romancing Vietnam   Justin Wintle

'Mr Wintle has written what may be the best account so far of life in post-war Vietnam' – *Economist*. 'An excellent traveller. Wintle is inquisitive, is not burdened by self-consciousness – and things happen to him' – *Daily Telegraph*

Travelling the World   Paul Theroux

Now, for the first time, Paul Theroux has authorized a book of his favourite travel writing, containing photographs taken by those who have followed in his footsteps. The exquisite pictures here brilliantly complement and illuminate the provocative, wry, witty commentaries of one of the world's greatest travellers.

READ MORE IN PENGUIN

A SELECTION OF FICTION AND NON-FICTION

My Secret Planet Denis Healey

An anthology of the prose and poetry that has provided pleasure and inspiration to Denis Healey throughout his life. 'His boyhood, days at Oxford, the war, politics, the arts, death and the spiritual life ... these are all pieces to be relished' – *Sunday Times*

Genie Russ Rymer

A compelling and searching history of Genie who, at thirteen, had spent her entire childhood in one room, caged in a cot or strapped to a chair. Almost mute, without linguistic or social skills, Genie aroused great excitement among the scientists who took over her life. 'Moving and terrifying ... opens windows some might prefer kept shut on man's inhumanity' – Ruth Rendell

Falling in Love Jacky Fleming

Brilliant, bawdy and irreverent cartoons about falling in love ... 'I couldn't put it down. My advice to anyone thinking of falling in love, about to fall in love or already in love is – Stop! Buy this book, a pound of chocolates and go home by yourself for the evening. You'll have a much better time' – Sandi Toksvig

A Place of Greater Safety Hilary Mantel

Hilary Mantel's award-winning fictional history of the French Revolution. 'She has soaked herself in the history of the period ... and a striking picture emerges of the exhilaration, dynamic energy and stark horror of those fearful days' – *Daily Telegraph*

The New Spaniards John Hooper

Few of the millions of visitors Spain receives each year see beyond the hotels and resorts of its coastline. In this completely revised edition, there are chapters on, among other things, Spain under Socialism, women's changing role, bullfighting, and what John Hooper calls 'the cult of excess'.

READ MORE IN PENGUIN

LANGUAGE/LINGUISTICS

Sociolinguistics Peter Trudgill

Women speak 'better' English than men. The Eskimo language has several words for snow. 1001 factors influence the way we speak. Professor Trudgill draws on languages from Afrikaans to Yiddish to illuminate this fascinating topic and provide a painless introduction to sociolinguistics.

Bad Language Lars-Gunnar Andersson and Peter Trudgill

As this witty and incisive book makes clear, the prophets of gloom who claim that our language is getting worse are guided by emotion far more than by hard facts. The real truth, as Andersson and Trudgill illuminate in fascinating detail, is that change has always been inherent in language.

Our Language Simeon Potter

'The author is brilliantly successful in his effort to instruct by delighting . . . he contrives not only to give a history of English but also to talk at his ease on rhyming slang, names, spelling reform, American English and much else . . . fascinating' – *Higher Education Journal*

Grammar Frank Palmer

In modern linguistics grammar means far more than cases, tenses and declensions – it means precise and scientific description of the structure of language. This concise guide takes the reader simply and clearly through the concepts of traditional grammar, morphology, sentence structure and transformational-generative grammar.

The Language Instinct Steven Pinker

'A marvellously readable book . . . illuminates every facet of human language: its biological origin, its uniqueness to humanity, its acquisition by children, its grammatical structure, the production and perception of speech, the pathology of language disorders and the unstoppable evolution of languages and dialects' – *Nature*

READ MORE IN PENGUIN

PSYCHOLOGY

Introduction to Jung's Psychology Frieda Fordham

'She has delivered a fair and simple account of the main aspects of my psychological work. I am indebted to her for this admirable piece of work' – C. G. Jung in the Foreword

Child Care and the Growth of Love John Bowlby

His classic 'summary of evidence of the effects upon children of lack of personal attention . . . presents to administrators, social workers, teachers and doctors a reminder of the significance of the family' – *The Times*

Recollections and Reflections Bruno Bettelheim

'A powerful thread runs through Bettelheim's message: his profound belief in the dignity of man, and the importance of seeing and judging other people from their own point of view' – *Independent*. 'These memoirs of a wise old child, candid, evocative, heart-warming, suggest there is hope yet for humanity' – *Evening Standard*

Female Perversions Louise J. Kaplan

'If you can't have love, what do you get? Perversion, be it mild or severe: shopping, seduction, anorexia or self-mutilation. Kaplan charts both Madame Bovary's "perverse performance" and the more general paths to female self-destruction with a grace, determination and intellectual firmness rare in the self-discovery trade. A most remarkable book' – Fay Weldon

The Psychology of Interpersonal Behaviour Michael Argyle

Social behaviour and relationships with others are one of the main sources of happiness, but their failure may result in great distress and can be a root cause of mental illness. In the latest edition of this classic text, Michael Argyle has included the latest research on non-verbal communication, social skills and happiness, and has extensively revised and updated the text throughout.

READ MORE IN PENGUIN

A SELECTION OF HEALTH BOOKS

The Kind Food Guide Audrey Eyton

Audrey Eyton's all-time bestselling *The F-Plan Diet* turned the nation on to fibre-rich food. Now, as the tide turns against factory farming, she provides the guide destined to bring in a new era of eating.

Baby and Child Penelope Leach

This comprehensive, authoritative and practical handbook is an essential guide, with sections on every stage of the first five years of life.

Woman's Experience of Sex Sheila Kitzinger

Fully illustrated with photographs and line drawings, this book explores the riches of women's sexuality at every stage of life. 'A book which any mother could confidently pass on to her daughter – and her partner too' – *Sunday Times*

The Effective Way to Stop Drinking Beauchamp Colclough

Beauchamp Colclough is an international authority on drink dependency, a reformed alcoholic, and living proof that today's decision is tomorrow's freedom. Follow the expert advice contained here, and it will help you give up drinking – for good.

Living with Alzheimer's Disease and Similar Conditions
Dr Gordon Wilcock

This complete and compassionate self-help guide is designed for families and carers (professional or otherwise) faced with the 'living bereavement' of dementia.

Living with Stress
Cary L. Cooper, Rachel D. Cooper and Lynn H. Eaker

Stress leads to more stress, and the authors of this helpful book show why low levels of stress are desirable and how best we can achieve them in today's world. Looking at those most vulnerable, they demonstrate ways of breaking the vicious circle that can ruin lives.

READ MORE IN PENGUIN

A SELECTION OF HEALTH BOOKS

Living with Asthma and Hay Fever   John Donaldson

For the first time, there are now medicines that can prevent asthma attacks from taking place. Based on up-to-date research, this book shows how the majority of sufferers can beat asthma and hay fever to lead full and active lives.

Anorexia Nervosa   R. L. Palmer

Lucid and sympathetic guidance for those who suffer from this disturbing illness and their families and professional helpers, given with a clarity and compassion that will make anorexia more understandable and consequently less frightening for everyone involved.

Medicines: A Guide for Everybody   Peter Parish

The use of any medicine is always a balance of benefits and risks – this book will help the reader understand how to extend the benefits and reduce the risks. Completely revised, it is written in ordinary, accessible language for the layperson, and is also indispensable to anyone involved in health care.

Other People's Children   Sheila Kitzinger

Though step-families are common, adults and children in this situation often feel isolated because they fail to conform to society's idealized picture of a normal family. This sensitive, incisive book is essential reading for anyone involved with or in a step-family.

Miscarriage   Ann Oakley, Ann McPherson and Helen Roberts

One million women worldwide become pregnant every day. At least half of these pregnancies end in miscarriage or stillbirth. But each miscarriage is the loss of a potential baby, and that loss can be painful to adjust to. Here is sympathetic support and up-to-date information on one of the commonest areas of women's reproductive experience.

READ MORE IN PENGUIN

A SELECTION OF HEALTH BOOKS

When a Woman's Body Says No to Sex Linda Valins

Vaginismus – an involuntary spasm of the vaginal muscles that prevents penetration – has been discussed so little that many women who suffer from it don't recognize their condition by its name. Linda Valins's practical and compassionate guide will liberate these women from their fears and sense of isolation and help them find the right form of therapy.

Mixed Messages Brigid McConville

Images of breasts – young and naked, sexual and chic – are everywhere. Yet for many women, the form, functions and health of our own breasts remain shrouded in mystery, ignorance – even fear. The consequences of our culture's breast taboos are tragic: Britain's breast-cancer death rate is the highest in the world. Every woman should read *Mixed Messages* – the first book to consider the well-being of our breasts in the wider contexts of our lives.

Defeating Depression Tony Lake

Counselling, medication, and the support of friends can all provide invaluable help in relieving depression. But if we are to combat it once and for all, we must face up to perhaps painful truths about our past and take the first steps forward that can eventually transform our lives. This lucid and sensitive book shows us how.

Freedom and Choice in Childbirth Sheila Kitzinger

Undogmatic, honest and compassionate, Sheila Kitzinger's book raises searching questions about the kind of care offered to the pregnant woman – and will help her make decisions and communicate effectively about the kind of birth experience she desires.

The Complete New Herbal Richard Mabey

The new bible for herb users – authoritative, up-to-date, absorbing to read and hugely informative, with practical, clear sections on cultivation and the uses of herbs in daily life, nutrition and healing.

READ MORE IN PENGUIN

A SELECTION OF HEALTH BOOKS

Twins, Triplets and More Elizabeth Bryan

This enlightening study of the multiple birth phenomenon covers all aspects of the subject from conception and birth to old age and death. It also offers much comfort and support as well as carefully researched information gained from meeting several thousands of children and their families.

Meditation for Everybody Louis Proto

Meditation means liberation from stress, anxiety and depression. This lucid and readable book by the author of *Self-Healing* describes a variety of meditative practices. From simple breathing exercises to more advanced techniques, there is something here to suit everybody's needs.

Endometriosis Suzie Hayman

Endometriosis is currently surrounded by many damaging myths. Suzie Hayman's pioneering book will set the record straight and provide both sufferers and their doctors with the information necessary for an improved understanding of this frequently puzzling condition.

The New Our Bodies, Ourselves
The Boston Women's Health Book Collective

To be used by all generations, *The New Our Bodies, Ourselves* courageously discusses many difficult issues, and is tailored to the needs of women in the 1990s. It provides the most complete advice and information available on women's health care. This British edition is by Angela Phillips and Jill Rakusen.

Not On Your Own Sally Burningham
The MIND Guide to Mental Health

Cutting through the jargon and confusion surrounding the subject of mental health to provide clear explanations and useful information, *Not On Your Own* will enable those with problems – as well as their friends and relatives – to make the best use of available help or find their own ways to cope.